Life Management Skills:
Taking Charge of Your Future

Joann Driggers

Delmar Publishers

an International Thomson Publishing company **I(T)P**®

Albany • Bonn • Boston • Cincinnati • Detroit • London • Madrid
Melbourne • Mexico City • New York • Pacific Grove • Paris • San Francisco
Singapore • Tokyo • Toronto • Washington

NOTICE TO THE READER

Cover photos courtesy of Images © 1998 PhotoDisc Inc.
Cover design: Carolyn Miller

Delmar Staff
Publisher: Susan Simpfenderfer
Acquisitions Editor: Jeff Burnham
Developmental Editor: Andrea Edwards Myers
Production Manager: Wendy Troeger
Project Editor: Carolyn Miller
Marketing Manager: Katherine M. Hans

COPYRIGHT © 1999
Delmar is a division of Thomson Learning. The Thomson Learning logo is a registered trademark used herein under license.

Printed in the United States of America
8 9 10 XXX

For more information, contact Delmar, 3 Columbia Circle, PO Box 15015, Albany, NY 12212-0515; or find us on the World Wide Web at http://www.delmar.com

International Division List

Japan:
Thomson Learning
Palaceside Building 5F
1-1-1 Hitotsubashi, Chiyoda-ku
Tokyo 100 0003 Japan
Tel: 813 5218 6544
Fax: 813 5218 6551

Australia/New Zealand:
Nelson/Thomson Learning
102 Dodds Street
South Melbourne, Victoria 3205
Australia
Tel: 61 39 685 4111
Fax: 61 39 685 4199

UK/Europe/Middle East:
Thomson Learning
Berkshire House
168-173 High Holborn
London
WC1V 7AA United Kingdom
Tel: 44 171 497 1422
Fax: 44 171 497 1426

Latin America:
Thomson Learning
Seneca, 53
Colonia Polanco
11560 Mexico D.F. Mexico
Tel: 525-281-2906
Fax: 525-281-2656

Canada:
Nelson/Thomson Learning
1120 Birchmount Road
Scarborough, Ontario
Canada M1K 5G4
Tel: 416-752-9100
Fax: 416-752-8102

Asia:
Thomson Learning
60 Albert Street, #15-01
Albert Complex
Singapore 189969
Tel: 65 336 6411
Fax: 65 336 7411

Spain:
Thomson Learning
Calle Magallanes, 25
28015-MADRID
ESPANA
Tel: 34 91 446 33 50
Fax: 34 91 445 62 18

Library of Congress Cataloging-in-Publication Data

Driggers, Joann.
    Life management skills: taking charge of your future / Joann
Driggers
       p. cm.
    Includes bibliographical references and index.
    ISBN 0-7668-0506-9
    1. Life change events—Psychological aspects. 2. Life change
events—Problems, exercises, etc. 3. Emotions. 4. Control
(Psychology) I. Title.
BF637.L53D75   1998
158—dc21
                 98-20900
                 CIP

Life Management Skills:
Taking Charge of Your Future

Contents

Preface

INTRODUCTION

Thank you for taking a glance at this book. You will find that it is filled with tips and suggestions on a broad spectrum of topics to help you get control of your life and to make the most of your special skills and talents.

This book is special because it is filled with over two hundred activities that allow you to immediately apply the information, making it a part of your life. It is based on the premise that what counts is what you do, not what you know, and so it takes a hands-on approach. For example, you could read about riding a bicycle, but would that mean you *could* ride a bike? Of course not. You need to get up on the bicycle seat, put your hands on the handle bars, and start to pedal.

If you have surveyed the book by flipping the pages from back to front, you have discovered that it has many blank spaces, allowing you to personalize the content to your particular needs and lifestyle. Just as we all will not choose the same bicycle, we do not all want to learn the exact same things. This book is organized so that you will design your own learning experience.

Who Should Read This Book

Anyone who wants to really make a change in how they run their life should read this book. It is different from other books because it does more than just present facts and data. It offers unconventional ways to learn information using unique hands-on activities and exercises. The activities are based on the latest in brain research and multiple aspects of human intelligence. This means that the activities are fun and interesting, and *they work*.

Some readers will use this book for self-paced self-improvement. Others may be using it as part of a class. Either way, your personal goal is probably the same, that is, to get better control of your life. Be assured that the format is flexible and intended to fit both of these circumstances.

Most of us have too many demands on our time and energy, from work and family to school and community or friends. It seems we run out of time before we run out of our "to do" list. The purpose of this book is to provide practical, personal experiences that will show you ways to get more out of life. You will learn to set goals, make better decisions, and improve your time management. Along the way you will also learn more about yourself and what is important to you. You will discover how the application of current brain research can make your learning easier and more fun. In short, you will gain more control over your life.

How to Get Started

It is not essential to use this book in the order it is presented. Feel free to start with any section or chapter. However, most people choose to learn about values and goals toward the beginning, since they are the foundation for the decisions we make and the actions we take.

About the Activities

Each chapter begins with a brief overview of the topic, then there are at least ten activities. *Don't do all the activities.* In each chapter there are two or three activities that have been created to provide different ways to attain the same knowledge or skill. The purpose statement that precedes each activity will give you a clue about what you would gain from that activity. Choose the activities that most appeal to you and teach you what you want to learn.

Some of the activities include additional content related to a specific topic or concept that has been presented in the chapter. Therefore, you will find it valuable to scan each activity even though you choose not to do it. For example, *value clarification* is explained in the text of Chapter 1, but *prioritizing values* is only presented in Activity 9 in that chapter.

Other Features of the Workbook

At the end of each unit is a section called Explorations that focuses only on one important issue, for example, on how to delegate. This allows more concentrated information to be presented on important life management skills.

At the back of the book in the Appendix is a Competency Matrix that lists major workbook topics to help you keep track of your progress. As you complete activities, you will want to update the matrix to indicate your new level of learning for each competency. Many employers want employees to have certain basic skills and competencies. The matrix provides a record of that for you, and can serve as the backbone of a skills portfolio to be shared with an employer.

OK, are you ready to get started?

ACKNOWLEDGMENTS

The author would like to thank Jeff Burnham, Acquisitions Editor, Delmar Publishers, Inc., for offering her the opportunity to write this book. Without Jeff's foresight and vision of this project, I would have missed a great deal of fun, a chance to grow as a teacher, and travel down an exciting road. Gratitude goes to the whole Delmar publishing team who brought this project to fruition, particularly Andrea Edwards Myers, Developmental Editor, as well as to Linda J. Ireland, Copyeditor, Gustafson Graphics.

A real debt of gratitude is owed to all of the California Community College Family and Consumer Science educators who have developed and shared instructional resources and teaching strategies for Life Management. Since 1984, the Chancellor's Office, California Community Colleges, has funded Life Management projects that have developed curricula, collected and disseminated instructional resources, trained faculty, and assessed student success. Although the contributors are too numerous to mention, special thanks go to Peggy Olivier, Specialist, and Pat Stanley, former Specialist, both of California Community College Chancellor's Office; Lynne Miller, Long Beach City College; and Kay Sims, Yuba College.

The author and Delmar Publishers would like to thank those individuals who reviewed the manuscript and offered suggestions, feedback, and assistance. Their work is greatly appreciated.

Lisa Hoover
ITT Technical Institute
Pittsburgh, Pennsylvania

Michael Mahoney
Drake Business School
Astoria, New York

Appreciation also goes to Jeanne Erskine, Rick Stepp-Boling, and Randy Wilson, all at Mt. San Antonio College, for their suggestions and encouragement.

Finally, without the day-to-day enthusiasm, help, encouragement, and support of Steve Collier, this book would not have been possible. Thank you!

Joann Driggers

UNIT ONE
Developing Your Emotional Potential

Chapter 1
Getting Started:
The Power of Self-Belief

Chapter 2
Setting Realistic Goals

Explorations
Understanding Systems

Chapter 1

Getting Started: The Power of Self-Belief

How many decisions do you think you have made today? Probably many, even dozens, beginning with deciding to get out of bed this morning. Decisions that you make are consciously or unconsciously based on your values.

VALUES AND THEIR SOURCES

Values are learned beliefs that arouse strong emotional as well as intellectual responses. They are our deepest feelings and thoughts about life. Although values themselves cannot be seen, their presence is felt in the way a person talks and acts. Values represent the ultimate reason people do what they do—their basic ideals, objectives, and aspirations. Examples of values include freedom, fairness, compassion, respect for elders, loyalty, challenge, privacy, flexibility, cooperation, fun, dependability, family closeness, courage, adventure, responsibility, spontaneity, and honesty.

All of us share some basic values related to sustaining life, yet there are differences between and among cultures and individuals. So, where do our personal values come from? The values that we hold dear are a result of our learning and life experiences. Value formation began in our earliest days and was influenced by our *family* and *culture*. The atmosphere in your family home, the way your parents treated you and each other, the family habits and procedures all played a role in your early value formation.

A second source of values had an impact on you when you were three or four years old, as you increased your *social* exposure and personal experiences. Childhood playmates, toys and games, play environment, and interactions with other people all presented opportunities for value formation. *Education* and the *media* also introduced you to new ideas and experiences. School expanded your learning in and out of the classroom. The media (television, radio, films, printed materials, and now the Internet) had an impact on your values as well, resulting in admiration or emulation of an athlete, comedian, or musician.

The final transmitter of values was the world of *work*. The importance of honesty, financial gain, family, spirituality, and other values varies from job to job and from one career field to another. What goes on at work, as well as our choice of work, reflects and influences our values.

All of our experiences affect what we value, and how much we value it. Between birth and age seven, people begin to form their preliminary value structure or system. During the early school years, ages seven to eleven or twelve, there is a testing and modification of this value system. By the age of fifteen or sixteen, values have been, for the most part, "locked in." From that point it is primarily the ranking of a particular value in relation to other values that is subject to change. For example, families with young children may decide that their highest priority is the time spent with the children and, therefore, may turn down overtime or a promotion at work that would diminish available family time. When those children are in their teens, the parents may welcome the extra work hours because of the financial benefits gained from them.

VALUE CLARIFICATION

People who are uncertain of their values do not have clear and consistent purposes. They lack criteria for making judgments and decisions. Knowing our own values increases our understanding of ourselves and increases our satisfaction with our decisions. But because value systems are complex, we sometimes have conflicting values. For example, you might value both adventure and safety, two values that conflict when you are deciding whether you should take up sky-diving.

Resolving these conflicts and avoiding others can be achieved by frequently reviewing, evaluating, and revising your values. This allows you to evaluate your ideas, thoughts, beliefs, and actions of the past in light of your current or future life. This process is called **value clarification**. It has three basic steps: choosing, prizing, and acting.[1]

Choosing
   choosing from alternatives
   choosing after consideration of consequences
   choosing freely
Prizing
   prizing and cherishing
   public affirming when appropriate
Acting
   acting
   repeating a consistent pattern

The first step, *choosing*, requires you to think about value-related issues, as we are doing in this chapter. Choosing means that you have a basic understanding of values and that you can identify some of your personal values. The second step, *prizing*, asks you to accept your values in a nonjudgmental way. It recognizes that not everyone has an identical value system. Prizing includes affirming that you have chosen your values and are proud of them. The final step, *acting*, means that you use your values consciously as the basis of decision making. You will find several value clarification activities in this chapter.

Think of value clarification as the certified public accountant (CPA), or the accounting system, for your values. Value clarification makes your actions more congruent with your values. As you learn more about values, you will become more aware of what you cherish, and you will increase the use of values as criteria for decision making.

---

[1] Howard Kirschenbaum, "A World of Confusion and Conflict," *Forum: Value Clarification* (New York, NY: J. C. Penney Co., Spring, Summer 1972).

SELF-BELIEF OR SELF-ESTEEM

In addition to values, your perception of your personal worth forms a frame through which you see the world. This perception is called **self-belief**, or self-esteem. It is an emotion—a measure of how loving and accepting you feel toward yourself. People with high self-esteem feel confident and capable, and so can reach their goals and fulfill their dreams.

One way to achieve and maintain high self-esteem is to use **positive affirmations**, sometimes called positive self-talk. How does it work? Well, in your mind you play audiotapes (or, if accompanied with mind pictures, videotapes) that help form your self-belief. These audio and videotapes have been collected by your mind in a haphazard way. Every day you "play" these tapes, reinforcing, adding to, or deleting items in the collection. Some of the tapes are positive in nature, but others are negative. Positive self-talk is a method of deliberately controlling this process to make it supportive of your goals.

Writing affirmations is easy. They need to be positive, in the present tense, and with a personal pronoun, usually "I." For example, "I am in perfect health." Notice that the condition desired (perfect health) sounds like it has already been achieved. That is what makes the statement present tense. You should also include positive, enthusiastic, descriptive words such as "easily," "happily," or "always."

Don't worry that the statements do not match the current situation. You are just using imagery to create a picture of what you want. Be aware that thought precedes action. "I think I'll enroll in school" comes before the deed itself. When we imagine and tell ourselves how we want things to be, our mind goes to work to create or attract situations, circumstances, and characteristics that will help us reach our goals.

VALUES AND THE WORLD OF WORK

Is **SCANS** familiar to you? No, it's not a new breakfast food, although in some circles it is as popular as hot cakes. Most school districts and many colleges in the nation are reviewing their curriculum with SCANS in mind. So, what is it? SCANS is an acronym for Secretary's Commission on Achieving Necessary Skills and is a result of thousands of interviews with business owners and managers, union officials, human resource officers, and workers in factories and offices.

The report produced by the commission identified foundation skills and workplace competencies that adults need for success in the workplace. In other words, it identified what skills an employer values in an employee. These skills and competencies were deemed essential regardless of the type, level, or location of work. They are listed in Figure 1–1.

Many SCANS skills are incorporated into this workbook, since they are essential life management skills. As you expand your knowledge and skills over the next few months, keep SCANS in mind. Plan to evaluate your current competencies and set some goals to advance them to a higher level. If you are particularly interested, ask your instructor for more details.

Knowledge about values, value clarification, and self-belief is good to have, but it is only the beginning, since it is our daily actions and habits that determine the quality of our lives. So now it is time to turn to the activities in this chapter. They have been designed to provide opportunities for practical application. Review all of them, then complete the

---

Foundation skills

Basic skills—Reading, writing, arithmetic, mathematics, listening and speaking

Thinking skills—Creative thinking, decision making, problem solving, mental visualization, knowing how to learn, reasoning

Personal qualities—Responsibility, self-esteem, sociability, self-management, integrity/honesty

Workplace competencies

Resources—Manages time, money, materials, facilities, and human resources

Interpersonal—Cooperates as a team member, teaches others, serves clients/customers, exercises leadership, negotiates, works with cultural diversity

Information—Acquires and evaluates, organizes and maintains, uses computers

Systems—Understands systems, monitors and corrects performance, improves and designs systems

Technology—Selects technology, applies it to tasks, maintains and troubleshoots technology

---

Figure 1–1 SCANS competencies

ones that address your needs and use an approach to learning that interests you.

INDIVIDUAL ACTIVITIES

1. Coat of Arms[2]

Purpose: To begin to identify personal values and to help answer these questions: "What is important to me?" "What am I doing with my life?" "Is my life making a difference?" and "What do I really value?"

You are probably familiar with the concept of a coat of arms, or shield. This exercise asks you to draw, in any shape and size, a Personal Coat of Arms. Divide the shape into six areas, and fill each area with an appropriate drawing, a picture clipped from a magazine, a photograph, or the like, according to the following guidelines:

First area:
Show something you are very good at and something you are struggling to get better at.
Second area:
Symbolize something about which you would never change your mind.
Third area:
Represent your most significant material possession.

---

[2] Sidney Simon, Leland W. Howe, and Howard Kirschenbaum. *Values Clarification: A Handbook of Practical Strategies for Teachers and Students* (Chesterfield, MA: Values Press, 1978).

Fourth area:
   Represent your greatest achievement of the last year and your
   greatest setback or failure of the last year.

Fifth area:
   Show what you would do if you had one year to live and you
   were guaranteed success in whatever you attempted.

Sixth area:
   What three words would you like people to say about you if
   your life ended today?*

*The only place words can be used is area number six. All ideas in other areas are to
be presented in picture or symbol form.

2. Twenty Things I Love to Do[3]

Purpose: To help identify personal values and to prize these values. Results
can also be used to motivate you and help you avoid procrastination.

As quickly as you can, in the lefthand column in Figure 1–2, list
twenty things in life that you really, really love to do. They can be big or
small, indoors or outdoors, perhaps something you do only during a particular season. Try to be specific, for example, name the sport, describe
the type of film or book, and so on. Don't worry if you cannot quite get
twenty. If you can think of more than twenty, feel free to include all of
them.

When you are finished recording the things you love to do in Figure
1–2, use the columns on the righthand side of that figure to code your
list in the following manner:

$	Check this column for any item that costs more than $5 each time it is done.
A or P	Place the letter A in this column for those items you prefer to do alone and the letter P for those you prefer to do with other people.
PL	Check this column for those items that require planning.
R	Use this column to indicate those items that may have an element of risk to them. The risk can be physical, emotional, or intellectual.
5	Check this column for any item that would not have been on your list five years ago.
Date	Finally, indicate in this column the date you last did each activity.

Now, take a minute to look over your list and the codings.

What patterns can you identify in the things you love to do?

What pleases you about the list?

[3] Adapted from Sidney Simon, Leland W. Howe, and Howard Kirschenbaum, *Values
Clarification: A Handbook of Practical Strategies for Teachers and Students* (Chesterfield, MA:
Values Press, 1978).

What I love to do	$	A or P	PL	R	5	Date
1.						
2.						
3.						
4.						
5.						
6.						
7.						
8.						
9.						
10.						
11.						
12.						
13.						
14.						
15.						
16.						
17.						
18.						
19.						
20.						

Figure 1–2 What I love to do

What did you learn about yourself?

List two or three values that are suggested by your list of activities.

Are there some things that you like to do that you haven't done lately? Why do you think that is?

Now that you know twenty things that excite and motivate you, use some of these activities as rewards for doing a task about which you have been procrastinating.

3. My Journal—Values

Purpose: To identify personal values and to evaluate the level of consistency with which you act on those values.

Journal writing can serve several purposes. First, it can serve as a record of your life, to be savored and enjoyed in the future. Second, it can provide a valuable of-the-time, true-to-your-life record of your experiences. Finally, it can be of immense help in clarifying values and solving problems, adding insight and richness to your life.

A journal is much more than a diary. It can be a record of conversations, dreams and aspirations, images and reflections, feelings and emotions, drawings and cartoons, song lyrics, poems, and pictures.

Your journal is private, and no one will be allowed to look at it without your permission. In a journal, a person can be totally free without infringing on the rights of anyone else.

Each journal exercise is independent and can be recorded on any paper of your choice. However, there is usually a journal activity in each chapter of this workbook, so if keeping a journal over the time span in which you work with this book appeals to you, select an attractive blank book for this purpose. They are readily available at drugstores and bookstores. Or consider a book that has been created for this purpose, such as *The Simple Abundance Journal of Gratitude* or the *Black Pearls Journal*.

This activity involves keeping a Values Journal over the next two weeks. Make notations in your journal about thoughts, feelings, and experiences whenever they occur, whether at school, work, or home. Jot down evidence of a particular personal value, or evidence of values that appears in the actions of those around you. Make note of your personal behavior when your actions are guided by your values (for example, you exercise because you value personal physical fitness), when your actions don't seem to match your values (you eat eight ounces of potato chips at one time even though you value being healthy), or when one value seems in conflict with another (you relax and watch television rather than study for your quiz).

After two weeks, reread your Values Journal entries. Then write one or two paragraphs in your journal discussing your value system or hierarchy. Include a list of two or three values that seem to be very important to you and a short list of values that seem to be less important. Also mention any situations in which you seem to hold competing or conflicting values.

4. Pictures of My Friends

Purpose: To identify your values and affirm your choices.

You have undoubtedly had many good friends throughout your life. Use the mind-mapping technique to create a picture of your friends and the pattern of your friendships. Figure 1–3 shows a model of a map of friendships. As you can see, information such as personal qualities, activities, and other memories can be included. Make several mind maps so that you can include friends from your earliest memories, elementary and middle school, high school days, young adulthood, and the present.

Then, in order to evaluate what you have learned from this activity, use the same technique to map out what you have learned about yourself, your values, past friendship patterns, and present friendship patterns.

Use this format as a model to map and analyze past and present friendships in relation to your values.

Figure 1–3 Mapping friendships

You may write your responses in the appropriate shapes on Figure 1–4 or create your own map.

5. Family Interview

Purpose: To identify values that are cherished by family members of a previous generation, and to see how those family members have acted upon those values. Then to compare those values and actions to yours.

Interview a family member who is not from your generation. Choose, for example, a grandparent or an older aunt or uncle. Ask them to tell you about your family history, where they lived in their early years, how they came to live where they are now.

Go prepared with some open-ended statements and ask them to finish each one. Consider statements such as the following: "I am proud of my parents because . . ." "The most important thing to our family is . . ." "The best part of my childhood was . . ." "What I wish I had that young people have today is . . ." Be sure to write down three or four more such statements of your own so that you won't forget them, or waste time during the interview.

You might want to make an audio or videotape recording of this interview, or you may prefer to take notes as you listen. After the interview, thank your relative for the time. Then, as soon as possible, review

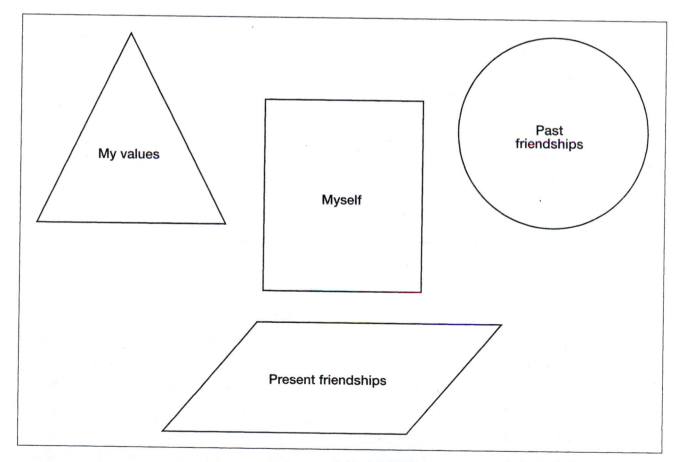

Figure 1–4 What I learned about my values and friendships

your notes or recordings. Consider what values the two of you have in common. Comment on how each of you would rank the importance of each of those values. Summarize your findings either in writing or at the end of your audio or videotape.

6. Musical Values

Purpose: To compare and contrast values presented in the music of one era to those presented in the music of another era.

Choose two distinct time periods that interest you and for which you can find recordings of songs. For example, locate recordings from the 1940s and the 1980s. (It is best to find recordings rather than just sheet music with words, since so much of communication is nonverbal.) Public libraries, campus music departments, and friends and family can be resources here.

Select five or six popular songs from each era, preferably from different song writers and performers. While thinking about values, listen to the songs of one era, and then to those of the other. What seems to be important to each time period? What issues or concerns are there? What language differences do you hear? In other words, compare and contrast the values presented in the music of the two eras.

Record your findings in Figure 1–5 or in audio format. Mention specific values that seemed prevalent and provide examples from the music.

Figure 1–5 Comparison of values found in the music of two eras

7. Source of My Values

Purpose: To identify the specific sources of your values.

Remember that there are five basic sources of values: family/culture, social, education, media, and work/career. Imagine that the drawing in Figure 1–6 (on page 14) represents your most important values. Under each of the five sources, list several values that you hold that came primarily from that specific source. For example, under family/culture you might list religion, and under education you might list responsibility. Try to stay focused on the *primary* source of each value, even though there may have been reinforcement from another source. List at least four values in each category.

8. Who Influences Me?

Purpose: To identify specific sources of your values and to analyze how these values affect your behavior.

Using Figure 1–7 (on page 15), identify and list in the lefthand column people, events, or experiences that have influenced your life. In the middle column, list a value that you have as a result, and in the righthand column, describe how this value influences, or has influenced, your behavior.

9. Clarifying and Ranking My Values Now

Purpose: To review what you have discovered about your personal values and to begin to rank or prioritize those values.

Review the definition of *values*, and reread the partial list of values found in this chapter as well as any similar list you have found. Then consider what you have learned from all the value clarification activities you have completed.

On the continuum shown in Figure 1–8 (on page 15), record your five most important values. Then record five more values that are also important, some that are somewhat important, some that have little significance for you, and some that are not important at all.

What you have done is to rank or *prioritize your values*. This allows you to consciously use your value system or hierarchy to make quality decisions. Because life events can influence the ranking, this process should be repeated periodically.

10. Values Action Record[4]

Purpose: To allow you to check the consistency of the match of your actions to your values.

Make a list of your top ten values (see Activity 9). Then keep a written record or "log" during the next week of the things that you do to support these values. Figure 1–9 (on page 15) provides you with an example.

Now on Figure 1–10 (on page 16) keep your own log. Be sure to identify what actions you take in support of your values. After one week, read

---

[4] Adapted from Carol Rupe, "Value Clarification Log," *SCANS: Teaching Life Management in California Community Colleges* (Sacramento, CA: Chancellor's Office, California Community Colleges, June 1996).

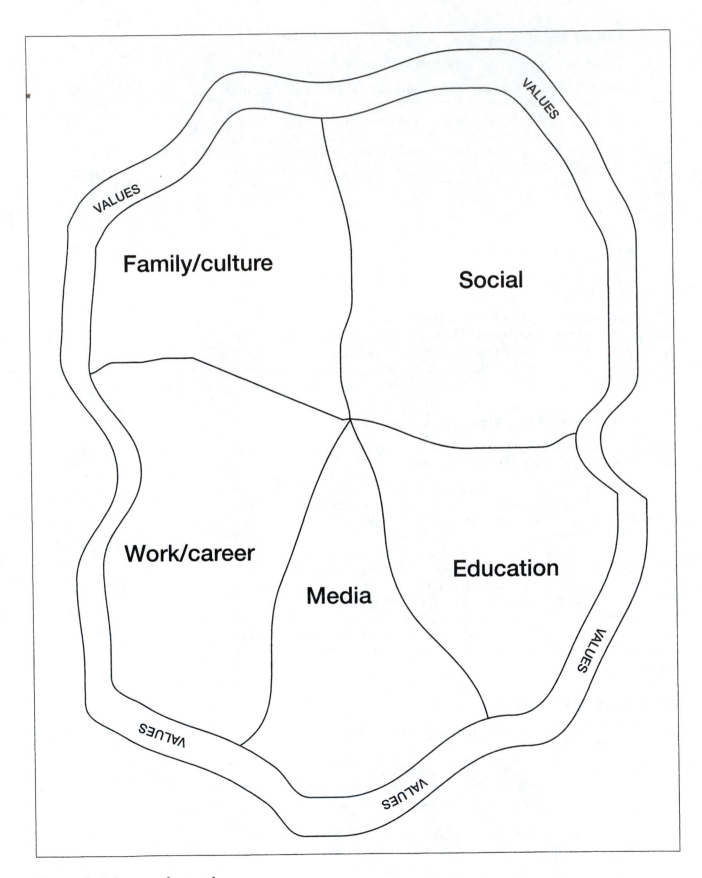

Figure 1–6 Source of my values

Influential person, event, or experience	What personal value is connected to this influence?	How did or does this influence my behavior?

Figure 1–7 Who influences me?

Most important	Also important	Somewhat important	Not very important	Not important

Figure 1–8 Ranking my values

Day	Value	Action
Monday	Health	Thirty minutes of aerobics
Tuesday	Education	Began "Family History" exercise by making an appointment with Grandpa

Figure 1–9 An example of a values action record

Day	Value	Action

Figure 1–10 Values action record

1. _____
   _____
   _____
   _____
2. _____
   _____
   _____
   _____
3. _____
   _____
   _____
   _____
4. _____
   _____
   _____
5. _____
   _____
   _____

Figure 1–11 My values in action

over your log. Then in Figure 1–11 identify five values that are important to you. Beside each one write two or three sentences explaining why that value is important and what you do to demonstrate that.

11. Affirmations

Purpose: To provide an opportunity to edit current self-talk and to write and use affirmations.

You will recall that positive self-talk, or affirmations, is a powerful tool to enhance one's success in life. Do you recall the three characteristics of affirmations? Write them here:

_____

_____

_____

One way to begin writing affirmations is to pick out a simple "change item" and then picture in your mind how you will act with the new habit. For example, a person could change "I never finish anything" to "I love completing each project in a timely way." Another approach is to listen to your self-talk for two days. Consider how you might deliberately improve your life by revising or deleting one type of statement and replacing it with a positive one. For example, "I am not good at taking tests" changes to "I am always prepared for tests and I do well."

Here are other examples of positive affirmations:

I choose to live life to the fullest.
Today I do what needs to be done with a sense of joy and a spirit of fun.
I always keep myself in shape—looking good and feeling great.
I can create and have the life I want.
Everyday, in every way, I am becoming more and more prosperous.
Today my enthusiasm is contagious.
Today things go easier when I'm easygoing.
No one else can make me angry or mad. I make the choice—I choose to be glad.
Today I lighten up. I have a great sense of humor.
In thought, word, and deed—I know I'll succeed.
I like who I am and where I'm headed.

Now it's your turn. Write one or two affirmations that fit your personal needs and circumstances. Check that they are positive, in the present tense, and use a personal pronoun. By including emotion words, your subconscious can better visualize the change, and that makes the desired change come faster. To reprogram yourself, you have several options (listed below). *Whichever option you choose needs to be done at least ten times each day for the next two weeks.*

Pause during the day and focus on your goal. Picture yourself having your desired result. Then

write your affirmations on paper, *or*
read each affirmation out loud, *or*
sing your affirmations aloud, *or*
record your affirmations in your own voice and play them back.

Sometimes you can read, sing, or listen while you are doing another task such as walking or driving, so make this enjoyable. The more feeling and emotion you have in your affirmation, the better. And remember, just as your subconscious has believed the negative, it will now believe the new situation is the truth.

At the end of two weeks, find a friend and describe this experience. Describe how your actions changed as you repeatedly affirmed your desired result. Tell about the total experience in Figure 1–12.

_____

_____

_____

_____

_____

_____

_____

_____

_____

_____

_____

_____

_____

_____

_____

Figure 1–12 My experience with affirmations

EXPAND YOUR LEARNING

For more information on topics covered in this chapter, consider reading one or more of the following:

Copage, Eric V. *Black Pearls Journal*. New York, NY: William Morrow and Co., Inc., 1995. This is a beautiful journal into which you can put your own thoughts.

Covey, Stephen R. *The Seven Habits of Highly Effective People*. New York, NY: Simon and Schuster, 1989.

Gawain, Shakti. *Creative Visualization*. San Rafael, CA: New World Library, 1978.

Peale, Norman Vincent, and Kenneth Blanchard. *The Power of Ethical Management*. New York, NY: Fawcett, 1989.

GROUP ACTIVITIES

1. What's in Your Wallet?[5]

Purpose: To identify personal values and to analyze your choices. We can learn a lot from simple aspects of our lives that we are inclined to take for granted.

_____

[5] Adapted from Sidney Simon, Leland W. Howe, and Howard Kirschenbaum, *Values Clarification: A Handbook of Practical Strategies for Teachers and Students* (Chesterfield, MA: Values Press, 1978).

Form a group of three or four people, no more than five. Go around the circle, one person at a time. Take out your wallet (or purse, or backpack, or the like). While looking through the contents, take out three things that might indicate your values. If you have trouble selecting something, you could show the most precious item, the most useful item, and the item that makes the biggest difference in your life.

When each person has finished, make a list of values that were indicated. Put your responses on the form provided in Figure 1–13.

If you have trouble identifying a value, check the list of values provided at the beginning of this chapter. Then ask yourself, "Why is this important?" You may have to ask "why" two or three times to get to a root value.

Notice if a value is mentioned more than once. This might be an indicator of its importance in your community or culture. Was the same item mentioned more than once? Could such an item, say a credit card, represent a different value to different people? Explain your answer.

2. Values: Sharing with Others[6]

Purpose: To provide an opportunity to synthesize your values by teaching others about values and value clarification. To expand your interpersonal and communication skills.

Choose a significant person in your life and have a planned discussion about values, including the following:

Item	What value could or does it represent?
1.	
2.	
3.	
4.	
5.	
6.	
7.	
8.	
9.	
10.	
11.	
12.	

Figure 1–13 What's in my wallet: Analyzing values

---

[6] Adapted from Carol Rupe, "Value Clarification," *SCANS: Teaching Life Management in California Community Colleges.* (Sacramento, CA: Chancellor's Office, California Community Colleges, June 1996).

1. First of all, explain the concept of values to this person and use an example of a value that *they* have and live by. (Naturally, this is really your perception of their values.)

2. Next, share your top two values. Explain why these values are pivotal in your life right now. Give examples of actions you have taken recently that are consistent with these values.

3. Next, ask the other person to write *their* understanding of *your* top two values and why they are important to you. They need to sign their name to the paper and identify their relationship to you.

4. Finally, read the other person's comments to see whether you made yourself clear to them. If so, initial the paper. If not, write a clarifying statement.

Chapter 2

Setting Realistic Goals

In Chapter 1, we looked at abstract concepts such as values and self-belief. Now we look at the specific and tangible, namely, goals. A **goal** is a result, or an achievement toward which effort is directed. Most often goals are tangible objects or observable results. We could say that values are the "why" of life, and goals are the "what"—what we want, what we do, what we want to have. From your own experience you undoubtedly realize that goals can change, that they do not stay the same for your entire life.

GOAL SETTING

Some goals are **long-term**, such as raising a family, becoming your own boss, owning a home. Others are **short-term**, like getting through this week. There are **intermediate** goals as well, goals that might be reached in two to five years.

Just like with values, a person will have many goals. Successful people can identify their goals and know which ones are more important. Many of the activities in this chapter will show you how to identify your goals, and will ask you to rank them in order of importance, a process that is called **prioritizing**.

Accomplishment and success is measured by your standards. Like goals, standards are based on your values. A **standard** is a measurable guideline or criteria. You could say that a standard is the "how" or "how much" of life. For example, let's say you want to eat a balanced diet (goal) to stay healthy (value) so you eat a minimum of seven grains, three vegetables, and three fruits each day (standard).

Groups and organizations have goals, values, and standards as well. For example, our highways have been built to move people from place to place (goal) safely (value) with speed limits of fifty-five or sixty-five miles an hour (standard).

Because of their close relationship, values, goals, and standards tend to act as a check-and-balance system. In setting your goals, you are indirectly examining, reinforcing, and strengthening your values. At the same time, you are assessing the validity of the standards you have established. Individuals who base their goals and standards on their values develop to their fullest potential and live effectively in a changing world.

Goal setting is easier for some people than for others. For some, setting goals for certain parts of life, such as at work, is feasible, but in other areas they just float and let the tide take them where it will. Knowing what you want and mapping out a plan to get there helps you to decide what to do next. This is very important for those of you who are inclined to want to catch as many opportunities as there are fish in the sea.

Let's digress a minute to discuss scarce resources in relation to goals. You have been making choices and decisions all your life. You recognize that you cannot be in two places at the same time, nor can you have your cake and eat it too. The reason for this fact of life is that our **resources** (money, time, energy) are limited, whereas the possible uses of these resources are unlimited. Thus we must make daily choices about the use of these resources. One strategy to help us in making choices is brainstorming, which is explained in greater detail in Figure 2–1.

THE DECISION-MAKING PROCESS

Choices are not made in a vacuum, and some of our choices are better than others. Our choices will be even better, however, if we are clear about our values, goals, and standards and use this knowledge as a basis for decision making. Given that our resources are scarce, good decision-making skills can help us to stretch those resources and thus get greater personal satisfaction out of the choices we make.

Some people have trouble accepting the idea of scarcity. They have endless ideas and would rather not set limits on using time, energy, or money. These people tend to be casual, easygoing, creative, and holistic in their thinking. Does this, perhaps, sound like you? All of these qualities are wonderful, but if taken to the extreme, they can lead to a life that is out of balance. A person, for example, may run out of energy and money before their most important goals are met. With a little effort, you can learn to pace yourself better and make better choices.

Decision making is a simple enough process:

1. Define the problem in light of your values, goals, and standards.
2. Set a deadline for solution.
3. Identify alternatives.
4. Weigh alternatives.

Brainstorming can be used by an individual or a group of people. It is used when a number of ideas are needed quickly. Most of you have probably tried this before, but you may have violated one important tenet of brainstorming: *evaluation of the ideas comes after all of them have been identified.* By waiting to evaluate the ideas, one suggestion often builds on another and the ideas become more creative and often better. There is plenty of time to evaluate after ideas and suggestions have been generated.

So, let's list the steps to a group brainstorming process:

1. Each goal or objective should be stated clearly.
2. Each person in the group has the chance to identify at least one idea.
3. A person can "pass" when it is their turn to contribute.
4. All ideas are good ones: no judging is done at this time.
5. Respect must be shown to all members of the group.
6. All the ideas should be recorded so everyone can see all of them.

Figure 2–1 Brainstorming

5. Make a choice.

6. Make an action plan to implement and evaluate your choice.

You may have seen or heard the steps described a little differently, but in all probability you can see similarities. So, pause and recall a decision you have made recently. Did you include all of these steps? Many people omit the first and the second step, often out of a sense of urgency, and jump into the process by identifying alternatives or solutions. That's all right, as long as you include steps 1 and 2 before you do step 4.

Step 1, which helps us stay focused on the problem, often mentions the action intended, such as "to buy a different car that will be more reliable." Step 2 asks us to think about how quickly a solution is needed. This is especially useful if we have more than one problem or decision, since it allows us to prioritize and direct our energy accordingly.

In step 3, the brainstorming technique is ideal, since the object is to look for tentative solutions. You may enjoy asking your friends and family to make suggestions. You may want to make a list of all the ideas, or you can put each idea on an individual sticky note and then rearrange or group them later.

At step 4 we temporarily stop production of ideas and begin to evaluate them. This step may be both the most fun and the most complex. Begin by having a sheet of paper for each alternative—list each idea, or put a sticky note with each idea, at the top of the page. Then gather information from knowledgeable sources (your own experience, books, current magazines, friends) about each alternative and write it on the appropriate paper. Include the time, money, and energy costs of each alternative.

Once you have the information, you can use one or more strategies to evaluate the ideas. One way is to consider the good points, or *pros,* and the bad points, or *cons,* of each possible solution. Another is to *forecast the future* by imagining the worst thing, the best thing, and the most likely thing that could happen if you made a particular choice. As you do the evaluation, you may discard one or more alternatives, or you may discover that you need more information. It is not uncommon to move back and forth between steps 3 and 4. Your goal is to make decisions more consciously, with the result being greater satisfaction and happiness.

Step 5 asks you to choose. If that thought makes you uncomfortable, ask yourself if you can change your mind later. Sometimes, if we don't like the result of a decision, we can make a different choice in the future. Also keep in mind that not choosing is a choice, since you have selected to "do nothing."

Step 6 involves creating a plan to implement your decision. Several activities in this and future chapters introduce a variety of planning formats for action plans. Regardless of the form, the first step is to be very clear about your goal or purpose. By thinking about your goal in SMART terms, you will start off on the right foot. The acronym **SMART** stands for specific, measurable, achievable, relevant, and time-framed. Activity 8 in this chapter shows you in detail how to use this concept.

PROCRASTINATION

Well, we have set goals, made decisions, and created action plans, so why haven't we seen the results we wanted? Sometimes it's because we have procrastinated. All of us do it, often resulting in a last-minute rush, poor quality work, and unsatisfactory decisions.

Procrastination is a strategy of delay, and the delay can continue to the crisis stage. It is a signal that there is a conflict of some sort. If we can understand that conflict, we can move forward. Jane Burka and Lenora Yuen, in *Procrastination: Why You Do It; What to Do About It,* have identified the major cause of procrastination as fear. This could be fear of failure or fear of loss of control. As a result of such a fear, we might procrastinate starting the task. In these situations, perfectionism frequently plays a role. There is a tendency to set standards that are unrealistically high, especially when a task is attempted for the first time.

Another possible cause of procrastination is fear of success. In this situation, we might begin the task, but then engage in self-sabotaging behaviors so that we ultimately fail. Thus we can absolve ourselves from having to be responsible or successful in the future.

Expecting ourselves to completely refrain from procrastination is unrealistic, but we can diminish it. Clear goals and realistic action plans start us off on the right foot. Knowing what will motivate us and using those things as rewards for incremental progress toward our goals is also a good strategy.

Now we need a few strategies that will just get us started. First, break the job into little pieces, so it is not so scary. Then establish a time to *start* the task. Try the five-minute plan—do the task for five minutes, and then you are free to stop. (Most people will select to continue with the task for at least awhile longer.) Some people like to do the easy part first, like a warm-up. Others like to do the hard part first in order to get it out of the way. Finally, give yourself a lot of rewards. A reward can be as simple as a cup of coffee, a bit of candy, watching a half-hour television program, or calling a friend on the phone.

You now have knowledge about types of goals and about the goal-setting process. You have discovered the relationship between goals, values, and standards. You have learned that there are steps to the decision-making process that, if followed, will lead to more satisfactory choices. And you know some strategies that can reduce procrastination. It's time to put these concepts and ideas into practice, so review the activities for this chapter and select several that meet your needs. Activities 1 and 2 focus on goal setting, an essential step to getting what you want out of life. Be sure to do at least one of them.

INDIVIDUAL ACTIVITIES

1. General Goal Setting

Purpose: To provide an opportunity for you to think about short-term, intermediate, and long-term goals, and to put those goals on paper.

Use the brainstorming process to imagine all the goals you have for a lifetime. Write your ideas in Figure 2–2. Include personal, family, and career goals—both the serious and the frivolous. Ready, set, go!

All right, good! If you forgot something (traveling, swimming with the dolphins, learning to paint, or whatever), feel free to add it at any time. Now, consider where you will be and what you will be doing five years from now. With that image in mind, brainstorm all the goals you have for the next five years. You will probably repeat some things from the previous list, but odds are that you will have some fresh ideas as well. Write these goals in the space provided in Figure 2–3.

Figure 2–2 Brainstorming all my goals

Figure 2–2 Brainstorming all my goals

Figure 2–3 My goals for the next five years

Great! Now, here's a bit of a change. Imagine that, for whatever reason, you have only six months to live, but that you will be healthy up until the last moment and that you do not have to worry about final arrangements. In Figure 2–4, write what you would do and how you would spend your time.

When you are finished, review the three lists in Figures 2–2, 2–3, and 2–4. Do you see a pattern? Does a particular goal appear on all the lists? Is the content of all the lists similar, except that perhaps they get progressively shorter? Or perhaps two are similar and one describes a different set of goals? Keeping in mind that there is no right or wrong pattern, write your observations about your lists in Figure 2–5.

Figure 2–4 If I only had six months

Figure 2–5 Reviewing my goals

Knowing your short-term, intermediate, and long-terms goals can help you make better decisions regarding education, family, and so on. Consider these lists as rough drafts, as a work-in-progress, to be expanded as you give more thought to your goals over the next few weeks.

But note particularly the short-term, or six-month, list. There are items on that list that are so important to you that you do not want to end your time on the earth without their accomplishment. What have you done lately to help you achieve those goals? Congratulations if you can answer with specific actions. If not, consider doing Activity 8, the Action Plan, and get going on one of your higher priorities.

2. Writing a Mission Statement

Purpose: To look at the "big picture" regarding your life's direction, and to articulate what you really want out of life.

A mission statement focuses on what you want to *be* and *do* based on your personal values. It is a verbal expression of your unique purpose. In *The Seven Habits of Highly Effective People,* Stephen Covey says that a mission statement is like your constitution and that, once written, it really does not change much.

Examples of missions statements include the following:

My mission is to be honest and just with all, and to leave the world a better place.

My mission is to balance work, family, and personal needs and to use my money and skills to the betterment of myself and others.

These simple statements take a great deal of thought. It may be easier to write more, than to be this concise. Many people prefer several statements, one to cover each area of their lives. To get started, think of your life as having seven categories: physical, mental, social, family, career, financial, and spiritual. Write at least one sentence for each category.

As you write, consider what will make you happy. Remember to include mention of your values too. It may take several rewritings over a period of time to be satisfied with your mission statements. The time spent will be worth it. Record your mission statements for each of the seven categories, as well as an overall mission statement, in the spaces indicated in Figure 2–6 (on page 28).

Read your overall mission statement once a day for three weeks. Use it as a basis for decision making and resource allocation. After three weeks, write about this experience in Figure 2–7 (on page 29).

3. My Journal

Purpose: To reflect upon the success of past goals and accomplishments.

If this is your first journal activity, read about the possible content of journals in Chapter 1, Activity 3. Then consider previous successes, both small and large. Over a period of four or five days, recall these successes and why they were important to you. Who helped you make them happen? Record these reflections and observations in your journal.

What insights do you have now that will facilitate your future accomplishments? Record those thoughts and ideas in your journal.

Overall mission statement

_____

_____

Physical

_____

_____

Mental

_____

_____

Social

_____

_____

Family

_____

_____

Career

_____

_____

Financial

_____

_____

Spiritual

_____

_____

Figure 2–6 My mission

4. Prioritizing Goals

Purpose: To use a simple strategy to rank goals in order of importance.

Most of us have many goals and, therefore, sometimes get distracted trying to work on all of them at once. A well-known strategy for prioritizing goals comes from Alan Lakein, *How to Get Control of Your Time and Your Life*. He suggests that you divide your master goal list into three columns labeled "A," "B," and "C," in order of importance. Do this by writing your goals in the appropriate columns in Figure 2–8.

Next Lakein recommends that you study the B column and redistribute all the B goals to either the A column or the C column. You

_____
_____
_____
_____
_____
_____
_____
_____
_____
_____
_____

Figure 2–7 My experience using my mission statement

A Goals	B Goals	C Goals

Figure 2–8 Prioritizing my goals

can redistribute the goals you have noted in Figure 2–8 by using arrows to show which column you want to move them to. To further refine this process, the A goals can be numbered by their relative importance, giving you an A-1 goal, an A-2 goal, and so on. Lakein's recommendation is that you direct all your energies to the A goals and ignore the C goals at this time, since you have designated them to be less important. Now you know to which goals your time, energy, and money should be devoted.

5. SMART Goals

Purpose: To learn to convert outcome goals into SMART behavior goals, so that they can be implemented by using an action plan.

Most of us have some idea what we want to do in life. Perhaps your list includes getting a better education, having a family, or being financially secure when you retire. All of these are outcome goals. The first step to turning dreams into reality is to convert an outcome goal into a SMART behavior goal.

As you may recall, the acronym SMART stands for specific, measurable, achievable, relevant, and time-framed. Let's say that your outcome goal is to be physically fit. There are many activities that you could do to reach that goal. You might jog, swim, bicycle, or dance. To be specific, the action should be clearly stated. So, for example, *jogging* would be indicated, rather than the more general term *exercise* (see Figure 2–9).

Once you have specified an activity, next you would measure the amount of that activity you wish to do—in our example, how far or how long you might jog. Then you would check to see that the goal is achievable, since to be successful, you must realistically evaluate your goals. It does no good to vow to run five miles a day when the most you have ever run is half a block. A goal is relevant if it suits your interests and needs.

The "time-framed" element requires you to indicate a time for the activity to occur. This may be a starting date, or it may be an indication of frequency. Thus, by following each of these steps, the outcome goal of physical fitness has become a SMART behavior goal.

All right, now it's your turn. Choose one of your goals with which you would like to get started. Write it here.

_____

_____

Now, brainstorm several activities, actions, or behaviors that you could take that would move you closer to accomplishing this goal. Write them here.

_____

_____

_____

S	(specific)	Jog
M	(measurable)	One mile
A	(achievable)	In 11–12 minutes
R	(relevant)	Yes, I like jogging around the track
T	(time-framed)	Every day, starting Monday

Figure 2–9 Creating a behavior goal

Next, choose only one of the actions you have noted. Criteria for that choice can be based on which action would be most effective, which one you would enjoy most, which would be easiest or cheapest—you get the idea.

Now, using the action you have chosen as a basis, write your outcome goal in SMART format:

S (specific) _____

M (measureable) _____

A (achievable) _____

R (relevant) _____

T (time-framed) _____

6. Formal Goal Setting

Purpose: To give you an outline or model for systematically looking at your goals. This exercise goes into greater depth than brainstorming.

If you did the brainstorming or the mission statement activity, keep those notes available. If not, spend a few minutes imagining what goals you would like to accomplish in the next five years. Consider what your most important goals are in the following areas: physical, mental, social, family, career, financial, and spiritual.

After creating a comprehensive list, you will have a better idea of what you want your life to be like. Then you can make plans to create that life. An important first step is to assess your views on life, that is, to consider your personal philosophy.

A. Assessing Your Views on Life. Give a few moments of thought to your beliefs about who controls you, your life, and the world around you. Then write several sentences to answer the following two questions in the space provided. Do not worry about having perfect or polished answers.

1. Do you believe in a power higher than yourself (that is, a Supreme Being, or God)? *Explain* your beliefs.

2. Who or what controls the events in your life?

B. Focusing on Your Goals. Next, do some brainstorming, focusing on your goals. Then answer the following three questions in the space provided.

1. What do you most want to accomplish in your life?
Lifetime:

Next Year:

2. What do you most want to experience in your life?
Lifetime:

Next Year:

3. What kind of a person do you want to be?
Lifetime:

Next Year:

C. Prioritizing Your Goals. After all this thinking, it is time to become more specific. Go through your previous lists of goals and organize them into the following seven categories: physical, mental, social, family, career, financial, and spiritual. In Figure 2–10, in the column labeled "Goal," list two or three short-term and intermediate goals for each category. Focus on goals that you want to reach within the next five years.

D. Evaluating Your Goals. After listing your goals in Figure 2–10, consider the level of importance of each. In the column in that figure labeled "Importance," rank your goals H, M, or L, according to the following criteria:

Category	Goal	Importance	Conflict?
Physical			
Mental			
Social			
Family			
Career			
Financial			
Spiritual			

Figure 2–10 My intermediate goals

H—This goal is *highly* important.
M—This goal is *moderately* important.
L—This goal is of *lesser* importance.

Finally, indicate in the last column in Figure 2–10 whether the attainment of one goal will conflict with your efforts to attain another goal on the list. (For example, will earning your college degree in two years conflict with getting married and starting a family in the next three years? Most people would say "yes.") If one goal does conflict with another, identify the conflicting goal in the righthand column.

You now have a clearer picture of your goals and your priorities. You have finished goal setting for the time being. Your next activity would be to create an action plan (see Activity 8) to obtain one or more of your goals.

7. Teaching Goal Setting

Purpose: To provide an opportunity to teach the skill of goal setting to someone else, and thereby achieve a higher level of knowledge.

If you have ever taught something to someone else, you know that it takes a high level of knowledge to do so. This activity provides those readers who have already achieved some degree of know-how in regard to goal setting to take their skills to an even higher level.

Your task is to find someone who is a goal-setting novice. This might be someone younger or older than yourself. It might be a sibling, spouse, friend, child—virtually anyone who has little skill in goal setting. After discussing goals with them, try to determine their level of understanding of the topic. Then, together with the other person, choose *one* of the previous activities (Activities 1–6). Clarify that the other person understands the process, and then have them complete the activity.

Once the activity has been completed, sit down with your student and review the results—not for content, but for process. Remember, your position is not to evaluate their goals but to evaluate whether they have expanded their understanding of the concept of goals.

Ask your student to write one paragraph in the following space to give you feedback on the experience:

8. Action Plan—Special Event or Project

Purpose: To expand skill in planning an event or project that consists of several different, unique steps. Some examples of events or projects include a party or special gathering, a vacation, a house project, or a major consumer purchase.

A. Select a Long-Term Project or Event. Choose an activity, event, or project that you want to do in the near future. You may want to consider the goals you listed in your goal-setting activity and choose one of them for this activity.

My goal is: _____

_____

B. Consider Your Outcome Goal. Write your goal in SMART terms.

S (specific) _____

M (measureable) _____

A (achievable) _____

R (relevant) _____

T (time-framed)_____

C. Break Down the Goal into Do-able Activities. Brainstorm a variety of activities or tasks that will advance you toward your goal. Include items such as a budget, the number of people involved, who will be involved, what you will expect from them, how much time is available, what equipment or supplies you will need, and how you will get those supplies. Do any appointments or reservations need to be made? If so, how far in advance?

These are just ideas. The list is *not* complete! You might organize your ideas in a list or several lists, or you might use sticky notes on a tabletop, which would allow you to move the notes around and group similar ideas or related tasks.

D. Sequence Tasks and Estimate Time. Rearrange all the tasks you have identified into the order in which they will be done (easy to do with sticky notes), and estimate the time the activities will take to do them. For example, one task might be to order engraved invitations, and the time needed to accomplish the task might be one day, plus two weeks of waiting for delivery. Record your tasks and the time they will take in the following space:

Task   *Time to accomplish the task*
                                              (including waiting time)

_____

_____

_____

_____

_____

_____

_____

_____

E. Set a Completion Date for This Project or Event. It is likely that when you started planning, you had a deadline in mind. You are now in the position to evaluate whether that time frame is realistic. If necessary, readjust your original deadline.

Date of completion _____

If date has changed from the original one, explain why.

_____

_____

F. Create Your Plan of Action. You are now ready to create your action plan. Your goal is to make this plan *so clear* that you could practically hand it over to someone else to implement. In fact, this is also the time to delegate as many tasks as possible. Consider *who* you need to help you and *what* you need to have done. As you set out your plan, it is possible that necessary tasks or activities that you have not yet considered will come to mind. Be sure to revise your plan to include them.

In Figure 2–11, list each activity or step of your action plan in *chronological order,* along with the person responsible for the task, the supplies needed, and the date by which that step is to be finished. Be sure that you allow buffer time, that is, time for something to go wrong, in this plan. Once you begin implementation, complete Activity 10.

Activity	Person responsible	Supplies	Completion date

Figure 2–11 My plan—In chronological order

9. Action Plan—Storyboard

Purpose: To expand skill in planning an event or project that consists of several different, unique steps. The final plan is in the form of a story-board, rather than the table format used in Activity 8. Some examples of events or projects include a party or special gathering, a vacation, a house project, or a major consumer purchase.

A through E. Follow the format for steps *A* through *E* provided in Activity 8, creating your own forms on separate paper if necessary.

F. Create Your Plan of Action. You are now ready to create your action plan. Your goal is to make this plan *so clear* that you could practically hand it over to someone else to implement. In fact, this is also the time to delegate as many tasks as possible. Consider *who* you need to help you and *what* you need to have done. As you set out your plan, it is possible that necessary tasks or activities that you have not yet considered will come to mind. Be sure to revise your plan to include them.

Present your plan in the form of a storyboard, which is a series of panels with sketches of important changes in action, with each major activity shown in chronological order. You can draw the sketches free-hand or on a computer. Be sure each panel, or page, of the storyboard includes the person responsible for the task, the supplies needed, and the date by which that step is to be finished. Once you begin implementation, complete Activity 10.

10. Action Plan Feedback

Purpose: To provide an opportunity to practice feedback or evaluation of a personal project.

Once you have a good start on your action plan, you need to pause and evaluate your progress. This will give you assurance that all is well or give you time to make corrections. Use the following form for that purpose, completing each open-ended statement:

So far, I have (accomplished) _____

_____

_____

_____

_____

What I liked about it was _____

_____

_____

_____

_____

What I forgot about was _____

_____

_____

_____

_____

What I will change or adjust is _____

_____

_____

_____

_____

As for the time schedule, _____

_____

_____

_____

_____

11. Visualizing/Charting Your Progress

Purpose: To provide a motivational tool to keep you going as you implement your action plan for a short-term goal.

Sometimes our goals seem like huge mountains that we must climb. We need to develop tools that encourage, inspire, and motivate us. One trick recommended by time management expert Alan Lakein[1] is to **swiss cheese** a task, that is, to break the task into small pieces. This makes it seem less daunting, especially if you then create a way to visually track or chart your success.

For this activity, select a short-term goal on which you are already working and that you will complete in the next few weeks. It may be a big report at work or school, a short-term savings goal, or a project around the house. Then analyze the task, imagining the small parts of it. For example, if you are working on a report, you might determine the purpose, set standards, outline the report into sections, and set a deadline for completion. If you have a short-term savings goal, you might divide the amount of money you need a month from now into four weekly amounts.

Once you have selected your goal and broken it down into small parts, you can chart your weekly progress. There are many possible formats that can be used. Examples of a checklist, a thermometer, and a graph are provided in Figure 2–12.

Write the goal you have selected at the top of Figure 2–13 (on page 40). Then, in the appropriate box in that figure, create a chart, graph, or similar tool to track your progress toward your short-term goal. Use this tool to provide motivation as you move toward success. Then, after you have used the tool awhile, write a paragraph or two, in the space provided in Figure 2–13, about how this strategy has worked for you and how you might use it in the future.

12. Procrastination

Purpose: To provide an opportunity to identify personal patterns of procrastination, and then to analyze them in order to diminish procrastination.

Over a period of several days, keep a record of every time you procrastinate, whether it is at work, home, or school. Include the activity about which you procrastinated, what you did instead, and how you felt. Record this information in Figure 2–14 (on page 41).

Write a paragraph or draw a picture in Figure 2–15 (on page 41) that explains what form your procrastination takes. In other words, show what pattern there seems to be in your procrastination.

Most experts believe that procrastination is usually caused by fear. What might you be afraid of in relation to the activities that you postponed?

---

[1] Alan Lakein, *How to Get Control of Your Time and Your Life* (New York, NY: Peter W. Wyden, Inc., 1973).

Try to remember what things have prompted you to finally get started on postponed activities. Describe them in the space provided.

What specific strategies will you take to overcome procrastination?

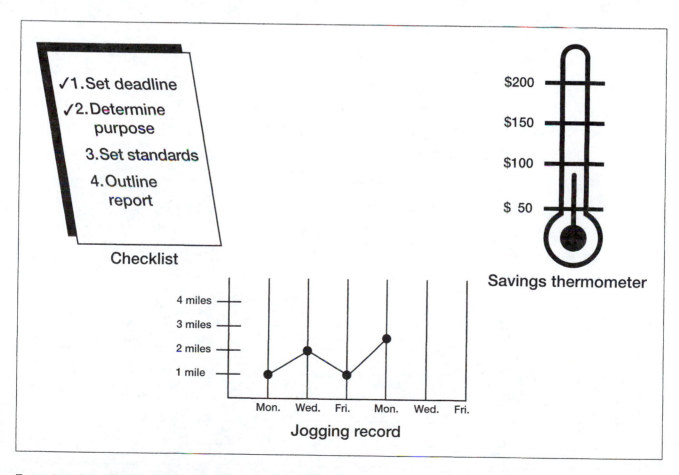

Examples of visualization tools that can help motivate you to reach a goal.

Figure 2–12 Check list, thermometer, and graph

My goal is _____

My visualization tool:

How visualization worked, and how it can be used in the future:

_____
_____
_____
_____
_____
_____
_____
_____
_____
_____
_____
_____
_____

Figure 2–13 Charting my progress

Activity	What you did instead	How you felt

Figure 2–14 My procrastination record

Figure 2–15 My pattern of procrastination

13. Slob for a Week

Purpose: To provide an opportunity for a perfectionist to evaluate personal standards for their effectiveness, and to consider possible changes.

Many people have unrealistically high standards and feel that every job must be completed to the highest standard possible. This is common thinking of perfectionists. The reality is that some tasks do not deserve this type of attention. Barbara Kerr, psychologist and specialist on creativity, recommends being a "slob for a week" to encourage a re-evaluation of standards and an expansion of flexibility and creative thinking.

This activity requires that you quit picking up after yourself and others. Perfectionists tend to do so in a slightly compulsive fashion. Slob for a Week means leaving other people's possessions where they have left them, other people's dishes where they have left them, and so on. It also requires *you* to leave your clothes on the chair, your books laying around, and so forth. Although the first couple days may be difficult, do it anyway. You will have more time to devote to your journal, your art, and your personal reading—time to take a long bath, dream, and do whatever else you want to do. You will be free!

After one week, write what the week has meant to you in Figure 2–16, or record your thoughts on it on an audiotape.

Figure 2–16 What it meant to me to be a slob for a week

EXPAND YOUR LEARNING

Covey, Stephen. *The Seven Habits of Highly Effective People*. New York, NY: Simon and Schuster, 1989.

Lakein, Alan. *How to Get Control of Your Time and Your Life*. New York, NY: NAL Dutton, 1989.

Porat, Frieda. *Creative Procrastination: Organizing Your Own Life*. Menlo Park, CA: New Life Books, 1980.

Sher, Barbara. *Live the Life You Love: In Ten Easy Step-by-Step Lessons*. New York, NY: Dell, 1990.

Sher, Barbara, and Annie Gottlieb. *Wishcraft—How to Get What You Really Want*. New York, NY: Ballantine Books, 1986.

GROUP ACTIVITIES

1. Expanding Your Brainstorming Skills

Purpose: To encourage your creativity, to provide an opportunity to practice brainstorming, and to discover the value of teamwork in generating ideas.

Creativity can be defined in many ways, yet definitions usually incorporate the concept of the production of something new or original. These new ideas usually come from our storehouse of experiences, observations, and knowledge. The following experiences will allow you to break out of the mold, get off the track, and have some fun at the same time.

Complete the following three exercises.

a. Write down as many ways as you can think of that an umbrella and a tree are alike.

b. In the next three minutes, write down as many different athletic sports as you can think of.

c. In the next two minutes, write down as many ways as you can think of to use a metal fingernail file.

Now find another person who did this activity and compare lists. Were there many similarities? Did the two of you come up with even more ideas as you talked?

2. Acting Out Decision Making

Purpose: To provide an opportunity to analyze and synthesize knowledge about goal setting and decision making.

As a member of a team of two or three people, write a short story, including dialog, that has goal setting and decision making as a key theme. Act out the story in front of a larger group.

Explorations

Understanding Systems

As much as we may strive to control our lives, none of us ever obtains complete control because we do not live in a vacuum. Rather, each one of us is influenced by and influences the society in which we live. Our society is a system, composed of many smaller systems. Examples of these smaller systems include families, businesses, cities, states, and so on. If we understand these systems, we can make purposeful changes in them and obtain the results we desire.

WHAT IS A SYSTEM?

You may have learned about systems elsewhere. Systems planning is commonly taught in computer programming, biology, and business management classes. Systems thinking and planning have also been important topics for employee training in large companies around the world, so perhaps you have encountered the concept at work.

This Explorations section will introduce you to the basic concept of systems thinking, apply this information to you as your own system, and show you how you fit into the system of school. Future sections of this workbook will refer to these basic concepts and expand upon them. Systems thinking is particularly helpful in decision making and in implementing plans. Employers are placing increasing value on people who understand systems, because there is an increased appreciation that problems and tasks tend to be more alike than they are different.

A **system** has three parts: members, procedures, and an environment. For example, in a classroom, the members are the students and the teacher. There are procedures about starting the class, the activities that occur, and dismissal. The environment includes the room, its temperature and lighting, as well as the equipment in the room such as chairs, desks, and blackboard.

The simplest system has four phases: input, transformation, output, and feedback (see Figure Explorations 1–1). **Input** can be described as the information entering the system. This information includes *demands* such as your goals, values, standards, and daily events. It also includes the *resources* that you have available to meet these demands such as time, money, and special skills. The **transformation** phase includes *analysis,* where information is reviewed, decisions are made, and a plan is created, and *action,* where the plan is implemented. **Output** is the end result. Within this phase, you measure the degree of success in attaining the goal and hopefully enjoy increased satisfaction and quality of life as a result of your efforts. **Feedback** is the last part of the system and represents new goals and information that have developed as a result of the output. The output thus becomes input and the system repeats itself over and over.

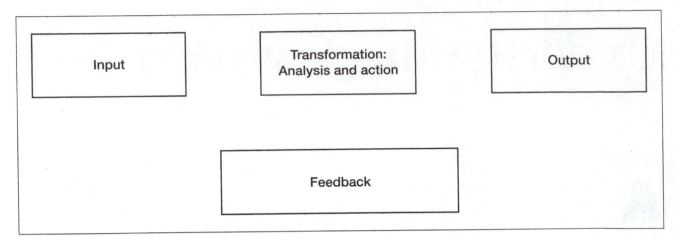

Key parts to a system include input, transformation, output, and feedback.

Figure Explorations 1–1 Basic system

Looking at Yourself as a System

Understanding systems is the basis for managing change and achieving success. When a change is made in one part of the system, there is a reaction or response in another part. Applying your understanding of a system gives you more control over the result.

Consider yourself as a system. You are the only member, your habits and routines are the procedures, and where you live and work is your environment. Imagine it is early morning, and the alarm goes off. This is input. Transformation is the analysis of this situation and the action you take, which is based upon your goals, values, and standards. Do you want to eat breakfast before going to work? Is being on time important? What exactly is "on time"? Let's say that you decide to push the snooze button, and you don't get up for another twenty minutes. The result, or output, is that you have to rush around the house, only get a banana for breakfast, and are five minutes late for work. Feedback is how you and other people felt about that experience, and it will influence your behavior the next morning.

Systems analysis is a reflective tool to help you gain insight on where to start improving the process for better results. Its five basic steps are:

1. State the aim of the process.
2. Indicate the source of input.
3. List the individual responsibilities or activities involved in this particular process.
4. Identify the result.
5. Include measurable feedback.

Now, in Figure Explorations 1–2, let's follow these five steps and diagram the morning wake-up that was previously discussed. To get started, remember that input is demands and resources entering a system. Some of the demands are reflected in the *aim* statement, such as beginning the day in an unhurried manner. This suggests that health and family are important values. A successful career is also probably important. The goals come directly from the aim statement. The desire for a nutritious breakfast eaten with family dictates the standards, as

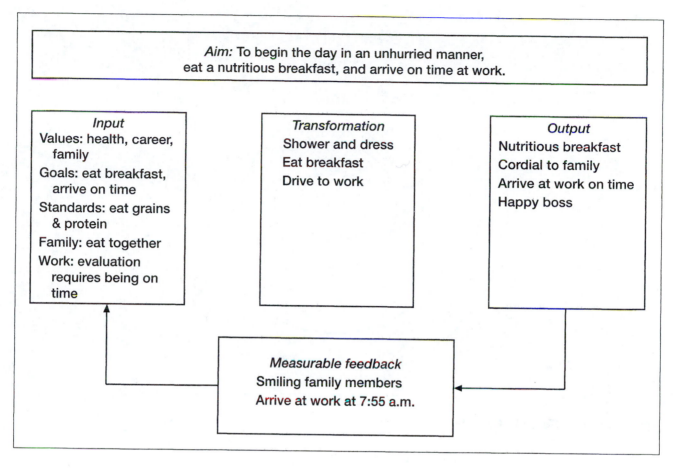

Figure Explorations 1–2 The morning wake-up

does the work evaluation. The transformation phase reflects the basic necessary actions, and the output is the anticipated result. Do you agree that the feedback in Figure Explorations 1–2 is measurable?

Your Personal Learning System

As previously mentioned, we are all part of many systems. Figure Explorations 1–3 shows that you also are a small system (a subsystem) within the larger ones: family or household, community, and so on. If all of your systems have not been listed in that figure, add them to the circle. This circle is sometimes called the **circle of influence**. It is a visual reminder that you have more control over the systems that are closest to you.

A key to personal success is to realize that you have a lot of control over your own system. For example, in regard to education, you can organize your own learning. You are not dependent upon your instructor, the authors of textbooks, or the school you attend. You can be your own change agent. You can control what you learn, how much you learn, and whether you apply what you learn.

So, let's see if you understand the basics of systems. To assess your understanding, diagram your personal learning system on Figure Explorations 1–4. When you are finished, find another person who has completed this activity and compare your systems diagrams.

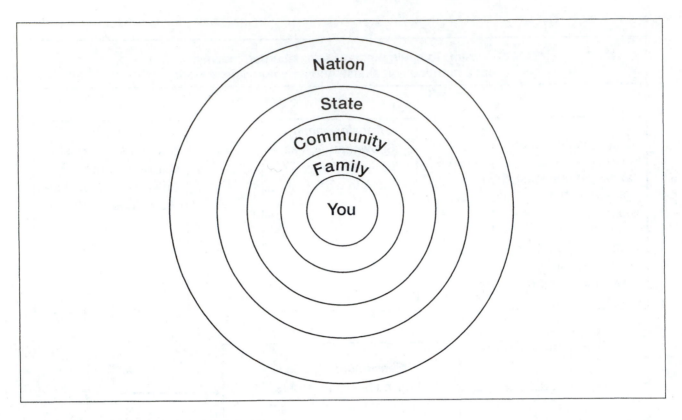

Figure Explorations 1–3 Circle of influence

Figure Explorations 1–4 Personal learning system

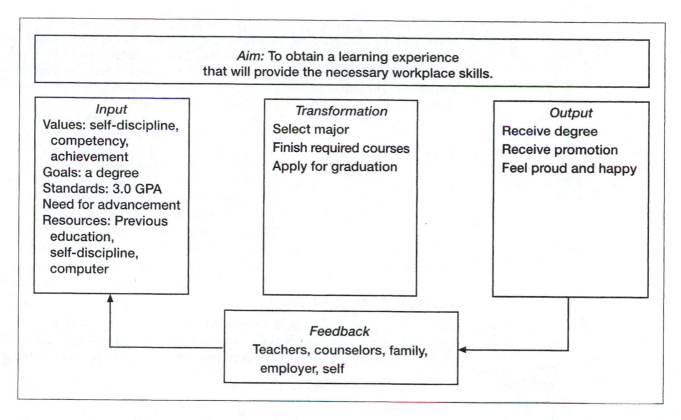

Figure Explorations 1–5 Learning systems flow chart

INTERACTION OF SYSTEMS

Now you know something about the most fundamental and simple of systems, yourself. Your personal learning system can change from day to day. In fact, change is a part of all systems. Some of these changes are within your control, while others are not. By understanding the interaction of systems that surround our own, we can better prepare for change and improve our personal results or output.

Let's begin with your diagram of your personal learning system and expand on that. It might look something like the one in Figure Explorations 1–5. Your aim is probably related to obtaining a learning experience that will provide necessary workplace skills. In the input section, you might have mentioned values such as self-discipline, competency, achievement, or success; goals such as a certificate or a degree; standards such as a particular grade point average. You also might have mentioned the need to get this training in order to advance in your career. All of these goals, values, standards, needs or wants, and events comprise the demands that enter a system.

Note that Figure Explorations 1–5 contains a part of input not in the previous example, resources. **Resources** are assets that are available for reaching goals. Your resources might be personal assets, such as your education, skills, and the quality of your character, or family assets, such as a computer or a car. So you can see that resources include people, services, and objects that are part of the system and that are available for accomplishing our goals.

Sometimes resources come from another system. If you are viewed as a learning system, then the classroom and the school are the next related systems. Some system analysts like to call people or organizations outside the system who provide input *suppliers,* as they supply products or services. In this example, suppliers could be teachers, counselors, the admissions office, or the placement office. Also included would be previous schools, such as high school and middle school, since they had an impact on your current resources. Suppliers are diagrammed on the left of the flow chart shown in Figure Explorations 1–6.

On the right side of the flow chart in Figure Explorations 1–6 are the recipients of the output, called *customers* by the business world. The recipient of your learning is your employer. This is important to remember, since your success (advancement) is dependent upon meeting the needs, criteria, and expectations of that employer.

People outside the system of yourself provide feedback. They include your teachers and counselors, your family, and your employer. If you meet or exceed their standards, your efforts will be rewarded. As you continue to apply life management skills such as systems analysis in the workplace and in your personal life, your results will improve.

RESOURCE ALLOCATION

Each time you identify a goal and make and implement a plan, you are using resources. The issue is how resources are selected and utilized. By examining classifications of resources you are better able to identify the

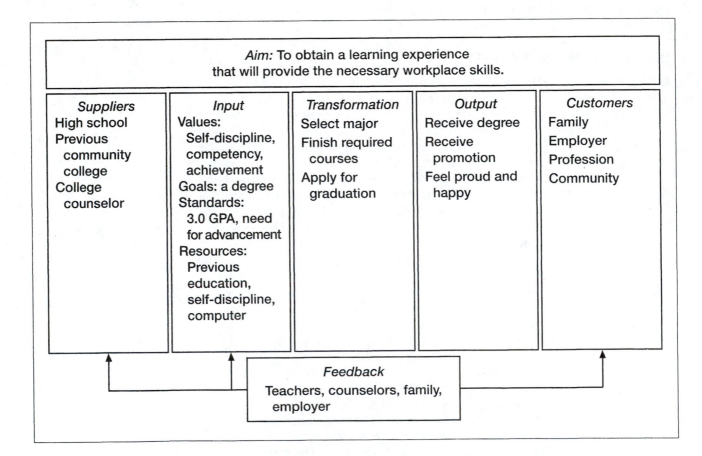

Figure Explorations 1–6 Interaction of learning systems

assortment of resources available, the cost of using certain resources, and probable ways each can be allocated.

One classification method categorizes resources into human, economic, and environmental. **Human resources** include time, energy, and the full range of a person's specific skills, talents, and knowledge. You also have access to the human resources of others. For example, you have access to your teacher's knowledge and skills. **Economic resources** include all forms of money such as checking accounts, credit, stocks, and the like. **Environmental resources** include *social resources* such as schools, places of worship, police and fire protection, as well as *natural resources* such as clean air and water, wildlife, trees, and so forth. Look at Figure Explorations 1–7 for more specific examples.

Notice that resources might be either internal or external to a system. Understanding the various classifications is an aid in identifying resources that might not have been previously considered. For example, many of us rely only on our own skills and abilities to solve problems or complete tasks. Yet all around us are friends and family members of all ages and with assorted talents who would be willing, indeed happy, to assist us. We just need to see these resources and ask for assistance or delegate a task.

Your success at goal attainment is largely a result of your recognition, allocation, and use of resources. Good management requires that you analyze the best use to which each resource can be put in order to achieve the highest degree of satisfaction.

SUMMARY

Now you have had an overview of the concept of systems. You have seen how you are a system of one person, and that you fit into other systems, such as family and community. You will find several activities in this chapter and other chapters that will provide more information on this topic and opportunities to gain greater proficiency in resource allocation.

Human resources	Abilities and skills, knowledge, attitudes, creativity, awareness, interests, energy
Economic resources	Personal possessions including house, furniture, computer, car; all forms of money (cash, savings, stock bonds) and access to credit
Environmental resources—Natural	Air, water, coal, oil, gas; trees, fields, plants, parks; animal life, both wild and domestic; recreation facilities
Environmental resources—Social	Social ties between individuals, family, friends; communal resources such as police, fire, government, school systems, religious institutions; services for consumption; employment and investment

Figure Explorations 1–7 Classification of resources

INDIVIDUAL ACTIVITIES

1. Identifying Personal Human Resources

Purpose: To provide an opportunity to identify personal human resources, including yourself and other significant people in your life.

Human resources are often overshadowed by the focus on economic resources. This exercise should help you expand your awareness of the pool of human resources available to you. We will begin with you and your special assets. In Figure Explorations 1–8, identify and list some of your specific assets. Categories have been provided for your convenience.

Now rank your personal human assets, using the appropriate column in Figure Explorations 1–8, in order of importance to your life now—that is, rank those that are most important in helping you reach your current goals the highest, and those that are least important for

Asset categories	Specific assets	Importance now	Importance in five years
Talent/skill			
Intelligence			
Energy			
Education			
Experiences			
Health			
Appearance			

Figure Explorations 1–8 Personal human resources

that purpose the lowest. Then, think into the future five years from now. Which assets will be most important at that time in regard to your goals? Use the righthand column in the figure to rank your assets accordingly.

Do you think you are using your own human resources to best advantage? Did some additional personal assets come to mind as you thought about the future? Write a paragraph about what you gleaned from this experience.

2. Identifying Human Resources Around Us

Purpose: To provide an opportunity to identify human resources in the significant people in our lives who help us meet our goals.

We rarely sufficiently appreciate the human resources available to us in the form of family, friends, colleagues, and community members. This exercise should help you expand your awareness of the human resources available to you. In Figure Explorations 1–9, identify and list the names of people who support you and who share their knowledge and talents with you. Categories have been provided for your convenience.

Asset categories	Specific names	Human resource assets	Importance
Family			
Friends			
Community			
Other			

Figure Explorations 1–9 Human resources around me

Now, identify the specific assets of those individuals that make them human resources in your life. List the assets in the "human resource assets" column in Figure Explorations 1–9.

Then, using the righthand column of the figure rank the importance of the contribution these people and their human resource assets make to your life now.

Write a paragraph regarding your conclusions about the human resources you have in other people in your life.

GROUP ACTIVITIES

1. Circle of Influence

Purpose: To gain a greater understanding of the multiple systems to which an individual belongs and which can provide resources to an individual.

Using the Circle of Influence shown in Figure Explorations 1–3, have a group of people brainstorm the many subsystems to which a person might belong in a family. For example, a person belongs to their immediate household; to an extended family, which might consist of parents or stepparents, aunts, uncles, cousins, and so forth; and to people who are not related but who have the importance or status of a family member. Then, brainstorm the many subsystems to which a person might belong in a community, state, and nation.

What have you learned from this experience?

UNIT TWO
Developing Your Intellectual Potential

Chapter 3
Improving
Your Thinking Skills

Chapter 4
Improving Your Study Skills

Explorations
Planning Your Education

Chapter 3 _____

Improving Your Thinking Skills

Each day most of us face a situation in which we have forgotten something important. As a result, we may have cereal in the house but no milk; we may be embarrassed because we flubbed an introduction; or, more seriously, we may have received a reprimand from our boss for missing a meeting or a critical deadline. Life would be more pleasant if only we could remember better. This chapter will show you how that is possible.

MEMORY BASICS

Before we go too far, let's give ourselves credit for what we do remember. Chances are you remembered to brush your teeth this morning; you were able to drive your car or take public transportation successfully to your destination; and you know the names of the people immediately around you at work. The key to your success is how you have used your brain for remembering this data.

Your brain is a pattern-seeking device. It is constantly trying to determine what is meaningful in what it experiences. Every new experience is quickly evaluated to see if it fits into the existing network, much like a piece of a puzzle is evaluated to see how it fits into the whole puzzle.

Current brain research indicates that a brain can store information on three levels, the sensory memory, the short-term memory, and the long-term memory. The first step is for your brain to sense or experience. The **sensory memory** is like a flash bulb that goes off in a very dark room. The image that your mind receives lasts only a second at the most, yet it is a perfect reflection of what you saw and heard. If this reflection is meaningful, it moves to the next stage, into short-term memory.

Short-term memory is a temporary storehouse of information, typically no longer than thirty seconds. To make the image last longer, you must extract meaning from it—that is, you must tie it to something you know. With repetition, the image moves into long-term memory.

Long-term memory capacity seems limitless. Much of what we forget is actually stored away in our brains in a system not unlike a filing cabinet, but we may have lost the key to access the information. This chapter is about forging the keys to access names, events, dates, and other data that we have stored in our long-term memory, whether for a test in school or for a business or social occasion.

Learning Modalities

Before we can store information, we must be aware of it or perceive it. We originally experience information through our sensory channels, that is, through sight, sound, touch, taste, and smell. In a classroom, most input comes from sight, sound, and touch. One of these senses is usually dominant in an individual. As people mature and their skills and experiences increase, they may become more "mixed." But under pressure, they usually resort to their dominant modality.

Input comes in four modes: visual, auditory, kinesthetic, and mixed. Your dominant modality is your most efficient way to receive information. Your challenge is to adapt the input to fit your strengths. You may already know which sense you prefer to use to receive input. If not, or to confirm your opinion, complete Activity 3 in this chapter.

Multiple Intelligences or Capacities

After perceiving information, we must extract some meaning from it in order to move it to short-term and eventually long-term memory. In the early 1980s, a new theory about learning was introduced that can assist us with our understanding of that process. This theory, presented by Howard Gardner (*Frames of Mind,* 1983), is called **multiple intelligences (MI).** Gardner proposes that rather than the two traditionally recognized forms of intelligence (linguistic and logical-mathematical), there are actually seven forms of intelligence. The additional capacities included in the MI theory are: musical, spatial, bodily-kinesthetic, intrapersonal, and interpersonal. Figure 3–1 briefly defines each capacity.

Each of us is born with all seven intelligences, or capacities, but as a result of choice or circumstances, we typically develop some of them

---

Howard Gardner, Harvard psychologist and author of *Frames of Mind* and *The Unschooled Mind,* has focused on how to make learning more productive and longer term. His theory is that there are seven capacities or intelligences that are available to facilitate remembering and learning.

1. **Linguistic:** The capacity to use words effectively in writing or in speech to persuade, to remember information, or to explain, as in a writer or orator.

2. **Logical-mathematical:** The ability to use numbers effectively and to reason well, and the ability to recognize and solve problems using logical patterns to categorize, infer, make generalizations and test hypotheses, as in a scientist or mathematician.

3. **Spatial:** The capacity to perceive the visual-spatial world accurately and to transform and recreate visual perceptions, as in an artist, architect, or designer.

4. **Musical:** The capacity to perceive, express, transform, or discern musical forms such as pitch, rhythm, and timbre, as in a composer or musical performer.

5. **Bodily-kinesthetic:** Expertise in using one's body to express ideas and feelings, often goal-oriented, as in a woodcarver, surgeon, or dancer.

6. **Intrapersonal:** The capacity for self-knowledge—to detect and discern among one's own feelings—and the ability to use that knowledge for personal understanding, as in a religious leader or psychotherapist.

7. **Interpersonal:** The ability to notice and respond appropriately to the moods, temperaments, motivations, and desires of other people, as in a salesperson or politician.

Figure 3–1 Multiple intelligences: Seven ways of knowing

more fully than others. Also, we use them in various combinations, depending upon the demands we face in our lives.

EXTRACTION AND INTERNALIZATION

When we begin to review information for meaning, we are at the **extraction**, or understanding, stage. As you may recall, this needs to occur before the information can be stored in memory. When the brain attempts to attach meaning and make sense out of information, it uses the linguistic, logical, or spatial capacities. If you know which one of these three capacities is your area of strength, you can prepare the information in the appropriate format. Utilizing the intelligences that are dominant for us as individuals can expand and quicken the pace of our learning.

Linguistics gain meaning through words and, therefore, need as many words as possible. They may want to write in margins of books and may prefer handouts with wordy details. They want extra reading on a topic.

Logical-mathematicals gain meaning by reorganizing information. They prefer outlines of their own making, and they create their own order.

Spatials gain meaning by drawings, maps, color, and simplicity. They need to reduce information to key words.

Once extraction has occurred, we can **internalize** the information and store it in long-term memory. At this point, we use musical, bodily-kinesthetic, intrapersonal, or interpersonal capacities. Again, we have a preference or dominance for one of these four, and if we are aware of that preference, we can learn accordingly.

Musicals can tap out a rhythm or play instrumental music as they repeat information (preferably out loud). They can set the information to music and sing it.

Bodily-kinesthetics can incorporate movement of any sort (swing a leg, tap a finger, pace the floor). They can do an experiment or demonstration, and they need frequent movement breaks when studying.

Intrapersonals can create mental images, teach one or two other people, practice on their own, and write about the meaning of the information in a journal.

Interpersonals can tell a story, teach a group of people, draw a picture, and do an experiment.

Figure 3–2 provides a graphic overview of the whole learning process.

With effort, a person can develop their weaker capacities. But learning will be more comprehensive and information easier to retain if you run with your strengths. If you have not yet determined your strengths, visit a campus counselor to take a multiple-intelligence assessment.

Memory Retrieval

As mentioned, the challenge is to retrieve information from long-term memory. Recognition and recall are the two basic ways to accomplish this. **Recognition**, your judgment that information presented to you is something you already know, provides easier access to memory. Perhaps you cannot state the name of the last film that you saw, yet

Input	Extraction	Internalization
Visual	Linguistic	Musical
Audio	Logical-mathematical	Bodily-kinesthetic
Kinesthetic	Spatial	Intrapersonal
Mixed		Interpersonal

Figure 3–2 Overview of the learning process

you recognize it when you see it advertised or hear others discussing it. On a test, many true/false and multiple-choice questions are at the recognition level.

Recall is a self-initiated search of long-term memory for information. This search can be triggered by an event, a question from a friend, a mental picture, or a short-answer test question. Recall can be facilitated by cues in the situation. For example, you may not immediately remember the name of the store where you bought the shoes you are wearing, but if you think of related information, such as when you bought them, which shopping area you were at, and who you were with, you probably can recall the store name.

Recall Strategies

It is highly likely that you have already used some recall strategies. Now you want to be more conscious of them and use them more frequently. Although there are many strategies for retrieving information, most of them are variations of repetition, organization, and mnemonics.

The reason you remembered to brush your teeth this morning is that when you were a child, a parent showed you how to brush, did it for you, and then reminded you every day until it became a habit. **Repetition** is also how you learned to drive a car; you practiced and practiced until you could practically do it in your sleep. Anyone who is proficient at a skill or sport can attest to the power of repetition. An effective repetition tool for learning information is flash cards, something you may recall using in primary grades. Be sure to look in the Individual Activities section for directions on creating flash cards in a variety of styles.

It is believed that most people find it difficult to remember more than five or six things at a time. One way to help yourself remember things is to *organize* long lists into small groups or chunks. For example, let's say that you are taking a nutrition class and are studying vitamins and minerals. Rather than studying each one independently, you could group all the fat soluble vitamins together (vitamins A, D, E, and K), and then group all the water soluble ones together (C plus all the B vitamins). This grouping process is commonly called **chunking.** You can categorize information by using any pattern that makes sense to you and applies to the subject.

Another organizing strategy is **mind-mapping.** A map is a drawing or verbal picture of ideas gained from reading or listening—a sort of visual outline. Look through the Individual Activities section in this chapter to learn this technique, especially if you enjoy drawing or making flow charts or diagrams.

Mnemonics is a category of strategies that includes rhymes, acronyms (a word formed by the initial letters of words in a phrase), and words or sentences that are artificial memory aids. Mnemonics does not replace understanding, but only aids retrieval. A rhyme commonly taught to aid in correct spelling, for example, is "I before E, except after C, or when sounded as A as in neighbor or weigh." Two acronyms used in music are *FACE* (for the spaces on the music staff) and *Every Good Boy Does Fine* (*EGBDF* for the lines on the music staff). It is common for businesses to turn a phone number into words (1-800-4MY-TAXI), which makes it convenient for customers and undoubtedly increases business. Several activities are provided in this chapter to help you apply these strategies to your learning.

CRITICAL THINKING

Learning is not just repeating information. Real learning takes place as you filter information through your own knowledge and experience. As you have seen, you need to make connections in a language and context that is both familiar and understandable to you. This process requires critical thinking. When you think critically, you make judgments about truth, you distinguish fact from opinion, and you use logic to draw conclusions.

The decision-making process is an example of critical thinking. You specify the problem, generate and evaluate alternatives, and choose the best alternative. This is active thinking, thinking of the highest order. This type of thinking requires you to ask questions, be inquisitive, and search for answers. You may need to compare and contrast features or characteristics. You probably will need to synthesize or integrate by bringing together separate aspects of a situation or topic.

You have probably used critical thinking in selecting a household appliance or a car, or in selecting your major field of study. By sharpening your critical thinking skills, you will make more confident and purposeful decisions about your future.

Brain Dominance

All of us can use critical thinking, although we may take different approaches. In the 1960s and 1970s, experiments performed on people whose two brain hemispheres were disconnected due to illness or accident showed that each side of the brain has distinct strengths. And just as most people are righthanded or lefthanded, people tend to favor one mode of thinking (left-brain or right-brain) over the other. Figure 3–3 provides a thumbnail sketch of each mode.

Certainly each of us has access to both left-brain and right-brain modes, and they function in a complementary way. For example, the right side of the brain is dominant when you are brainstorming alternatives, and the left side is dominant when you evaluate them. The question is, which mode do you favor? Review Figure 3–3, and make an educated guess about yourself.

This brief introduction to this topic is somewhat oversimplified, but anyone interested in learning, problem solving, and creativity needs to be aware of the performance of each mode of consciousness or perception. The mode in which we operate affects how we perceive the world, our

Left side of the brain	Right side of the brain
Word-oriented, verbal	Image-oriented, nonverbal
Analytical, logical	Grasping wholes
Sequential	Simultaneous
Deals with time	Deals with space
Responsible for verbal and mathematical functions	Responsible for spatial, artistic, musical, and bodily-kinesthetic functions
Remembers words and numbers	Remembers objects, people, places, music
Seat of reason	Seat of passion and dreams

Figure 3–3 Left-brain and right-brain characteristics

preferences in organization and time management, and our decision making.

SUMMARY

Now that you have been introduced to memory, learning modalities, multiple intelligences, extraction and internalization of information, retrieval of information, and critical thinking skills, it's time to choose activities that will allow you to practice and apply what you have learned.

INDIVIDUAL ACTIVITIES

1. As I Remember It

Purpose: To provide practice in recalling personal experiences, and to gain know-how regarding the use of cues.

Find a partner who will assist you for fifteen to twenty minutes. Instruct your partner to prompt you with at least eight statements, beginning each with the phrase "Tell me from your childhood about." Your partner should allow gaps in between each statement so you have time to respond. You should keep your eyes closed the whole time. The following are phrases your partner can use to complete the statement that prompts your memory:

    a rainy day
    your favorite pet
    a memorable smell
    a teacher
    your bedroom
    a favorite toy
    your favorite pair of shoes
    a birthday party
    a family trip
    a favorite relative
    a secret place

a family celebration
your favorite television program
a book or story
a favorite song

Write a paragraph about how cues allowed you to remember.

2. Sound Log[1]

Purpose: To increase your awareness of how your brain selectively receives and stores information from audio sources.

Sound accompanies us everywhere. In addition to environmental sound, we often program our own sounds with radio, television, and the like. Many of us wake up to a sound of our choosing and, as the day goes by, are exposed to layer upon layer of sounds. As a result, we have learned to hear selectively. This is a necessary and valuable skill that you may not realize you possess.

Keep a sound log of each different sound you hear. Begin the log when you wake up in the morning and end the log when you arrive at work or school. The intent is that you will have about an hour of listening in more than one environment. Record each sound in Figure 3–4 as you hear it.

a. How long was the given time, and how many total sounds did you hear?

Time	Sound 1	Sound 2	Sound 3	Sound 4

Figure 3–4 Sound log

[1] Minrose Quinn, "Our Mediated Environment," *Forum* (New York, NY: J. C. Penney Co., November 1982).

b. What sounds overlapped, requiring you to hear them all at once?

c. How many sounds were you hearing at the same time?

d. How many sounds could you really *listen to* at the same time?

3. Check Your Channels[2]

Purpose: To increase awareness of your personal preferences and skills for information input.

The words that we choose often refer to our input preferences—auditory, visual, or kinesthetic. For example, a person with an audio preference might show understanding by saying "I hear you."

1. To check your understanding of this concept, name the preference for each word listed in Figure 3–5. Write your anwers in the appropriate column in that figure.
2. Now monitor your own language for at least a day. Keep track of which of the words listed in Figure 3–5 you use by making hash marks next to those terms each time you use them. You may add

Word	Preference	Word	Preference	Word	Preference
Active		Dim View		Observe	
Announce		Discuss		Pressure	
Appear		Dream		Pronounce	
Boisterous		Feel		Scope	
Catch on		Firm		See	
Clarity		Foresee		Sketchy	
Concrete		Listen		Tongue-tied	

Figure 3–5 Checking channels

[2] Roger Bailey, "Neurolinguistics: Information Processing in the Human Biocomputer," *Forum* (New York, NY: J. C. Penney Co., November 1982).

words to the list if you discover other terms are prevalent in your vocabulary.

3. Into which of the three categories—auditory, visual, or kinesthetic—did the words you used most often fall? How about the words you used least often?

4. Changing Channels[3]

Purpose: To provide you with an opportunity to apply what you learned in Activity 3.

Effective communication depends upon understanding the input modalities and multiple intelligences of others around you and adapting your language and actions to meet their strengths.

Think of something you want or need, a project you want to try, a place you want to go, something you cannot achieve or acquire without the help of someone else (employer, employee, friend, spouse, child). Let's call that person an *enabler*. Now monitor the enabler's language to identify their probable input preferences, just as you did for yourself in Activity 3.

Next, devise a persuasive presentation using the enabler's mode, keeping in mind that the actions and form of delivery need to match the mode. In other words, use pictures or charts for the visual enabler, provide a hands-on demonstration for the kinesthetic, and supply sounds or music for the audio person.

After you have made your presentation, write in Figure 3–6 about your experience and what you have learned from it.

Figure 3–6 What I learned about changing channels

[3] Adapted from Roger Bailey, "Neurolinguistics: Information Processing in the Human Biocomputer," *Forum* (New York, NY: J. C. Penney Co., November, 1982).

5. Mapping for Memory and Comprehension

Purpose: To learn how to create a visual rather than a strictly verbal outline of a unit of information by mapping the components.

If you have ever diagrammed a sentence or created a flow chart, you have some understanding of mapping. There are three steps to this process:

1. Select the author's main idea.
2. Select the most important supporting information.
3. Add remaining details.

As you may have surmised, mapping requires judgment, conciseness, and organization. It also includes creativity as you design the map itself. Figure 3–7 provides an example of a map of *memory retrieval* that can be used as a guide to create a mind map of your own. (See section entitled "Memory Retrieval" earlier in this chapter.)

In examining Figure 3–7, do you agree that the two main points or topics of memory retrieval are recognition and recall? Do you see how the supporting information was diagrammed first, and then the details were added? Pictures or drawings, such as the one in this figure, can be very useful, especially for spatials.

Now it is your turn. Choose something that you want to learn, such as two or three pages of information from a text, manual, or class notes.

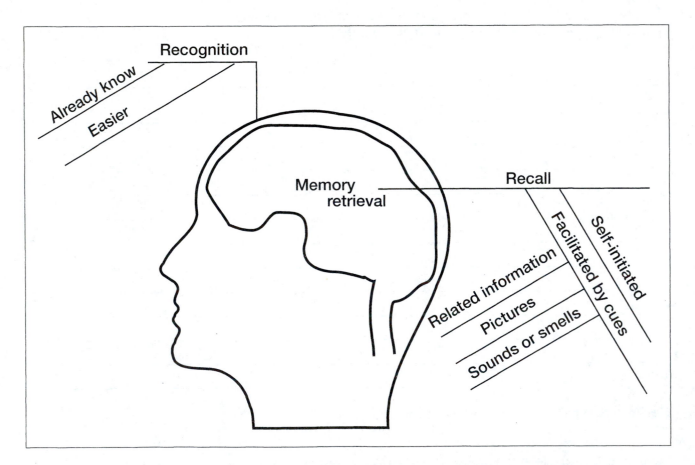

Figure 3–7 Mind map of memory retrieval

Figure 3–8 My mind map

Create a map of the information in the space provided in Figure 3–8. If you hand this into your teacher, include a copy of the actual text pages or class notes from which you drew your map, so that your know-how can be evaluated.

6. Flashy Flash Cards

Purpose: To create a learning tool that will be fun and interesting to use during repetition exercises.

There is no doubt that repetition is effective for learning symbols like vocabulary or the periodic table in chemistry. Those with strong linguistic skills may enjoy flash cards in their traditional form, which uses words, but those of you who are able to draw or who have good visual-spatial skills might find it productive to use pictures or nonverbal symbols. For example, in a history of art class, the artist's name could be on one side of a card and the famous painting on the other. Or in an applied art class, where you need to remember the colors of the spectrum, the colors could be painted on one side and the acronym *Roy G. Biv* (red, orange, yellow, green, blue, indigo, violet) on the other.

Now it's your turn. Create a minimum of five flash cards that are either in the traditional linguistic format or contain pictorial representations of the concepts you are learning. Use these cards to study, and

_____
_____
_____
_____
_____
_____
_____
_____
_____
_____
_____
_____
_____
_____
_____
_____
_____
_____
_____
_____

Figure 3–9 My experience using flash cards

then find someone to test your knowledge. Write about your experience with flash cards in the space provided in Figure 3–9.

7. Story Time

Purpose: To create an organizing tool for a short list that will be easy and interesting to use during repetition exercises.

One type of mnemonic is called narrative chaining. The premise is that you create a sentence or group of sentences that form a series of links to help you recall the items on your list. For example, you can remember the primary division of the animal kingdom by remembering the sentence "Kings Play Cards On Fairly Good Soft Velvet" (Kingdom, Phylum, Class, Order, Family, Genus, Species, Variety). With this technique, the first letter is often all it takes to trigger recall.

Using a narrative chain, create a tool that will help you remember a short list of things, perhaps the steps to the decision making process. Write your original list and your narrative chain in the space provided.

8. Repetition with a Twist

Purpose: To demonstrate how effective repetition can be as a way to enhance memory, especially when combined with personal learning strengths and preferences.

To many people, repetition sounds dull, boring, or tedious. Mental pictures of writing a sentence twenty-five times—over and over—come to mind, and we lose interest. Yet you probably used repetition to learn the Pledge of Allegiance, multiplication tables, and the words to popular songs. Clearly, repetition works. To make it more fun and easier to internalize, what we need to do is tie the data to a personal strength, such as music or athletics. In other words, you can use your dominant multiple intelligence for internalization.

Identify a chunk of material that you need to recall in the future. It might be information from your textbook for a test, something related to work, or a personal interest. Organize the material in a way that is meaningful to you, such as an outline, mind map, or flash cards. The trick to this process is to recite the information *out loud* while you are listening to compatible instrumental music or while you are physically active, such as walking, jogging, using a treadmill. Your musical or bodily-kinesthetic skills will put you on the fast track to learning and will make the process more enjoyable.

Describe the results of this activity in the following space. You may also want to demonstrate to class members what you did, providing a testimonial for the effectiveness of this strategy.

What I did was _____

_____

_____

What I liked about it was _____

_____

_____

It reminded me that _____

_____

_____

Next time I will _____

_____

_____

9. Extraction and Internalization

Purpose: To create an opportunity to practice learning utilizing your dominant extraction and internalization modes.

Determine your dominant mode for extraction (linguistic, logical, or spatial) and your dominant mode for internalization (musical, bodily-kinesthetic, intrapersonal, or interpersonal).

Then select one appropriate extraction activity and one appropriate internalization activity.

Use these activities to learn something new. For example, perhaps you need to prepare to write and present a speech, or take a quiz or a test. Prepare for the task by using an activity that suits your dominant mode for extraction and internalization. Provide documentation that you did so. Such documentation might be the extraction tool you created, such as an outline, mind map, or flash cards. Internalization documentation might be a testimonial note from your study buddy or a picture of yourself studying to teaching others.

How did it feel to use an activity that really suits you?

What did you think of this exercise?

10. Personality as a Clue to Learning

Purpose: To take an abbreviated assessment of your personality, likes, and dislikes in order to provide more knowledge about your preferred learning style.

There are several assessment instruments that are available through school counselors to determine personal temperament and learning style. One tool frequently used is the Myers-Briggs Type Indicator (MBTI). An abbreviated version has been created called *True Colors*. By taking this assessment, you will have some insight into your preferred learning style. Follow the process described in Figure 3–10 (on page 71).

You should now have four scores, each matched to a color. By plotting them on the Color Wheel provided in Figure 3–11 (on page 73), you will get a better picture of yourself. This information can help you improve interpersonal relationships and choose a career. It also provides direction for your preferred learning style. Those of you with the highest score in *orange* tend to be imaginative, adventuresome, and fast-paced. Many "oranges" favor visual or kinesthetic input, spatial extraction, and kinesthetic or interpersonal internalization. *Golds* are systematic, organized, structured, and detailed. Many golds seem to favor kinesthetic input, logical-mathematical extraction, and intrapersonal internalization. *Blues* are sociable, harmonious, and adaptable. They might prefer audio input, linguistic extraction, and musical or interpersonal internalization. *Greens* are theoretical, analytical, and precise. They are inclined to prefer visual input, logical-mathematical extraction, and kinesthetic or interpersonal internalization.

If you are interested in a more detailed assessment, or for further information on the True Colors program, contact your school counselor or True Colors directly (see address and phone number in Figure 3–10).

Step 1: Rank each of the following four paragraphs from most like you (4) to least like you (1). If two describe you equally well, assign the same number twice.

a. I need to feel unique and authentic. I look to contribute, to encourage, and to care. I value integrity and unity in relationships. I am a natural romantic, a poet, and a nurturer.

Score: ☐

Step 2: Rate each of the following words according to how well it describes you: 3 = a lot, 2 = somewhat, 1 = very little.

a. warm ☐

   compassionate ☐

   sympathetic ☐

   enthusiastic ☐

   idealistic ☐

   sincere ☐

   flexible ☐

   harmonious ☐

   romantic ☐

   imaginative ☐

   Score: ☐

Grand Total
☐
Blue

b. I act on a moment's notice. I consider life as a game, here and now. I need fun, variety, stimulation, and excitement. I value skill, resourcefulness, and courage. I am a natural trouble-shooter, a performer, and a competitor.

Score: ☐

b. spontaneous ☐

   impulsive ☐

   physical ☐

   immediate ☐

   bold ☐

   optimistic ☐

   generous ☐

   charming ☐

   energetic ☐

   adventurous ☐

   Score: ☐

Grand Total
☐
Orange

Source: Courtesy of True Colors, 30812 S. Pacific Coast Highway, Laguna Beach, CA 92677, 888-558-2577.

Figure 3–10 Learning styles and personality types

c. I seek knowledge and understanding. I live life by my own standards. I need explanations and answers. I value intelligence, insight, fairness, and justice. I am a natural nonconformist, a visionary, and a problem-solver.

Score: ☐

c. curious ☐

logical ☐

calm ☐

independent ☐

inventive ☐

analytical ☐

perfectionist ☐

rational ☐

abstract ☐

hypothetical ☐

Score: ☐

Grand Total ☐

Green

d. I need to follow rules and respect authority. I have a strong sense of what is right and wrong in life. I need to be useful and to belong. I value home, family, and tradition. I am a natural preserver, a parent, and a helper.

Score: ☐

d. loyal ☐

dependable ☐

prepared ☐

thorough ☐

sensible ☐

punctual ☐

stable ☐

caring ☐

concrete ☐

faithful ☐

Score: ☐

Grand Total ☐

Gold

Step 3: Add your scores in each section from Step 1 and Step 2 and place the number in the box provided. Your highest total score indicates your strongest personality type and affects your learning preferences. Your second highest total score is your secondary style and is also important. The lowest score is least like you.

Plot your scores on the color wheel provided in Figure 3–11, using the appropriate colored pens or pencils.

Figure 3–10 Learning styles and personality types (cont'd)

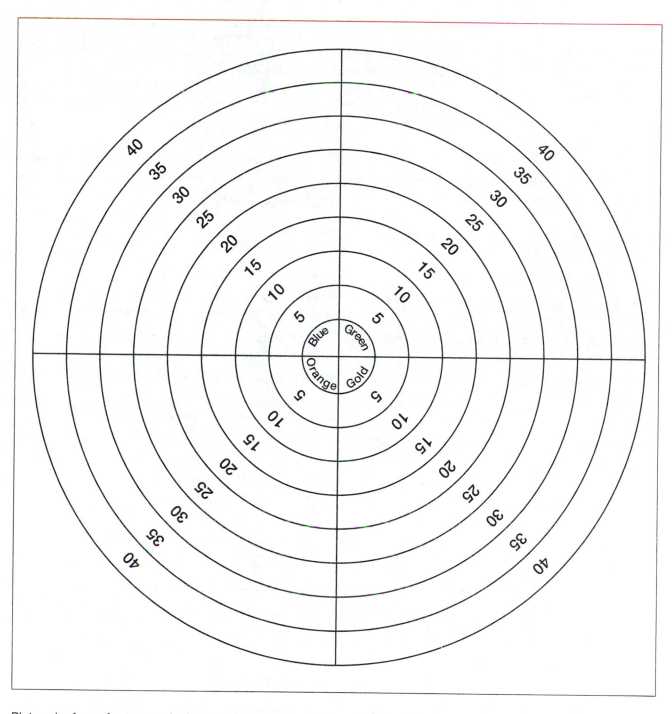

Plot each of your four scores in the appropriate section of the color wheel. Color the wheel with the appropriate colored pencils or markers.

Figure 3–11 My color wheel

11. Make It Left and Right in Your Life

Purpose: To explore the concept of left-brain and right-brain thinking, and to encourage greater use of the less dominant mode.

More often than not I probably use my _____ brain.

Now, from the list in Figure 3–12, select at least one activity from your *nondominant* mode. As you complete the activity, remember that it may feel awkward at first, like writing with your opposite hand. Stick with it, regardless of any such feeling.

Now, move to your more dominant mode and summarize how this experience felt. You can do this with words, pictures, numbers, or even sounds. Record your response in Figure 3–13.

Left-brain skill

Make a sequential list of everything you need to do today and follow it.

Complete a crossword puzzle.

Evaluate a recent decision, listing positive and negative results.

Pick out two chairs and make a list of their differences.

Use the decision-making process to solve a problem.

Right-brain skill

Name three or four ways that a cat and a refrigerator are alike.

Follow a hunch or your intuition.

Find a simple line drawing, turn it upside down, and draw it thinking only about shapes.

Compare the meaning of life to a particular food and explain the similarities.

Do something out of order, or spontaneously.

Figure 3–12 Left-brain and right-brain skills

Figure 3–13 Left and right: What I did and how it felt

12. The News and Critical Thinking

Purpose: To use critical thinking skills to analyze the presentation of one single event.

Select a current news event that interests you and that has been broadly covered. Briefly describe the event.

News event: _____

_____

Now compare and contrast the treatment and coverage of that event by *four* forms of media: your favorite television news program, the radio station that you use to get the news, a newspaper, and a news magazine. Use Figure 3–14 to record the data.

Summarize briefly how each form of media handled the facts.

How did the actors or announcers, the lighting and camera angles, the ink and paper influence your understanding of this event?

How did the opinions expressed influence your understanding of this event?

Source	Length	Placement	Facts	Opinions	Other comments
Television					
Radio					
Newspaper					
News magazine					
Other					

Figure 3–14 Media data collection

What conclusions did you draw from this exercise?

13. The Spot Quiz

Purpose: To critically view a television commercial and analyze some of the processes used that could influence decision making.

Watch a television commercial for a product or service or one from an organization promoting an idea. Then analyze it by answering the following questions.

What were the attention-getting strategies used?

What was said or what action was shown to stimulate desire?

Was there a sense of urgency portrayed? If so, how?

Who was the target customer?

What response was hoped for? (*Hint:* Commercials usually urge you to buy something but sometimes try to influence your opinion.)

What did this experience teach you?

14. Comparing the Cost of Convenience[4]

Purpose: To evaluate allocation of resources as a way of practicing critical thinking skills, particularly comparing and contrasting.

Individuals and families need to determine which tasks they will do themselves and which ones they will pay others to do. This is one part of deciding how to use household resources. Your exercise is to select a service, such as lawn care, house cleaning, child care, or car washing. Compare the cost of doing the task yourself with the cost of buying the service. Use the form provided.

Service compared: _____

_____

Description of the service: _____

_____

Do it yourself:

a. How long does it take you to accomplish the task? When do you usually do it?

b. What costs are involved?

c. What equipment is needed?

d. Are you satisfied with the results when you do the task yourself?

Professional service:

a. Who would you pay to do the service?

b. How would you locate this person or company?

c. What would be the cost for the service?

d. What would be included?

e. How would the results compare with those you get when you do the task yourself?

[4] Adapted from Lynn Miller, "Cost of Convenience," *SCANS: Teaching Life Management in California Community Colleges* (Sacramento, CA: Chancellor's Office, California Community Colleges, June 1996).

Evaluation: What are your conclusions? Will you do the task next time or look for outside professional help? Why? _____

_____

_____

_____

_____

_____

15. My Journal

Purpose: To reflect upon your strong personal intelligences and modalities and how they can lead you to future success.

Consider what you have learned about memory, learning modalities, multiple intelligences, and critical thinking. Comment in your journal about past experiences with these capacities. Forecast how you will be able to use this information about yourself to reach goals and turn dreams into reality in the future.

EXPAND YOUR LEARNING

Cameron, Julia. *The Artist's Way: A Spiritual Path to Higher Creativity.* New York, NY: G. P. Putnam's Sons, 1992.

Folger, Janet, and Lynn Stern. *Improving Your Memory.* Baltimore, MD: The Johns Hopkins University Press, 1994.

Keirsey, David, and Marilyn Bates. *Please Understand Me.* Del Mar, CA: Prometheus Nemesis Book Co., 1978. Discusses the Myers-Briggs Type Indicator assessment and contains a full explanation of the theory and sample text.

Ornstein, Robert. *The Right Mind: Making Sense of the Hemispheres.* Orlando, FL: Harcourt, Brace & Co., 1997.

von Oech, Roger. *A Whack on the Side of the Head: How You Can Be More Creative.* New York, NY: Warner Books, Inc., 1990.

GROUP ACTIVITIES

1. Mapping for Memory and Comprehension

Purpose: To learn how to create a visual rather than a strictly verbal outline of a unit of information by mapping the components. This is like Individual Activity 5 but is performed in a group of two or three.

If you have ever diagrammed a sentence or created a flow chart, you have some understanding of mapping. There are three steps to this process:

1. Select the author's main idea.
2. Select the most important supporting information.
3. Add remaining details.

As you may have surmised, this process requires judgment, conciseness, and organization. It also includes creativity as you design the map itself. Take a look at the map of memory retrieval provided in Figure 3–7. Use that map as a guide in creating your group mind map.

Now, as a group, choose something that you want to learn, such as two or three pages of information from this text. Create a map of it in the space provided in Figure 3–15. If you hand this into your teacher, indicate the text pages from which you drew your map, so that your know-how can be evaluated.

Figure 3–15 Our group mind map

2. Thinking About Debit Cards

Purpose: To use your critical thinking skills in a group to determine the advantages and disadvantages of a combination ATM/debit card, and then to decide if it is a good practice for you and your family.

The goal of this exercise is to gather information about electronic funds transfer and to determine how you feel about these services. Electronic funds transfer includes using (1) a card to obtain cash and make deposits at an automated teller machine, (2) a debit card to make purchases at grocery stores and gas stations, and (3) automatic bill paying.

First, answer the following questions based on your current knowledge. Then, compare notes with others in the group to expand your information.

Which forms of electronic funds transfer have you used?

What do you like about using these services?

What don't you like about using these services?

What do you know about the safety rules and features of a debit card?

Make a list of advantages and disadvantages to electronic funds transfers.

How do you feel about privacy issues related to these services?

What recommendations do you have for anyone shopping for electronic funds transfer services?

As a group, identify which critical thinking skills you used to perform this exercise and record them here: _____

_____

_____

_____

_____

_____

Write about whether you think a debit card is a good idea for your family, and why or why not: _____

_____

_____

_____

_____

_____

Chapter 4

Improving Your Study Skills

As you have previously seen, you are the primary member of a learning system. In the last chapter, you discovered more about your personal resources. In this chapter, we will look at your environment, that is, where you study, and at the procedures or organization that you use when you study. We will also explore the human resources available to you from friends, family, and your school. Thus, the goal of this chapter is to analyze your personal learning system in order to enhance your results, so that you improve your studying and learn in an easier and more comfortable fashion.

THE "GIVENS" IN THE SYSTEM

In any system there are a number of assumptions, or **givens**. One is that change is constant, and another is that there is increasing complexity as a system develops. You probably understand and accept the former, so let's consider the latter.

When you were a child, you learned the names of colors, the sequence of numbers, and the alphabet. As time went on, you were expected to know how to select and mix colors, solve mathematical problems, and write grammatically correct sentences. Now your course work is even more complex, on a much higher order of thinking.

Your life is more complex as well, since you must meet your economic needs, fulfill family obligations, and still find time to study. Learning is not always easy or comfortable, but being clear about your goals can help you remain focused. So, what is your ultimate goal with learning? Is it to pass a class and earn a grade? Or is it to expand your ability to think for yourself and improve your life? Which is a "given" for you?

Even though certain required courses may bore you or seem irrelevant, the act of thinking about the information and mulling over the problems is worth the effort. It's like exercising your brain muscles. How well you do in any course depends on your attitude and method of study. Learning may at times be frustrating, and even intimidating, yet by making the effort you will gain enrichment and rewards.

STUDYING ENVIRONMENT

Setting aside the *ideal* space may be only a dream if you share your household with several other people. Regardless, it is important to find a space where you can stay alert and concentrate. And you need access to this place frequently, as studying in the same place each time increases learning. This may entail going to a library or study center, or it may mean making some changes at home. It is up to you to brainstorm until you have a place that you can use regularly with success.

Since the study site may not be perfect, think about ways that you can overcome its limitations. If there are visual distractions, how can they be reduced? Removing a television, screening off an area, or arranging the furniture so that your back faces the distraction are all possibilities.

Noise is often an issue, whether too much or too little of it. Some people, particularly those with strong musical or bodily-kinesthetic capacities, might work better with background sound or instrumental music. Use of headphones allows you to create such an environment without disturbing others. For the noisy environment, closing a door or wearing earplugs may be a solution. If the noise comes from interruptions, setting up an "open door" policy only at certain times may work. Have a talk with friends and family, let them know when you will be available, and ask for their cooperation in not disturbing you at other times. Use of an answering machine can also be beneficial.

Comfortable furniture suited to your body size and height can make studying easier and less tiring. Be sure to have your computer keyboard lower than a writing surface to avoid wrist pain and discomfort. And select a light suited to the task, whether it be reading, writing, or drawing.

STUDYING PROCEDURES

All systems have procedures and organization. Study procedures include the use of study aids and selected study techniques and scheduling time. If thoughtfully chosen, the procedures or routines that you have in regard to study can allow you to learn faster.

Study Aids

Study aids include items such as dictionaries, manuals, and office supplies. They also include the type of study aids discussed in Chapter 3 such as mind maps, flash cards, and flow charts. These could be self-created, from a text or study guide, found on the Internet, or supplied by your instructor. You should have all of your study aids conveniently located in your study environment.

Study Schedule

There are many factors that can lead to your success as a student, but learning to plan and organize your study schedule is one of the most important. This means setting priorities, and then planning a study routine that includes choosing a study environment and selecting regular times to study.

Set Priorities. Let's consider two examples. The student who is just out of high school is certainly very busy with assignments and, perhaps, a part-time job. A major difference from earlier in life is that young high school graduates are now much more on their own. No one watches to see if assignments have been read, homework turned in, or even if they have been attending class. All of this has become the student's personal responsibility.

For adults who have been out of school for some time, there is an equally challenging situation. Your schedule may already have been full with your job, parenting, chauffeuring children, and household maintenance. You have to plan for events of a personal significance, such as family holidays. School obligations will compete with all these commitments, and all have an urgency about them.

So, as you can see, all students, regardless of age or lifestyle, need to prioritize. No matter what, everyone has 168 hours in a week. The challenge is to use this time most effectively, and to diminish or eliminate less important activities. These skills will prove to be useful for a lifetime.

The lack of student success in scheduling is often caused by underestimating the amount of time necessary to complete assignments, read textbooks, and finish projects. A widely accepted formula is to reserve two hours of study time for every hour of course time per week. Take a moment to add these hours up *now* according to your current commitments. Then plan on completing at least one of the scheduling activities at the end of this chapter.

Establish a Study Routine. If you select the same environment and have a regular study schedule, your mind will recognize that it's time to learn and will concentrate faster. In other words, if it is Tuesday night after dinner and you are in your study space, you will be able to get down to business faster if this is a routine for you.

Your study environment should suit your personal study style and should be a place where you can easily concentrate. Some people will find the perfect spot at home. For others, it might be the school or public library. A library can be free of distractions such as phone calls or the temptations of leisure activities like the television. Parents of young children may find it well worth paying for child care so that they can complete assignments without interruptions. Individual Activity 1 focuses on evaluating and organizing a study space.

Having a regular study time will also diminish the number of interruptions, as people will be expecting you to be unavailable to them. They will be expecting a "closed door" at this time. As you develop the habit of regular studying, it will become easier. You will fined that it is more effective than cramming, since it allows opportunities for repetition and organization of the material to be learned.

It is best to initially create your schedule at the beginning of the term. Use a large monthly calendar and plot out deadlines such as tests, mid-terms, projects, and papers. As you plan your study time each week, set short-term goals. Break big assignments into smaller pieces and set a completion time. Write the short-term deadlines on your calendar as well. Use of a daily "To Do" list can also be helpful. The list could include family or community obligations as well as school tasks.

As you plan your schedule, be sure to be realistic and allow enough time for friends, family, and sleep. Yes, sleep! Because of the multiple demands on time and energy, many people are sleep-deprived. Although there are variations, scientists have discovered that most adults need eight and one-quarter hours of sleep each night. If you are still in your teens, you may need as much as nine and one-half hours of sleep. When you get less sleep, your cognitive functioning and emotional stability decrease. In other words, your brain power diminishes and you get irritable with an inadequate amount of sleep.

When to schedule study time is dependent upon your preferences and lifestyle. Some of you will prefer to study late at night and others early in the morning. People who have a peak of energy in late evening are nicknamed "owls," while those who burst into activity in the morning are called "larks."

Study Techniques

There is more to studying than reading the text from front to back. Actually, reading a text front to back may not be the best way to read it. Active reading involves previewing sections before reading them by looking at chapter headings, lists of key terms, and questions at the end of chapters. Then the reader needs to ask his or her own questions. What do I know about this information? Why was this assigned? What are two or three key topics? Finally it's time for reading and review. This process can be remembered by using the acronym PQR for Preview, Question, Review or SQ3R for Survey, Question, Read, Recite, Review. In either case, you can see that active reading is involved.

Many students find reading aloud increases concentration and understanding. Take notes while you read. The notes can be an outline, a list of key terms and concepts, or a mind map. Jot down any questions you have about the material. If there are questions at the end of the section, write out the answers. All of this requires you to be active, uses more of your senses, and involves more of your intelligences. And, as you have already learned, this is how information gets into long-term memory and becomes available for retrieval later.

By using appropriate techniques and materials, learning will be easier and more fun, and retention will increase. If the learning modality (visual, audio, kinesthetic) used most often in a class does not match yours, you may need to create study tools that match your learning modality.

Each modality benefits from a particular group of study tools. Visual learners often learn best with written directions, note taking, dictionaries, card files, flash cards with words or pictures, puzzles, and charts. Audio learners prefer listening, reading aloud, talking about information, audiotapes, music, puppet conversations, and poetry. Kinesthetic learners prefer tactile experiences, demonstration tasks, role plays, art, math manipulatives, pantomime, and movement activities. Although you may not be able to control all the input, be creative and get involved.

RESOURCES AROUND YOU

Many of us have a family member or friend that encourages our learning. If you do, be grateful and accept their encouragement and offers of assistance. Make a point of surrounding yourself with those who support you and your endeavors.

Your school also provides many resources. Get to know your teachers and counselors. Take an orientation tour of your library. This can be especially important if you are unfamiliar with the computerized information retrieval systems used in most of them today. At most schools, there is a space or laboratory that provides computers for word processing and access to the Internet. Investigate services provided by the learning assistance or tutoring center, career center, transfer center, and placement office.

INDIVIDUAL ACTIVITIES

1. Organizing Your Study Space

Purpose: To analyze the space where you currently study, and to improve it.

Changes in the environment can enhance or diminish output. Your task is to analyze your study environment so that changes can be made that will increase your effectiveness as a learner. Evaluate the visual distractions, noise and interruptions, furniture and supplies in the space you have selected. Summarize your findings in the space provided.

My study location is: _____

- Visual distractions

_____

_____

_____

- Noise situation

_____

_____

_____

- Furniture and lighting

_____

_____

_____

- Supplies

_____

_____

_____

What will you change or add to your environment? _____

_____

_____

_____

After two weeks, re-evaluate your study space to adjust it further if needed.

2. Study Schedule

Purpose: To establish specific times each week that you will study.

Review commitments for classroom time, work, and sleep. Mark these commitments on the form labeled "A Typical Week," found in Figure 4–1. Then determine how many hours each week you need to devote to study. Do you recall that you will need two hours for every hour in class? Plan for these hours to occur at regular intervals across the week, and mark them on the "A Typical Week" form. You still need time for eating, personal hygiene, driving or commuting, and some time for social or leisure activities would probably be welcomed.

A TYPICAL WEEK							
	Monday	**Tuesday**	**Wednesday**	**Thursday**	**Friday**	**Saturday**	**Sunday**
AM 5							
6							
7							
8							
9							
10							
11							
PM/Noon 12							
1							
2							
3							
4							
5							
6							
7							
8							
9							
10							
11							
AM 12							
1							
2							
3							
4							

Figure 4–1 A typical week

1. The degree to which I followed my schedule was (check one)

    ❑ poor ❑ fair ❑ good ❑ excellent

2. The easiest part to follow was _____

    _____

    _____

3. The things I would change about my schedule are _____

    _____

    _____

4. Answer Yes or No to the following:

    As a result of scheduling my time for a week,

    I was more effective in the use of my study time. _____

    my studying was more successful. _____

    my studying was more enjoyable. _____

    I felt that I had more free time. _____

5. Other comments: _____

    _____

    _____

    _____

    _____

    _____

    _____

Figure 4–2 Evaluation of my one-week schedule

Follow your study schedule for one week. Review it for its effectiveness and appropriateness by answering the evaluation questions found in Figure 4–2.

3. Adjusted Study Schedule

Purpose: To learn from your experience and create an adjusted study schedule.

After one week of using a new schedule, it is likely that some adjustments will be necessary. Create an adjusted schedule that incorporates your ideas from Activity 2. Follow the schedule for two weeks. Then describe in Figure 4–3 the results of this improvement to your learning system.

_____
_____
_____
_____
_____
_____
_____
_____
_____
_____
_____
_____
_____
_____
_____
_____

Figure 4–3 Summary of improvements to my personal study schedule

4. Setting Short-Term Goals for Learning

Purpose: To set realistic short-term goals for learning over the next few months.

A key to avoiding procrastination and successfully reaching goals is to divide large tasks into small ones. Begin by gathering together your records of due dates for major projects and exams. These are typically announced in the first few days of school, perhaps on a course outline or assignment sheet.

Create a project plan for each assignment. Figure 4–4 provides an incomplete example to demonstrate how the format works.

Now, create a project plan for one of your classes that will cover at least the next three weeks. Write your plan in Figure 4–5. Then follow that plan.

Did breaking the tasks into smaller pieces help you to feel better about studying?

Were you able to meet the deadlines?

Course title	Project	Action	Start	Complete
Life Management	*Exam 1*	*Read Ch. 1*	*9/10*	*9/10*
		Review and recite—Ch. 1 flash cards	*9/14*	*9/15*
		Read Ch. 2		

Figure 4–4 Incomplete example of a project plan

Course title	Project	Action	Start	Complete

Figure 4–5 Project plan form

Will you continue to use this process?

Summarize your experience of using a project plan.

5. Establish an Advisory Committee

Purpose: To create a support group who will encourage, advise, and help you accomplish your educational goals.

Identify four or five people whom you trust and respect and who want you to succeed in your educational goals. Ask them to be your Advisory Committee, to share their human resources so that you might more easily reach your goal. Bring them together, share your feelings and concerns with them, and ask them if they are willing to help and, if so, what they are willing to do.

Make sure that each Advisory Committee member has a distinct task or contribution. They may, for example, take over one of your chores, monitor the noise while you study, assist with child care, or provide encouraging words.

After four or five weeks, call your Advisory Committee members together. Report to them about your progress and ask for their comments and reactions. Seek their continuing support and encouragement.

6. Affirmations to Enhance Learning

Purpose: To create positive affirmations that are related to learning and education.

As you know, affirmations can be a powerful tool to maintain motivation and encourage success. Your task is to write five affirmations related to studying and three related to test taking. Write them in Figure 4–6.

Figure 4–6 Learning affirmations

_____

_____

_____

_____

_____

_____

_____

_____

_____

_____

_____

_____

_____

_____

_____

_____

Figure 4–7 Results of using affirmations

Use your affirmations for two weeks, saying them out loud several times a day. Then write a paragraph about the results in Figure 4–7.

7. Experiment with a Study Technique

Purpose: To try a study technique that is new to you, such as mind-mapping, PQR or SQ3R, flash cards, or outlining.

Results come from application of knowledge. This activity asks you to select one study technique that is new to you and commit yourself to using it in all your courses for the next three weeks.

The technique I have selected is: _____

_____

I began using it on _____

I've been using it in the following courses: _____

_____

_____

As a result, _____

_____

_____

_____

_____

Skills needed	My current skill level	My desired skill level

Figure 4–8 Analysis of current skills

8. Evaluation of Current Skills

Purpose: To identify the skills you currently possess that can contribute to your school and career success, and to determine what skills you need to develop.

Throughout your life you have been developing basic skills such as reading, writing, math, listening, and speaking. You have developed abilities to make decisions, solve problems, think creatively, visualize, and apply critical thinking. You have also gained competencies that are valued in the workplace. These include managing resources (time, money, equipment, and people) and interpersonal skills (including leadership and cooperating as a member of a team). You have developed some research skills and may know how to use a computer. And you know something about systems and technology (tools, machines, and audiovisual equipment).

You may have recognized this description of skills from the discussion of SCANS competencies in Chapter 1. Your task is to identify eight specific skills that are needed on your current job (or the next job you would like to have), identify your level of competency in those skills, and then prescribe a new skill level for yourself. Write your ideas in Figure 4–8.

9. Funny Studies

Purpose: To use humor to examine how students study, and to use that examination as a basis for improving your own study habits.

Collect a series of cartoons, comics, and jokes that relate to study habits. Organize them by common themes or issues, and make a list of those issues. For example, they might focus on procrastination, the dog eating the homework, or falling asleep in class. In Figure 4–9, write one or two suggestions that could improve each situation.

Theme or issue	Suggestion for improvement

Figure 4–9 Funny studies

10. Lifesavers: Buoy Up Your Study Habits[1]

Purpose: To demonstrate that our brain muscle needs to be warmed up before use, just like our body muscles.

It usually takes a few minutes to have our brain working at full capacity and to have our concentration focused on a task. One way to accomplish this is through brain warm-ups such as creating metaphors or solving puzzles. So, here's your first one. Imagine a roll of Lifesavers. In Figure 4–10, record all the ways that Lifesavers are like life. One example has been provided for you.

Other similes might be used in creating metaphors, such as: life is like fishing, life is like surfing, life is like a banana, life is like eating a grapefruit. Or you might begin from the other direction: Eating a fine dinner is like . . ., raising a child is like . . ., learning to drive is like. . . .

Lifesavers are like life because

life and Lifesavers are both sweet.

Figure 4–10 Lifesavers are like life because . . .

---

[1] Adapted from Mary Nelson, "Lifesavers," *SCANS: Teaching Life Management in California Community Colleges* (Sacramento, CA: Chancellor's Office, California Community Colleges, June 1996).

11. Goldilocks[2]

Purpose: To learn to distinguish higher level thinking so that you will more consciously use these levels when studying.

As noted in Chapter 3, well-developed critical thinking skills are essential. The purpose of this assignment is to apply progressively higher levels of thinking to a familiar story. This exercise is based on a classification of thinking called Bloom's Taxonomy that identifies six levels of knowledge. Beginning with the most fundamental level, they are: knowledge, comprehension, application, analysis, synthesis, and evaluation. You might recall that your learning matrix is based upon this classification system.

Read the story of *Goldilocks and the Three Bears,* and then answer the following:

Knowledge: Recall the items used by Goldilocks in the three bears' house.

Comprehension: Explain why Goldilocks liked Baby Bear's chair best.

Application: Specify what Goldilocks would use if she came into your house.

Analysis: Compare the story to reality. What incidents could not have happened?

Synthesis: Propose how the story would be different if it were *Goldilocks and the Three Fishes.*

[2] Adapted from Sandi Anderson, "Bloom's Taxonomy and Maslow, Goldilocks and the Three Bears," *SCANS: Teaching Life Management in California Community Colleges* (Sacramento, CA: Chancellor's Office, California Community Colleges, June 1996).

Evaluation: Judge whether Goldilocks was bad or good, and defend your opinion.

Now, gather together with other students who did this activity and share your responses. See if you can reach consensus.

12. Polishing Your Research Skills

Purpose: To improve your skills at finding current information on a topic that interests you.

The traditional search method for finding current information on a topic is to look through the *Reader's Guide to Periodicals.* Your task is to pick a topic, any topic, whether it relates to this class or another class, or is just personally interesting to you. Then visit your school or public library and find two articles via the traditional search mode. It's very likely that you will start with a keyboard and computer terminal, and then find a hard copy of the periodical stored somewhere in the library.

Next, find two more articles on the same topic by using the Internet. You might have access to the Internet at home. If not, check with your teacher, as many campuses and communities now provide access in computer labs or libraries. When you have finished, discuss what type of information seems to be available from the two research sources. Then, in Figure 4–11, compare and contrast these two methods and indicate when each might be preferable.

Figure 4–11 Current topic—Compare and contrast two methods of research

13. Career Analysis[3]

Purpose: To provide a framework for analyzing a career field.

You may already have a career in mind. If not, be sure to participate in the activities in the Explorations section, Planning Your Education, that follows this chapter. If you *do* have a career in mind, either your current or future one, it deserves to be carefully evaluated for its impact on your life and lifestyle.

Look at Figure 4–12, the Career Wheel. It graphically presents the factors that matter when a career is selected. Certainly some of these issues are more important to you than others. However, comment on each one of them in Figure 4–13 (on page 100), the Career Wheel Table.

14. Competency Matrix

Purpose: To review the Competency Matrix in the Appendix and rate your current knowledge and skills in regard to life management.

To this point, you have learned a lot about yourself. You have also expanded your knowledge of important skills such as goal setting, value clarification, decision making, and study skills. As you practice these skills, you will continue to expand your level of competency.

The intent of this activity is that you will evaluate your current level of competency. Then, as you continue to read and apply the knowledge presented in this workbook, you will re-evaluate your level.

Turn to the Appendix, review the matrix, and check off your current levels. Remember that many of these skills are desired by employers. The matrix can be the backbone of your proof of competency, and it can be fleshed out by your completed activities in this workbook.

EXPAND YOUR LEARNING

Botstein, Leon. *Jefferson's Children: Education and the Promise of American Culture.* New York, NY: Doubleday, 1997.
Pauk, Walter. *How to Study in College.* Boston, MA: Houghton Mifflin, 1996.

GROUP ACTIVITIES

1. Career Center Visitation

Purpose: To visit the campus career center with a group of students to learn to use the various print and computer resources available.

Arrange for an appointment at your campus career center for yourself and fellow students. Ask for an orientation to the available services and a demonstration of the computer resources.

---

[3] Elizabeth Stark, "The Career Wheel," *SCANS: Teaching Life Management in California Community Colleges* (Sacramento, CA: Chancellor's Office, California Community Colleges, June 1996). Developed by Home Economics teachers for a California Department of Education project in the 1960s.

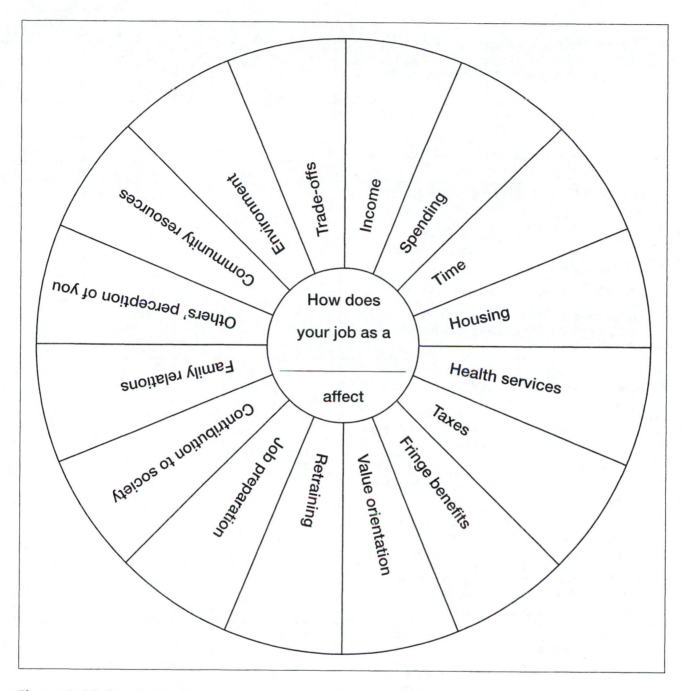

Figure 4–12 Career wheel

Then each student should identify one career area to research. Working together whenever the same career is selected, gather information and then complete Figure 4–14 (on page 101), the Career Search.

2. Establish a Student Support Team

Purpose: To create a support team of fellow students who will work together to encourage, advise, and help each other accomplish their educational goals.

Income: How much will you make? Will your income increase as you stay with the job? Can you support yourself and your family on this income?	
Spending: What are the costs of the job?	
Use of time: What will your schedule be? Will it vary? Will overtime be required? Will you need to take work home with you?	
Housing: Will you be required to live in a particular geographic area? Will you need space at home to work or entertain?	
Health: What are the health risks? Is health insurance provided?	
Taxes: In what income bracket will you be?	
Fringe benefits: What are the economic, social, and educational fringe benefits of the job? Who will pay for them?	
Value orientation: Is the job compatible with your values? Will the job clarify or alter your value system?	
Retraining: What are future projections for your job? Are there provisions for retraining?	
Job preparation: How long will it take you to prepare for this job? Where can you do that? What are the costs?	
Contribution to society: Does the job make a positive one? Does it improve the quality of life for yourself, your family, and society?	
Family relations: How does the job impact on your family life? On your home responsibilities? On your spouse's expectations?	
Others' perceptions: How will others regard you because of this job?	
Community resources: What community resources will you need as a result of the job? Are they available?	
Environment: What effects will your job have on the environment? What environmental resources will you consume because of this job?	
Trade-offs: After considering all of the above facts, what must you give up to have this job?	

Figure 4–13 Career wheel table

Career: _____

_____

_____

_____

Educational requirements: _____

_____

_____

_____

Personal qualifications: _____

_____

_____

_____

Job outlook and projections: _____

_____

_____

_____

_____

Likely employers: _____

_____

_____

_____

_____

Why are you interested in this career area? _____

_____

_____

_____

What resources were helpful in this search? _____

_____

_____

_____

Figure 4–14 Career search

Identify four or five fellow students who are willing to work together to enhance the scholastic success of everyone in the group. They do not all need to be enrolled in the same class. Bring them together to discuss their feelings and concerns about their education, particularly focusing on their needs this term.

Each member of the group needs to identify what assistance they need. It might be help with computers, encouragement to continue with school, sharing child care or transportation, or help with an assignment. Within the group, each member should volunteer help with one or more items. Everyone should keep a list of who agrees to do what. Be sure to keep the contributions balanced, so that one person is not overburdened. Remember, the object is to make being a student easier and more pleasant.

Plan to meet regularly to assist each other. Expect to be flexible, adapting as new needs arise. After three weeks, evaluate how effective the support team has been and determine what changes could make it better. Make a plan to implement those changes.

3. Evaluating Internet Sites

Purpose: To work with another person to learn how to evaluate the accuracy and validity of an Internet site.

Since anyone can create a Web page and can include whatever information they prefer, it is important to learn to evaluate the validity of the information. This activity asks you to find another person who is interested in a topic that also interests you.

Find a Web site on that topic by searching for key words or by asking a librarian for assistance. Then answer these four questions about the site.

1. Who mounted the information?
2. What special knowledge or credentials does the author have?
3. Does the site exhibit a bias or a slant?
4. When was the site last updated?

After you have answered the questions, develop a list of criteria that you will use in the future to evaluate a Web site. Compare your list to the one created by librarians at the University of Albany, SUNY. You can find that list at http://www.albany.edu/library/internet/evaluate.html.

Share your results of this activity with others in your group.

Explorations

Planning Your Education

Some people seem to decide on their career very early in life, while others struggle with the choice. Most of us know that if we do not feel happy and fulfilled with our work, the rest of our life won't be satisfactory either. This Explorations section focuses on assisting you in the selection of a career that will provide you with satisfaction, recognition, financial fulfillment, and a balanced life. This selection entails self-exploration—that is, determining what you like to do and your strengths and weaknesses, and matching this assessment to a career. Then occupational research can help you to discover the education and training required of that desired position. This process will allow you to select a major. Although some of you have already made these decisions, a quick review of this material is still valuable, as it can validate your choice. The second part of this section describes how to make an educational plan based on your major, which may lead to a degree, and how to transfer to another institution for those who wish to pursue more advanced work.

CLARIFYING YOUR VISION

As a child Melissa enjoyed collecting insects and bugs, seashells and autumn leaves. She loved learning about animals and plants, and she excelled in science, especially biology, in high school. She earned an Associates degree at the community college nearby, and then transferred to the state university as a microbiology major. Her goal is to be an entomologist.

Few of us have such a linear career search. Take Edward, for example. He graduated from high school feeling uncertain about his goals. Since he had little direction, he applied for a sales job at a small retail store near his home. He enjoyed the job, developed his sales skills, and soon was made store manager. Six years later he realized that he had gone as far as he could at the job without more education. Besides, he wasn't certain that he wanted to continue there. He was starting to feel restless and bored, and wanted more out of a career. He took a job selling bottled water to businesses, and although he increased his income, he still wasn't satisfied.

Like Edward, you may have found that decisions about education and jobs need to be made by the young, even while personalities and interests are still changing and developing. Many readers of this workbook can attest to the fact that we might be thirty-five or forty years old before we clarify our career vision. It is important to know that there is nothing wrong with being uncertain or slow to make a decision. However, it is very important to make a commitment to the process of career decision making, which includes clarifying your desires and researching the topic.

103

The purpose of this section is to provide a structure for that research and clarification. It is intended for those who are changing career direction as well as for those making their first career choice.

DETERMINING WHAT YOU WANT TO DO

Most people who read this workbook are attending a school or college. Now is the time to take advantage of the services offered by the assessment or counseling department, career center, and job placement center, available at most colleges for free or very low cost. Most schools offer personalized help to evaluate students' interests and research careers. Staff can also give you advice on shortcuts that will make planning easier. Make an appointment with a counselor or advisor and request tests on aptitude, interest, and personality. (You may have already begun that process as part of this unit.) Then make a follow-up appointment for interpretation, which is essential, since sometimes tests yield differing results. Create a file of test results and interpretations as part of this research.

Remember, though, that tests are limited in their ability to measure motivation, aspirations, and commitment. Also, they do not reflect work history, education, or life experience. All of these must be factored together as you continue with your self-appraisal.

The United States Department of Labor Dictionary of Occupational Titles lists over 20,000 job titles and descriptions. We could begin there to choose a career, but most of us would quickly tire or become bored with this process. A shortcut is to think about job titles as falling under two categories: field and function. Most of us recognize **fields**, such as law, health care, art, or business, that emphasize a major category of information. We are accustomed to hearing about fields and, in all likelihood, have organized our previous educational choices around fields. For example, the broad field of Human Services offers many job choices, depending upon an individual's interest and specialized training. Job titles in the field of Human Services include parole officer, social worker, recreation therapist, career or employment counselor, family services worker, financial services advisor, child care worker, and creative arts therapist. Becoming more familiar with the options in the field of your choice is an essential part of choosing a career.

A job's **function** is its major activity or responsibility. Cohen and De Oliveira, in *Getting to the Right Job,* identify six functions: sales, marketing, creative, production, finance, and administration. There are jobs in every function in each field. Your task is to select a function that most suits you and identify the various fields that appeal to you. Before pursuing these tasks, however, review the following descriptions of each function:

> *Sales:* Responsible for convincing people to buy a product or service, a person in sales must establish contact, pitch the product, close the sale, and follow up with customer support.
>
> *Marketing:* Responsible for defining the image of a product or service and formulating a sales strategy, the person in marketing might have duties that would include conducting market research, selecting pricing strategies and packaging, and planning advertising and promotion.
>
> *Creative:* Responsible for the initial creation of a product or service, a creative position might include writing (books, articles, songs,

legislation) or something three-dimensional (painting, use of tools, building a house).

Production: Responsible for generating a product or service, production duties include coordinating the purchase and delivery of raw materials, the actual manufacturing, and the distribution of the finished product.

Finance: Responsible for monetary matters, people in finance may be involved with borrowing, spending, counting, billing, and analyzing the results.

Administration: Responsible for expediting the mission and goals of the company, administrators perform tasks such as corresponding, recordkeeping, advising, negotiating, and arranging.

This is the big picture of the world of work. You have now learned about functions, and you have refreshed your memory regarding potential fields. Now it is time to gather information about your interests, skills, and preferences.

Assessing Fields and Functions

The first few activities are visionary in nature. Their purpose is to help you dream and to let your ideas soar. Begin by imagining your ideal job. Don't worry if your picture of it is a little fuzzy, and don't concern yourself with the realism of your vision. Concrete issues can come later.

In Figure Explorations 2–1, write a paragraph that describes the ideal job for you. No matter how difficult this is to imagine, write something about a job you would like.

Figure Explorations 2–1 My ideal job

In Figure Explorations 2–2, try to list ten tasks that are commonly part of the ideal job you've selected. The degree of clarity with which you view this job will be evident here. If you cannot do this part completely or easily, you will still have learned something of value, which is that you need more information.

Next brainstorm all the reasons your ideal job appeals to you. Be sure to include ideas such as "I will make a difference in someone's life" as well as "I will get to eat out on an expense account." Record your ideas in Figure Explorations 2–3.

1. _____
2. _____
3. _____
4. _____
5. _____
6. _____
7. _____
8. _____
9. _____
10. _____

Figure Explorations 2–2 Ten tasks

_____
_____
_____
_____
_____
_____
_____
_____
_____
_____

Figure Explorations 2–3 What I would like about my ideal job

It's time to analyze your job and to begin to see other job alternatives. Fill in the chart in Figure Explorations 2–4, categorizing your ideal job by title, field, and function. Refer back to Figures Explorations 2–1 and Explorations 2–2 if you need to do so.

Now, we will rearrange the chart in Figure Explorations 2–4 by moving the "Field" column so it appears first, followed by the "Function" column and then the "Job title" column. In Figure Explorations 2–5, write your chosen field opposite each function. If done correctly, your field will appear six times in the lefthand column. Then, search your memory banks for appropriate job titles to match your field and each of the six functions, and fill in those titles on the chart. Make up titles if necessary. Next, consider how appealing each job sounds to you and, using a rating scale of 1 to 10 (with 10 being the best), rate each job. You will use your results in just a minute. First, we will focus on alternative fields.

Rearrange the chart a second time by moving the "Function" column so it appears first, followed by the "Field" column and then the "Job title" column. In Figure Explorations 2–6, write the appropriate function of your ideal job on each line. If done correctly, your function will appear six times in the lefthand column.

Job title	Field	Function

Figure Explorations 2–4 My ideal job

Field	Function	Job title
	Sales	
	Marketing	
	Creative	
	Production	
	Finance	
	Administration	

Figure Explorations 2–5 Matching fields and choosing job titles

Function	Field	Job title

Figure Explorations 2–6 Matching functions, fields, and job titles

Now come up with a minimum of four fields in which you could perform the duties related to that function. For example, if marketing is the function, you could promote products in the fields of health care, art, publishing, sports, and so on. Next identify a job title for that field and function. For example, you might be an advertising director, public relations manager, and so on. Rate each job as you did before.

Which fields seem most interesting to you? Why?

Review all your lists to determine whether a specific function or a particular field is more interesting to you. If the function is your preference, you have the freedom to consider any number of fields. If a field interests you the most, then you need to match your skills and aptitudes to a particular function within that field.

Gathering More Information

Now it is time to look at jobs in detail. Use at least two of the strategies described below to clarify the responsibilities of two or three jobs that you have been considering.

1. Make a list of anyone you know who does the job. Be sure to ask friends, family, and teachers in case they know someone. Then set up several five- to ten-minute interviews with these people to hear about their tasks.

2. Watch a documentary film or read a biography about someone who has or had this job.

3. Read at least one book or watch a documentary film about the field that is your preference.

4. Read several articles in professional or trade journals and business publications about people who are doing the job you want.

5. Read several articles in professional or trade journals and business publications about the field and function that you prefer.

6. Look through the want ads to identify job titles that fit your field and function. Make a career ladder for the field.

7. Take an introductory class that focuses on your chosen field or function.

8. Volunteer at a local business or nonprofit organization that relates to the jobs that interest you.

9. Visit your transfer or career placement office to learn about the future demand for your proposed job.

10. Interview a recent graduate from your current school who has a career goal similar to yours.

11. Complete Individual Activity 13 in Chapter 4 regarding the Career Wheel.

After this research, you should be able to select a major based on your preferences for fields and functions. You should also know something about the career ladder you might follow.

MAKING AN EDUCATION PLAN

Some readers of this book already have a field and a function selected. You may even already know the specific job that you want. At any rate, all of you have a common goal—to get the job that will be appropriate to your needs and interests. It can be both expensive and time-consuming to change your mind about a career. If you have come this far and have not completed at least two of the activities in the preceding section, "Gathering More Information," go back and do that now.

You will need the catalog of the school where you are currently enrolled. This will provide you with the list of certificate and degree requirements, course titles, the units or credit hours, and descriptions. Review the section appropriate to your major as well as the section on General Education courses, which are classes required by most schools that are outside of your major. Check off the classes that you have already completed. Arrange to have transcripts from other schools sent to the Records Office so that you can receive full credit for previous coursework.

Make an appointment with a counselor or advisor to verify your selection of major and degree. They can help you sort through curriculum requirements and create a plan that will move you toward a timely graduation. If you plan to transfer, they can alert you to prerequisites specific to your major.

It is very important to plan in advance which courses you want to take each semester. At some schools, certain classes are offered infrequently, yet they are a prerequisite to other required classes. If you miss the class, you could get behind as much as a year. It is also essential that you be realistic about the number of courses you can take each term. Be sure to factor in enough time for study, work, and family.

Now you are ready to list the courses you will take, term by term, including any prerequisites. Use Figure Explorations 2–7 for that purpose.

Where to Transfer?

For those who wish to pursue advanced work, this is the perfect time to apply the decision-making process. You will need to set a deadline to select your preferred schools. Then you will want to identify alternatives by comparing your present school requirements for certificates or degrees to requirements at other campuses. Most students can eliminate

NAME

| Summer | Year | Units |
| Total |

| Fall | Year | Units |
| Total |

| Spring | Year | Units |
| Total |

| Summer | Year | Units |
| Total |

| Fall | Year | Units |
| Total |

| Spring | Year | Units |
| Total |

| Summer | Year | Units |
| Total |

| Fall | Year | Units |
| Total |

| Spring | Year | Units |
| Total |

| Summer | Year | Units |
| Total |

Key:

✓ = Course for Major

X = General Education Course

O = Elective Course

P = Pre-requisite

Major:

Transfer Institution:

Total Units ☐

Total Transfer Units ☐

Educational Advisor _____ Date _____

Comments _____

Figure Explorations 2–7 Education plan

some schools based on their size, location, or cost. Again, ask an advisor in your transfer or career center for help.

Gather information from various sources. Talk with as many people as possible, such as teachers, previous alumni, and members of advisory committees. Perhaps your school invites representatives from visiting colleges to your campus. Study the school catalogs and other written materials. Many schools have videos available in campus transfer centers. Plan to visit other colleges and talk with counselors and faculty there. Check for Web pages for the campus or department.

FINALIZING YOUR ACTION PLAN

Periodically you will need to review your progress and success. If you do not take the courses in the expected sequence, adjust your plan. If you plan to transfer, review your education plan to confirm that you have taken all the prerequisites and that you have completed the minimum number of transferable units. Be sure to meet all deadlines for application to the new institution. (You may be able to do this via the Internet.) Your advisor can help you with this evaluation.

During the term before completion, visit your advisor for a graduation review. This will confirm that the school records match your own expectations for course credit. In the final term, you may need to apply for graduation, arrange for transcripts to be sent, and other such requirements. Congratulations, you have completed a major goal!

EXPAND YOUR LEARNING

Bolles, Richard. *What Color Is Your Parachute?* Berkeley, CA: Ten Speed Press, 1991.

Cohen, Steve, and Paulo de Oliveira. *Getting to the Right Job: A Guide for College Graduates.* New York, NY: Workman Publishing, 1987.

Hartman, Kenneth E. *Internet Guide for College-Bound Students.* New York, NY: Guidance Publishing, 1997.

http://www.ca.gov/commerce/newecon/html. This Web site explores emerging industry clusters including telecommunications, health care, environmental technologies, entertainment, fashion, and manufacturing.

UNIT THREE
Developing Your Physical Potential

Chapter 5
Eating Well

Chapter 6
Staying Healthy

Explorations
Changing Habits: The Self-Change Model

Chapter 5

Eating Well

Eating well is a matter of knowing and applying nutritional information and utilizing food labels as an information source. This is an especially important area in which to apply decision-making skills. Readers who have already taken a course in nutrition will recognize the important role nutritional information plays in food selection. For the less informed, some nutrition basics are presented here.

Sometimes it might seem that we are preoccupied with food—buying it, eating it, and exercising or wishing it away. Food does deserve our attention, since it provides us with energy to keep our hearts pumping, our lungs breathing, and our bodies functioning in a normal healthy way. It also provides some people with a hobby, as in gourmet cooking, and it accounts for fifteen to twenty percent of family spending (groceries and eating out).

There is a growing concern about the one-third of the American adult population that is overweight, and their children who tend to take after them. By knowing about the nutritional value of food, we can begin to understand the research on weight and health, maximize our economic resources, and expand our human resources.

SIX ESSENTIAL NUTRIENTS

All foods contain one or more **nutrients**, major elements that nourish our bodies. There are six major nutrients: carbohydrates, protein, fat, vitamins, minerals, and water.

Carbohydrates provide energy for the body, particularly the brain and nervous system. Complex carbohydrates come from breads, cereals, and grain products. They provide fiber, which aids the digestive system. Simple carbohydrates are found in fruits and vegetables and all forms of sugar. Because sugar provides only simple carbohydrates with almost no other nutrients, it is considered the least desirable source.

Protein has many functions but is of primary importance for growth and maintenance of bodily systems, and for the repair of tissue. Major sources include meat, fish, poultry, beans, eggs, nuts, and dairy products. Insufficient protein is rare in the typical American diet.

Fats provide a concentrated store of energy in the body and insulation for the body. They also assist with the utilization of certain vitamins. Fat can be consumed as a pure product, such as butter or safflower oil, or as part of a food like marbled beef or avocado.

Research has linked diets high in fat to increased risks of certain cancers, heart disease, and obesity. To make sense of that information, it is important to know that there are two classes of fat. Unsaturated fats are liquid at room temperature and include oils derived from corn, soybeans, peanuts, and olives. Saturated fats are those that are solid at room temperature. They often come from animal sources, such as meat or dairy products, but they also can come from palm and coconut oils. It is the consumption of these saturated fats that poses a particular health risk.

Another issue in regard to fat is dietary cholesterol. **Cholesterol** is a fatty acid that is particularly high in eggs, dairy products like cheese and ice cream, fatty or marbled meat such as beef steaks, and organ meats (liver and kidney). Although research on this topic is still controversial, those people at risk of developing heart disease probably should reduce their intake of cholesterol.

Vitamins is a nutrient classification that provides trace amounts of elements essential for life and growth. Vitamins A, D, and K are mobilized by fat and are essential for healthy bones and teeth. Vitamin C cannot be manufactured by your body; hence, it must be eaten daily. It holds your cells together, helps you resist infection, and keeps your teeth and gums healthy. The B vitamins (thiamin, riboflavin, and niacin, for example) allow your body to utilize protein and carbohydrates.

Minerals provide trace elements essential for strong bones and teeth, healthy muscles, and blood and nerves. They also assist with the formation of many enzymes and hormones. Calcium and iron levels need special monitoring in the American diet to avoid deficiencies, and sodium needs to be reduced in most such diets.

Water is found in every cell of the body and is essential for transporting other nutrients and for waste removal. It regulates body temperature, and it cushions and lubricates parts of the body. Water is present in most liquids that we drink and in most foods that we eat, but it is recommended that we drink sixty-four additional ounces of water daily.

THE FOOD GUIDE PYRAMID

How can you tell whether you are making good food choices—choices that will include all the essential nutrients? Researchers have provided us with simple visual systems, much like study aids. In the past, you may have learned about the four food groups, or even the basic seven. In the mid-1990s, those plans were updated in order to help us make healthy food choices. Now we have the **Food Guide Pyramid** (see Figure 5–1).

The Food Guide Pyramid recommends a range of servings from five major food groups to achieve a healthful combination of nutrients. The range of servings is provided to suit individual needs, such as age and physical activity levels.

The items listed on the lowest level of the Food Guide Pyramid are to be eaten in the highest amounts. They are referred to as the **bread group** and include whole grain breads, cereals, tortillas, pastas, and brown rice, which provide complex carbohydrates and fiber. Other grain products, such as donuts, cookies, and muffins, may contain so much fat, sugar, or salt that they are less desirable.

Vegetables contain specific vitamins, minerals, and fiber. They have a high nutritional value, and you can eat as much as you want of most of them with a few exceptions, such as fried vegetables (potatoes, zucchini) because of the high fat content and most canned vegetables because of their high sodium content.

Fruits also contain specific vitamins, minerals, and fiber. They can be a primary source of vitamin C. Canned fruits often contain added sugar, and dried fruits are very high in sugar. Later in this section is a

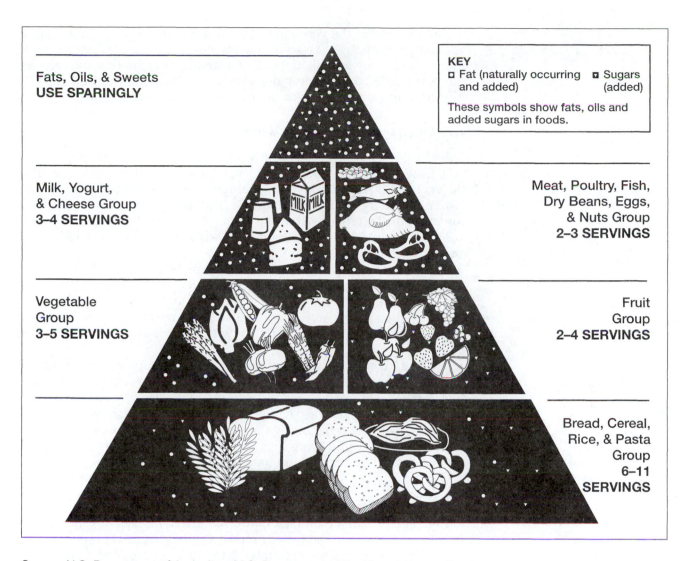

Fats, Oils, & Sweets
USE SPARINGLY

KEY
☐ Fat (naturally occurring   ◪ Sugars
   and added)   (added)

These symbols show fats, oils and
added sugars in foods.

Milk, Yogurt,
& Cheese Group
3–4 SERVINGS

Meat, Poultry, Fish,
Dry Beans, Eggs,
& Nuts Group
2–3 SERVINGS

Vegetable
Group
3–5 SERVINGS

Fruit
Group
2–4 SERVINGS

Bread, Cereal,
Rice, & Pasta
Group
**6–11
SERVINGS**

Source: U.S. Department of Agriculture/U.S. Department of Health and Human Services

Figure 5–1 Food Guide Pyramid

discussion of how to read labels, so you will learn how to determine
these differences.

The milk group provides calcium, vitamin D, protein, and fat.
Most people eating a typical American diet will need to monitor it for
calcium. As already noted, most of us get enough protein, and many of
us get too much fat. The foods with the highest fat content in this classification include whole milk, cream, sour and whipped cream, most
cheeses, and ice cream. Better choices for many people are two percent
(reduced-fat) milk, one percent or low-fat milk, nonfat yogurt, and
ricotta cheese.

The next classification, the major source of protein, is called the
meat group. It includes meat, poultry, fish, dried beans, eggs, and nuts.
An important caveat is to select low-fat versions of these foods wherever
possible, since this category contributes a lot of fat as well as protein.
Many people overestimate the quantity of food needed from this section. A person needs only five to seven ounces daily.

Items listed at the very top of the pyramid are to be eaten sparingly because, even though fats, oils, and sweets add a lot of flavor to food, they provide only a small amount of nutrients compared to the calories they contain. Figure 5–2 provides a list of common foods in this classification. It may surprise you to discover what is included.

HOW MUCH FOOD FOR ME?

The number of servings in each food classification is dependent upon your gender, age, size, and activity level. The same factors affect the calorie level that is needed for you to maintain your present weight. A *calorie* is a unit of energy. It is the amount of heat needed to raise the temperature of one kilogram of water one degree Centigrade. As you make food choices, consult Figure 5–3 for guidance with the number of servings you need in each food group.

So, now you need to know what a serving is for various foods. If you cannot visualize measuring units such as a quarter cup, half cup, or a teaspoon or tablespoon, you may need to visit your kitchen or your grocery store's kitchen gadget section to familiarize yourself with quantities. See Figure 5–4 (on page 120) for a list of typical serving sizes for a variety of foods.

Notice that daily servings for the meat group are expressed in ounces. This ensures accuracy because labeling information is presented that way. As you purchase items from the meat group, you will need to look at the weight on the package of meat. You also might find it useful to know that a chicken thigh or breast weighs about 3 ounces, a drumstick 2 ounces, and a wing 1 ounce. Regular hamburgers at fast-food restaurants are 2 ounces, and quarter-pounders are, of course, 4 ounces.

SELECTING HEALTHY FOODS

On a typical trip to a supermarket, we choose from more than 25,000 items that range from fresh foods to canned goods to packaged products of all types. There is an increasing array of mixtures of foods and chemicals

Fats	Sweets
bacon, sausage	candy, cakes
butter/margarine	cookies, doughnuts
chips (potato, corn, tortilla)	fruit drinks, punch
creams, cream soups, sauces	gelatin desserts
French fries, onion rings	honey, sugar, syrups, jams
gravy	lemonade/Kool-aid
mayonnaise, salad dressings	pies
pastries, croissants	soft drinks/sodas

Figure 5–2 Fats, oils, and sweets: Use sparingly

	Less active women, older adults	Children, teen girls, active women, less active men	Teen boys, active men
Calories	1,600	2,200	2,800
Bread group	6 servings	9 servings	11 servings
Vegetable group	3 servings	4 servings	5 servings
Fruit group	2 servings	3 servings	4 servings
Milk group	3–4* servings	3–4* servings	3–4* servings
Meat group	2–3 servings	2–3 servings	2–3 servings
Total Fat Grams**	53 grams	73 grams	93 grams

*Pregnant or breast-feeding women, teenagers, and young adults to age twenty-four need four servings.

**Based on lowfat and lean choices with minimal amounts of added fats and oils.

Source: U.S. Department of Agriculture/U.S. Department of Health and Human Services.

Figure 5–3 Sample diets at three calorie levels

offered to us as a result of advanced food technology. Over the years, the government has worked with industry to create food labeling regulations. Labels tell us what the food is, what has been added to it, and what nutritional value we can expect from it. All labels must use a standard format and follow certain specifications for terminology. In other words, if a product claims to be low-fat, it must meet a certain criteria.

More and more packaged foods carry nutritional labeling, and soon we may see such labels on fresh foods as well. Label information can be a major source of product information and comparison. As you practice gathering product information from labels, your skill level and understanding will increase.

After reading this information, you may have decided to change some of your eating habits. As you have discovered, the typical American diet needs to have more calorie control; reduce consumption of fat, salt, and sugar; and increase consumption of foods with high nutrient value. The Dietary Guidelines for Americans provide us with criteria for eating well:

1. Eat a variety of foods daily.
2. Maintain a healthy weight.
3. Choose a diet low in fat and cholesterol.
4. Choose a diet with plenty of vegetables, fruits, and grain products.
5. Use sugars in moderation.
6. Use salt and sodium in moderation.
7. If you drink alcohol, do so in moderation.

By following these guidelines, we will have the basis for good health. Being overweight or underweight is a health issue as well as an appearance issue. Both groups have higher risks of certain diseases and a shortened life. Weight control is the focus of ongoing scientific research and

Bread group	Serving size
Bread	1 slice
Bun (hamburger)	1/2 bun
English muffin, bagel	1/2 muffin or bagel
Tortilla, chapati	1 (7-inch)
Pancake, waffle	1 (4-inch)
Rice, macaroni, oatmeal, grits, bulgur, couscous	1/2 cup cooked

Vegetable group	Serving size
Vegetables, cooked, canned, or chopped raw	1/2 cup
Vegetable juices	3/4 cup (6 ounces)
Vegetable soup	1/2 cup
Lettuce or raw salad greens	1 cup
Cole slaw	1/2 cup
Tomato, green pepper, potato, corn on the cob	1 medium

Fruit group	Serving size
Fruit, cooked, canned, or chopped raw	1/2 cup
Fruit juices	3/4 cup (6 ounces)
Orange, apple, banana, peach, pear, kiwi	1 medium
Apricots	3
Grapes	1 cup
Plums, prunes	2
Sliced strawberries	1/2 cup

Milk group	Serving size
Milk, all fluid types	1 cup (8 ounces)
Parmesan cheese	1/4 cup
Cheese	1 1/2 ounces (2 slices)
Cottage cheese	2 cups
Yogurt	1 cup
Milkshake	1 cup
Tofu (soybean curd)	1/2 cup

Meat group	Serving size
Hot dog	1
Nuts	1/4 cup
Eggs	1 or 2 egg whites
Tuna fish	1/4 cup
Peanut butter	2 tablespoons
Canned beans	1/2 cup

Figure 5–4 Typical serving sizes

is affected by many variables. A full discussion of this topic is beyond the scope of this workbook, so consult a nutrition book for more details.

Generally, if you want to lose weight, you will need to consume fewer calories and increase your level of activity. An easy way to decrease calories is to decrease fats and sweets. If you want to gain weight, you will need to consume more calories, perhaps by eating more grains and dairy products.

Although it is appropriate to be concerned about maintaining a healthy weight level, some people go to extremes in order to become or remain thin. When that desire becomes an obsession, some people resort to self-induced denial of food, called *anorexia nervosa*. Others binge on food, consuming thousands of calories and then purging their bodies by vomiting or using laxatives *(bulimia)*. Both of these conditions cause life-threatening physical effects. Because eating disorders encompass both psychological and nutritional aspects of a lifestyle, professional treatment should be sought.

INDIVIDUAL ACTIVITIES

1. Compare Your Food Intake to the Food Guide Pyramid

Purpose: To compare what you ate for three typical days to the Food Guide Pyramid classification.

As with any system, it is best to assess your current behavior in order to know if you need to create a plan for change. On the form provided in Figure 5–5, keep track of all the food you eat for the next three days. Remember, this exercise will be of no use to you if you are not honest with yourself. It is especially important to be accurate as you estimate the number of servings. Estimate to the nearest ounce, quarter cup, tablespoon, or other common measure.

As you fill out the form, you may have to break down mixed dishes into ingredients. For example, a bologna and cheese sandwich would be listed as two servings of bread, one serving of meat, and one of cheese. The mayonnaise or mustard would fit into the "other" category.

Once you have completed the form in Figure 5–5 and have a grand total for each column, divide the grand total of each column by three to give you an average daily intake. Chart your results in Figure 5–6 (on page 125).

Where do you lack essential foods?

Where are you eating too much?

2. Learning About Labels

Purpose: To practice reading a food label so that labeling information will be familiar and more clear, with the goal of using this information as a basis of selecting food.

Select a food label from a packaged food product such as a frozen dinner, cookies or crackers, or boxed entree. Complete Figure 5–7 (on page 126), the Label Worksheet, for this product.

List the food you eat each day under the meal or snack heading, and indicate the number of servings from each food group in the appropriate columns. Total each column for each day. Then add the results together in the Summary of Results section at the end of the form.

Day 1

	Bread and cereals	Fruit	Vegetables	Meat	Milk	Other fats, sugars, alcohol
Breakfast						
	___	___	___	___	___	___
	___	___	___	___	___	___
	___	___	___	___	___	___
	___	___	___	___	___	___
Lunch						
	___	___	___	___	___	___
	___	___	___	___	___	___
	___	___	___	___	___	___
	___	___	___	___	___	___
Dinner						
	___	___	___	___	___	___
	___	___	___	___	___	___
	___	___	___	___	___	___
	___	___	___	___	___	___
Snack						
	___	___	___	___	___	___
	___	___	___	___	___	___
	___	___	___	___	___	___
Total	___	___	___	___	___	___

Figure 5–5 Record chart of three days' food intake

Day 2

	Bread and cereals	Fruit	Vegetables	Meat	Milk	Other fats, sugars, alcohol
Breakfast						
	___	___	___	___	___	___
	___	___	___	___	___	___
	___	___	___	___	___	___
	___	___	___	___	___	___
Lunch						
	___	___	___	___	___	___
	___	___	___	___	___	___
	___	___	___	___	___	___
	___	___	___	___	___	___
Dinner						
	___	___	___	___	___	___
	___	___	___	___	___	___
	___	___	___	___	___	___
	___	___	___	___	___	___
Snack						
	___	___	___	___	___	___
	___	___	___	___	___	___
	___	___	___	___	___	___
Total	___	___	___	___	___	___

Day 3

	Bread and cereals	Fruit	Vegetables	Meat	Milk	Other fats, sugars, alcohol
Breakfast						
	___	___	___	___	___	___
	___	___	___	___	___	___
	___	___	___	___	___	___
	___	___	___	___	___	___

Figure 5–5 Record chart of three days' food intake (cont'd)

Day 3 (cont'd)

	Bread and cereals	Fruit	Vegetables	Meat	Milk	Other fats, sugars, alcohol
Lunch						
	_____	_____	_____	_____	_____	_____
	_____	_____	_____	_____	_____	_____
	_____	_____	_____	_____	_____	_____
	_____	_____	_____	_____	_____	_____
Dinner						
	_____	_____	_____	_____	_____	_____
	_____	_____	_____	_____	_____	_____
	_____	_____	_____	_____	_____	_____
	_____	_____	_____	_____	_____	_____
Snack						
	_____	_____	_____	_____	_____	_____
	_____	_____	_____	_____	_____	_____
	_____	_____	_____	_____	_____	_____
Total	_____	_____	_____	_____	_____	_____

Summary of Results

	Bread and cereals	Fruit	Vegetables	Meat	Milk	Other fats, sugars, alcohol
Day 1	_____	_____	_____	_____	_____	_____
Day 2	_____	_____	_____	_____	_____	_____
Day 3	_____	_____	_____	_____	_____	_____
Grand total	_____	_____	_____	_____	_____	_____

Figure 5–5 Record chart of three days' food intake (cont'd)

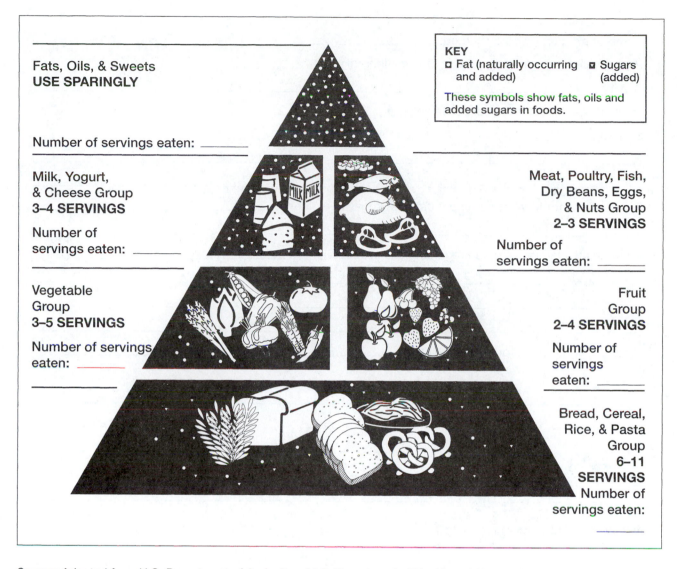

Fats, Oils, & Sweets
USE SPARINGLY

Number of servings eaten: _____

Milk, Yogurt,
& Cheese Group
3–4 SERVINGS

Number of
servings eaten: _____

Vegetable
Group
3–5 SERVINGS

Number of servings
eaten: _____

KEY
▫ Fat (naturally occurring   ▫ Sugars
and added)   (added)
These symbols show fats, oils and
added sugars in foods.

Meat, Poultry, Fish,
Dry Beans, Eggs,
& Nuts Group
2–3 SERVINGS

Number of
servings eaten: _____

Fruit
Group
2–4 SERVINGS

Number of
servings
eaten: _____

Bread, Cereal,
Rice, & Pasta
Group
**6–11
SERVINGS**
Number of
servings eaten:
_____

Source: Adapted from U.S. Department of Agriculture/U.S. Department of Health and Human Services

Figure 5–6 Comparison to Food Guide Pyramid

3. Compare and Contrast Cereals[1]

Purpose: To use label understanding to choose a cereal high in nutritional value.

Many breakfast cereals provide a good source of nutrients and fiber. Cereals are located on the lowest level of the food pyramid and can make an important contribution to eating well if they are not too high in fat or sugar. Labeling and fortification of breakfast cereals has had a long history, so the standardization in the industry makes comparisons relatively easy. In this activity, you will compare eight ready-to-eat

[1] Adapted with permission from "Consumer Comparison—Ready-to-Eat Cereals," Family and Consumer Sciences Nutrition faculty, Mt. San Antonio College, Walnut, CA.

Name of product being evaluated: _____

Predominant ingredient by weight (the first ingredient): _____

Serving size: _____

Total number of servings per container: _____

Special nutrient information (fortified, good source of), if any: _____

_____

_____

Reduction or removal of a nutrient (fat free, sugar free), if any: _____

_____

What health claims are made regarding this product? _____

_____

_____

_____

What did you learn about reading labels? _____

_____

_____

_____

_____

_____

Figure 5–7 Label worksheet

Cereal brand name	Serving size	Calories	Fat grams	Sodium milligrams	Total carbohydrate grams	Fiber grams	Sugar grams
1.	1 oz = ___ cup						
2.	1 oz = ___ cup						
3.	1 oz = ___ cup						
4.	1 oz = ___ cup						
5.	1 oz = ___ cup						
6.	1 oz = ___ cup						
7.	1 oz = ___ cup						
8.	1 oz = ___ cup						

Figure 5–8 Comparison of cereals

cereal products. The easiest way is to begin this assignment in a grocery store.

In Figure 5–8, record the name brand and cereal name of eight products, plus the serving size, calories, total grams of fat, milligrams of sodium (Na), and grams of total carbohydrates, fiber, and sugar for each product.

Use the form provided in Figure 5–8 to compare label information for eight brands of cereal. Once the form is completed, use a colored highlighter to identify the cereals that are low in fiber, fat, and sodium. With a different color, indicate the cereals that are high in those items.

Select two cereals that you would recommend as being high in nutritional value. Explain why you selected them.

Select two of the cereals examined that you felt were of the lowest nutritional value, and explain why you selected them.

4. Comparison of Packaged Food Products[2]

Purpose: To use label understanding to choose a packaged product with low-sodium and low-fat content.

The selection of frozen, packaged, or canned food products has grown immensely as consumers have opted for convenience products. The purpose of this assignment is to practice label reading and to make comparisons of nutrient and ingredient levels. Special attention will be paid to sodium and fat content.

Choose one classification of prepared food products from the following list:

Frozen entrees/dinners
Canned entrees (chili, stew)
Boxed entrees (macaroni and cheese)
Luncheon meats (sandwich meats, hot dogs)
Soups
Spaghetti sauces
Cheese products
Frozen desserts
Cookies
Crackers

Go to the grocery store and find ten competing products in the classification you have chosen. Some products may be made by the same manufacturer, for example, in the frozen entree classification, you might select three Budget Gourmet entrees, two Lean Cuisine entrees, and so on. For

---

[2] Courtesy of the Family and Consumer Sciences Nutrition faculty, Mt. San Antonio College, Walnut, CA.

Product name	Serving size in ounces or grams	Percent sodium	Fat calories	Calories per serving	Percent of calories from fat
1.					
2.					
3.					
4.					
5.					
6.					
7.					
8.					
9.					
10.					

Figure 5–9 Packaged food products comparison

each product, use Figure 5–9 to record the serving size in ounces or grams, the percentage (% of Daily Value) of sodium, the fat calories, and the calories per serving. Calculate the percentage of calories from fat for the right-hand column of the figure by taking the number of fat calories and dividing them by the total number of calories per serving, then multiplying by 100. For example, if the number of fat calories is 60 and the total number of calories is 180:

$$60/180 = .333 \times 100 = 33\%$$

So the percent of calories from fat is 33%.

What is your reaction to your research?

How will you use this information in the future?

5. Fatty Fast Foods[3]

Purpose: To analyze the fat and sodium content of various fast-food meals in order to make better nutritional choices.

Many people eat at fast-food restaurants as often as once a day. Many of these typical meals contain more than one full day's allotment of fat

---

[3] Courtesy of the Family and Consumer Sciences Nutrition faculty, Mt. San Antonio College, Walnut, CA.

and sodium in just one meal. You will need to use some research skills to obtain information, since labeling is voluntary at restaurants. However, some fast-food restaurants have calculated this information and will provide it to you if you ask for it. Other sources of this information include consumer publications such as *Consumer Reports* and *Nutrition Action Newsletter.* Use your library or the Internet to find this information.

Choose fast-food restaurants that you frequent. For each location, select a meal that you might typically eat. In Figure 5–10, record the serving size in ounces or grams, the percentage (% of Daily Value) of sodium, the fat calories, and the calories per serving. Calculate the percentage of calories from fat for the righthand column of the figure by first taking the number of fat grams and multiplying by 9:

$$\text{Fat grams} \times 9 = \text{fat calories}$$

and then taking the number of fat calories and dividing them by the total number of calories per serving, which is then multiplied by 100. For example, if the number of fat calories is 60 and the total number of calories is 180:

$$60/180 = .333 \times 100 = 33\%$$

So the percent of calories from fat is 33%.

How often do you choose fast foods?

What does your research imply in regard to your health and diet?

Fast-food meal	Serving size in ounces or grams	Percent sodium	Fat grams	Calories per serving	Percent of calories from fat
1.					
2.					
3.					
4.					
5.					
6.					

Figure 5–10 Comparison of fast foods

What changes are you willing to make in regard to the specific selection of foods at fast-food restaurants? For example, will you cut your visits by one-third? Will you select a different product when you eat there? If so, what?

Share your results with someone else, preferably someone who eats with you in fast-food settings. What was that person's response to your investigation? Did you inspire them to make any changes?

6. Teaching Nutrition to Others

Purpose: To provide you with an opportunity to teach others about basic nutrition, while advancing your own understanding to a higher level.

Select a group of people younger than yourself. Perhaps they are at a school where you previously attended or where you have a child who is a student. Offer to be a visiting teacher, and prepare a short lesson on some aspect of nutrition. Remember to include audio, visual, and kinesthetic opportunities if possible. And be sure to make it clear what action or change you want your audience to make. When you conclude, ask the students for feedback.

7. Evaluate a Weight Loss Program/Product

Purpose: To apply understanding of necessary nutrient levels and weight loss principles to the selection of a safe and effective weight loss program.

There is a plethora of weight loss systems available at the grocery and drug store, through magazines, and on cable television. The purpose of this assignment is to apply critical thinking skills to evaluate the safety and cost-effectiveness of a product or program.

Find at least two readings or articles that discuss in an objective way the issue of weight loss and weight loss programs. Then begin to list specific criteria that a program or product should meet to be both safe and effective. See how many criteria you can identify and record them on Figure 5–11.

1. _____
2. _____
3. _____
4. _____
5. _____
6. _____
7. _____
8. _____

Figure 5–11 Criteria for evaluating weight loss programs

Now let's check your thoroughness. Some of the points on your list could be that the program (1) provides a reasonable number of calories, not fewer than 1200; (2) provides adequate protein, fat, and carbohydrates; (3) includes a selection of foods from the breads and cereals, fruits, vegetables, milk, and meat groups; (4) includes easy to obtain foods; (5) features gradual weight loss; (6) encourages permanent lifestyle change; (7) is created by qualified doctors and dietitians; (8) informs customers about risks and side effects; and (9) makes claims that are scientifically proven.

8. Give Us Our Daily Water

Purpose: To survey and assess the average of water intake and make a recommendation for future goals.

Many people do not consume the recommended daily average of sixty-four ounces of water. Your task is to determine what is typical for you and, if you are not consuming enough, to set a new standard for yourself. Remember that this needs to be pure water. Fruit juice, coffee, and tea do not count. Record your water consumption on Figure 5–12 for five days, noting both the time of day and the quantity of water consumed.

What did you conclude about the amount of water you consume?

If you need to drink more, would you be willing to add eight ounces? Sixteen ounces? When would you drink that water? What would make this change easier? Write your responses on Figure 5–13.

9. Evaluating the Dining Atmosphere

Purpose: To evaluate the stress level related to personal dining and to determine whether changes are needed.

The food we select certainly has the most impact on our health. But the environment in which we eat and the pace at which we eat

Time of Day	Day 1	Day 2	Day 3	Day 4	Day 5

Figure 5–12 Record of my water consumption

Figure 5–13 Thinking about changing my water consumption habits

also has an effect on the body's ability to properly digest nutrients. The purpose of this activity is for you to measure the variation in stress levels that you experience when you eat. Use the following scale for this exercise:

1—Relaxed, calm, thinking, reading, pleasant conversation
2—Semirelaxed, thinking, concentrating, focused conversation
3—Somewhat hurried, time for limited conversation
4—Hurried, little time to talk
5—Very rushed, shoving food in mouth, eating while driving or standing

Obtain a piece of graph paper (or make your own). Label the vertical axis *Stress Level,* marking the number 1 on the bottom line and progressing up to 5. Label the horizontal axis *Meals.*

Now, give the next meal that you eat a rating from 1 to 5. Starting from the left side of your graph, put a dot at the corresponding location. After each meal for the next week, repeat this process.

You now have plotted information over time. Next, connect the dots. What was your average rating for a meal? What was your highest, most stressful level? Your lowest? Interpret and analyze your results in Figure 5–14. Indicate if you would like to make some changes and, if so, what changes you would like to make.

10. The Media and the Food Guide Pyramid

Purpose: To increase awareness of how advertisements influence our awareness of food choices.

The advertising industry in the United States spends over $130 billion each year, over $400 for each average consumer. This money is incorporated in the price of each product or service sold. Your task is to increase your awareness of the types of foods that are advertised on television and radio, and to consider what product information you gain that might be used in decision making. Finally, consider the influence of these commercials on your eating habits.

_____
_____
_____
_____
_____
_____
_____
_____
_____
_____

Figure 5–14 Interpretation and analysis of the stress levels in my eating environment

Food product	Information	Claim or appeal	Manipulation	Other

Figure 5–15 Gathering data on food advertisements

Begin by choosing radio or television as your data source. Then listen for a minimum of three hours—not three consecutive hours, but at different times of the day. Listen for specific product information and for any claims of performance or appeals to your needs and desires. Also determine whether you are manipulated by emotional approaches or testimonials. Record your data in Figure 5–15.

The next step is to examine the foods on the Food Guide Pyramid to see if any particular category of food groups is advertised most often. Using the pyramid provided in Figure 5–16, make hash marks in the sections that match the advertisements.

Now, in light of your research and considering the Dietary Guidelines, what conclusions can you draw? How do you think these commercials affect your food desires and choices? Write about these reactions in Figure 5–17 (on page 135).

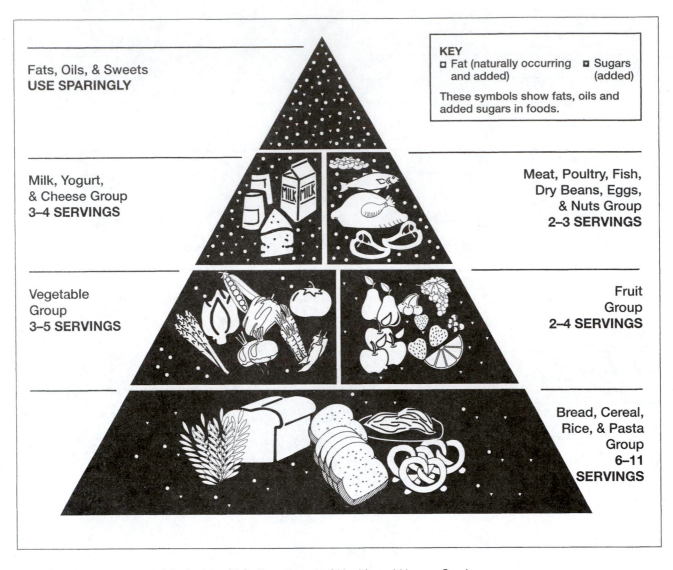

KEY
□ Fat (naturally occurring and added)   ■ Sugars (added)

These symbols show fats, oils and added sugars in foods.

Fats, Oils, & Sweets
USE SPARINGLY

Milk, Yogurt,
& Cheese Group
3–4 SERVINGS

Meat, Poultry, Fish,
Dry Beans, Eggs,
& Nuts Group
2–3 SERVINGS

Vegetable
Group
3–5 SERVINGS

Fruit
Group
2–4 SERVINGS

Bread, Cereal,
Rice, & Pasta
Group
**6–11
SERVINGS**

Source: U.S. Department of Agriculture/U.S. Department of Health and Human Services

Figure 5–16 Advertisements and the food guide pyramid

11. Clipping Coupons

Purpose: To heighten awareness about the types of foods that are promoted with coupons, and to forecast the cost of such foods.

A primary way to introduce a new food product and to promote its purchase is through food coupons. Many of these foods are highly processed and are high in fat, sugar, and sodium. Your task is to gather data about this issue, and then to draw some conclusions that can direct your future choices.

Search through a Sunday newspaper for the coupon section. It is usually six to twelve pages, and the dimensions of a comic book. Go through this section and clip out every coupon for a food product. Then organize the coupons based on the food pyramid classifications. In other words, put all the bread, cereal, pasta, and rice coupons together; all the cheese, yogurt, and ice cream coupons together; and so forth. Be careful

Figure 5–17 The media and the food guide pyramid

Figure 5–18 Clipping coupons to nutritional advantage

as you classify mixed products, so that they most accurately reflect their major nutrient. In other words, a coupon for a cake mix probably belongs in "other," rather than in the bread and cereal group.

Now compare the number of foods in each classification with the Dietary Guidelines and with the principles taught by the Food Guide Pyramid. Is there a classification that is overrepresented by coupons? Is there one that is underrepresented? What do you know about the relative cost of some of the prepared, packaged foods? What conclusions can you draw about coupon shopping? In Figure 5–18, write some guidelines for using coupons to nutritional advantage.

Foods I commonly ate ten years ago		Foods I regularly eat today	
1.	7.	1.	7.
2.	8.	2.	8.
3.	9.	3.	9.
4.	10.	4.	10.
5.	11.	5.	11.
6.	12.	6.	12.

Figure 5–19 My changing food intake

12. Changing Food Intake

Purpose: To recall the types of foods you ate ten years ago, to compare them to the kinds of foods you eat today, and to identify factors that have influenced any change.

Most people have changed the types of foods they eat when compared to what they ate ten years ago. One factor is the globalization of food sources, resulting in a broader supply of fresh fruits and vegetables. Another is the increasing cultural diversity in many North American communities. But there are other factors, some that are regional, and some that are personal.

Begin by recalling foods that you commonly ate ten years ago. Make a list of them in Figure 5–19. Then make a similar list for the foods you eat today.

Compare the two lists. Identify foods that you no longer eat frequently, and foods that are new to your regular diet. Consider why these differences exist, and identify factors that have influenced this change. Write your thoughts in the following space:

13. Eating Disorders: An Interview

Purpose: To gain empathy for and insight into why people have eating disorders.

It has been suggested that one out of five young women in college is a victim of eating disorders. This sad situation deserves our attention, and those who suffer from eating disorders would benefit by our empathy. Your task is to interview someone who has, or has had, an eating disorder. In preparation, you might need to read more about anorexia nervosa and bulimia. Articles are available of a general nature, as well as ones that feature well-known sufferers such as gymnast Cathy Rigby and the late Princess Diana.

Prepare a set of questions that would enable you to understand how the individual became involved in the eating disorder. Open-ended questions might be most comfortable for your interviewee. Write a one-page summary of your results, or present your results orally in class.

EXPAND YOUR LEARNING

Bailey, Covert, and Ronda Gates. *Smart Eating: Choosing Wisely, Living Lean.* Boston, MA: Houghton Mifflin Co., 1996.

Clayman, Charles B., ed. *Diet and Nutrition: The American Medical Association's Medical Library.* Pleasantville, NY: Pegasus, 1991.

Duyff, Roberta. *The American Dietetic Association's Complete Food and Nutrition Guide.* Minneapolis, MN: Chronimid Publishing, 1996.

Mayer, Jean, and Jeanne P. Goldberg. *Dr. Jean Mayer's Diet & Nutrition Guide.* New York, NY: Pharos Books, 1990.

GROUP ACTIVITIES

1. Safety and the Globalization of Food Sources

Purpose: To apply understanding of systems and critical thinking to the issue of the safety of the nation's food supply.

Consumers have grown accustomed to a wide variety and year-round availability of fruits, vegetables, entrees, and condiments from around the world. This country is also a major supplier of fruits, vegetables, meats, and grains to other nations. Occasionally there have been safety issues related to United States imports or exports.

In a group, use the systems approach to analyze this situation. Identify major concerns and interests. Come to consensus regarding two or three significant actions that the United States could take on its own to enhance the safety of the food supply. What would your group like other countries to do? Do you all agree that these are realistic ideas?

2. Health and Budget Friendly Meals

Purpose: To participate with a group to plan meals that are nutritious, yet economical.

Join with two other people to plan a nutritious dinner meal for a family of four within a limited budget. Consider what equipment and how much time would be needed to prepare the meal.

Share your menu with other groups in the class and have them evaluate your success.

Chapter 6

Staying Healthy

Most of us would place health high on our list of values. Staying healthy certainly is connected to our genes, which, of course, are beyond the scope of our control. However, making wise food choices, getting regular exercise and sufficient rest and relaxation, and not abusing our bodies with tobacco, alcohol, or drugs are things that are within our control. Wise choices in these aspects of our lives, and good investments of time and energy here, will yield huge dividends.

EXERCISE

No amount of exercise can guarantee a long, healthy life. However, even moderate amounts of exercise can improve the likelihood of staying healthy. Most of us don't exercise regularly because we do not see that it is urgent. We believe it can be postponed. The consequences of this thinking, however, are health problems and costs in both the immediate and distant futures.

You do not need any special equipment or a formal exercise program based at a gym, nor must you use weight-lifting equipment or participate in step aerobics. All you need to do is consistently flex your muscles and engage in an activity that strengthens your heart and lungs, back and limbs. Since you know the importance of motivation in behavior change, let's consider why you might want to exercise.

Regular exercise makes you stronger, more energetic, and in better overall health. This means you will feel like doing all the activities you wish to do.

People come in all shapes and sizes. Our genetics play an important role in how tall we are, and whether our silhouette is tubular, pear-shaped, shaped like an inverted triangle, or another shape altogether. Regardless of basic body shape, eating and exercise habits can affect our appearance. It's not feasible to totally change our body shape, but regular exercise can make our inherent body shape look as good and be as toned as possible.

Exercise helps build your lean muscle mass. One of the biggest problems of diets is that if you don't exercise while you diet, you will lose both fat and lean muscle mass. Diet without exercise is less effective than diet and exercise combined.

Personal Fitness Plan

A good fitness plan has three parts: aerobic fitness, muscle strengthening and endurance, and flexibility. Although the heart is a muscle, it cannot be exercised directly, so we need aerobic exercises to drive our large muscle groups to make our heart and lungs work at their top capacity. Effective **aerobic exercises** include brisk walking, running, stair climbing, biking, swimming, and dance. A test for checking to see whether you are working hard enough to have an aerobic benefit is to see if you can talk while exercising. If you can talk, then you are going at an appropriate pace. If you cannot talk, you are going too fast. If you can sing while you exercise, however, it would be safe to exercise a bit faster.

Muscle strengthening and endurance improves your work and athletic performance, prevents fatigue, improves your posture, and helps you feel more energetic. It also can protect your body from movement injuries and reduce chronic back pain. You are probably familiar with several traditional endurance and strengthening exercises, such as chin-ups, push-ups, side leg lifts, and similar calisthenics. Resistance training with free weights, weight-training equipment, or inexpensive rubber tubing is another way to increase muscle strength.

Flexibility is the ability to move a joint through its full range of motion. Stretching can increase your range of motion and reduce stiffness and pain. It is an essential component of any fitness plan, particularly during a cool-down phase as you conclude your exercise routine.

Getting Started

Begin your fitness program slowly. This way you will avoid injury. If you haven't been exercising, you may experience discomfort during your workout and sore muscles afterward. But little by little this will diminish, and you will feel increased strength and capability.

Your fitness plan does not require you to set aside a large chunk of time. It can be accomplished in short periods throughout the day. And it can be part of your daily activities. For example, aerobic exercise can be a daily walk around the neighborhood with your dog, friend, or neighbor. Muscle strengthening can occur purposefully as you exercise while watching television, as well as when you carry the groceries into the house or do the gardening. You can fit flexibility into your life by substituting a coffee break or eating break with stretching. Some stretches can be done at your desk while you are talking on the phone, or in the car while you are driving home from work.

Sports or recreational activities provide fitness benefits as well. Tennis, basketball, golf, and dancing all enhance endurance, strength, and flexibility while providing social benefits and pleasure. These activities may have been a part of your life in the past. Which ones, or similar ones, did you enjoy? Put them back into your life for fitness and fun!

REST, RELAXATION, AND RENEWAL

In *Seven Habits of Highly Effective People*, Stephen Covey tells a story about a man who is working in the woods feverishly sawing down a tree. A second man comes upon him, comments that he "looks exhausted," and asks how long he has been at it. The reply is "five hours." When the second man suggests that the first one stop and sharpen his saw, the reply is "I don't have time, I'm too busy sawing!"

We all need to stop to sharpen the saw, that is, to renew our physical, mental, and emotional energies. We need rest, relaxation, and time to reflect. Although we may believe we do not have the time, we need to reconsider. Isn't it time to sharpen the saw, to make life easier?

Rest

When people get stressed and schedules are too full, many people cut back on **rest**. Does this sound like your lifestyle? As noted in Chapter 4, most adults need at least eight hours of sleep each night in order to function properly mentally, emotionally, and physically. This amount of sleep allows us to feel rested.

Relaxation

Relaxation is an opportunity to reduce tension and anxiety by having a slower pace and incorporating a sense of joy into our lives. Many people try to squeeze relaxation into the weekend because our weeks are filled with forty-five hours of work, long commutes, dinner, homework, and children's baths. But then we get to Saturday and find we need to clean the house, do the laundry, shop for groceries, and attend the children's soccer practice.

Over the centuries, humans have experienced much more leisure time than that which most of us currently experience. Living patterns were tied to the seasons, allowing for less productive times in the winter months. In some societies, as many as one hundred and fifty days per year were spent on public holidays and festivals, creating much time for leisure. When coupled with the diminished light and the cold of winter, there was a great amount of time spent on rest and relaxation. The Industrial Revolution caused this cyclical pattern to become more linear, but the amount of leisure was still present.

Today we have conflicting feelings about leisure. On the one hand, we say we don't have enough of it, yet studies repeatedly indicate that over three-fourths of us watch at least three hours of television each day. Families with children watch even more. Is television-watching really providing us with a sense of relaxation and freedom?

Those who regularly engage in a hobby, team sport, or fitness program need to keep it in perspective. It is important to do these activities for the joy of them, and not feel obligated to have a high degree of mastery, for once we demand that standard of ourselves, we have turned fun into work.

Many people are busy with activities they neither enjoy nor want to do. Sometimes frenzied activity prevents us from clarifying values and goals. Do you feel the obligation to be engaged in some activity all the time? Are you frustrated because you are so busy, yet you seem to lack what you really want out of life?

Renewal

As you learned earlier, in every system, change is constantly occurring. Your personal ability to deal with change depends upon your flexibility and your willingness to be open and inquisitive. Most of us fear change; even when our minds tell us it is normal, our stomachs turn over at the prospect.

Consider those little Chinese finger tubes where the harder you push and pull, the more they constrict. Life is like that—the harder you push, the more constricting your life feels. We need **renewal**, time to pause so that we can hear and listen to the inner voice, our spiritual self. This spiritual dimension deals with finding meaning through purpose or contribution.

To handle change, you need inner strength. To have that, your inner self needs exercise and rest, just like your physical self. It needs to be nurtured and provided with opportunities for renewal, so that you can maintain intrinsic motivation. This means that you need time alone to read, to meditate, to think and contemplate, to look inward.

We all need an opportunity for contemplation and reflection. Our species seeks meaning and patterns in life. We need time to do that. We need time to reflect on what is really important to us, and how we are making our values manifest in our everyday lives. As we bring our lives into balance and our actions become consistent with our values, we gain an inner calmness and can better hear our inner voice, our intuition.

Balanced renewal is synergistic. What you do to sharpen the saw mentally enhances your physical and spiritual dimensions. What you do spiritually enhances your mental and physical states. And what you do to renew your physical dimension allows you to improve your life in all other areas.

SUBSTANCE ABUSE

The discussion in this chapter has focused so far on things that will help you maintain your good health. Many people use substances that detract from optimal health and performance, including legal substances such as tobacco and alcohol, and illegal ones such as heroin, cocaine, and marijuana.

Tobacco Use

Consumption of tobacco products has been debated since their first use. As early as 3500 B.C., Indians in what is now Mexico reportedly chewed tobacco to alleviate hunger pains. Native Americans used it to relieve pain from toothaches. After the first European settlers sent tobacco to Europe, its use and trade spread rapidly around the world.

The association of cigarette smoking with cancer, heart disease, and a host of other maladies has led to perhaps the most rapid turnaround in American values in recent memory. Smoking is banned in many government offices, business offices, schools, and airplanes. Restaurants that have not banned smoking have at least provided nonsmoking sections. As a result, tobacco use is on the decline in most groups.

The exception to this pattern is the teenage group. Young people in eighth through twelfth grade have shown an increase in smoking beginning in 1991. When queried, over thirty percent of seniors reported using cigarettes in the last month. Females were as likely to smoke as males. This does not bode well for the health or longevity of this generation. Research indicates that adolescents initially try cigarettes for reasons related to social norms, advertising, social pressure, and curiosity.

Teens who smoke regularly report that they smoke for pleasure and because they are addicted. Thus, their reasons parallel the reasons adults smoke. Tobacco contains nicotine, a stimulant. A stimulant is a drug that increases energy and makes the user feel more awake. Smokers become addicted both physically and psychologically to nicotine. When they try to give up smoking, they experience irritability, headaches, anxiety, and depression.

The paradigm shift against smoking occurred because of the overwhelming evidence of the negative impact of smoking on the health of the smoker. The Centers for Disease Control and Prevention has attributed twenty percent of all deaths to smoking. (Overall, twice as many men die as women, because of the proportion of men to women who smoked in previous generations.) As the cost of health care rose sharply in the late 1980s, the general public balked at paying the high costs of caring for those who brought premature illness and death upon themselves.

A 1994 Gallup Poll[1] found that seventy percent of the smokers interviewed said they would like to quit. Some people quit on their own. Some use a nicotine patch or replacement. Many use a combination of approaches, including assistance from a support group.

Alcohol Use

Contrary to popular belief, alcohol is a depressant. Although many who drink alcoholic beverages feel relaxation, pleasure, and stimulation, these feelings are in fact caused by the depressant effects of alcohol on the brain and central nervous system. The effect of drinking alcohol depends upon the rate at which alcohol is absorbed by the bloodstream.

The rate of the absorption of alcohol into the bloodstream is influenced first by body weight. The greater the body *muscle* weight, the lower the blood alcohol concentration (BAC). Alcohol is burned at the rate of about one drink every two hours in a one hundred and sixty pound man. Speed of drinking is also a factor, as the faster alcohol is swallowed, the faster the peak BAC level is reached. The presence of food in the stomach slows down absorption of alcohol. Drinking history has an impact as well, since tolerance can be developed so that it will take longer to get "high." And beverages vary in their concentration of alcohol from beer with four and one-half percent alcohol to a shot of spirits at forty percent alcohol.

As you know, too much alcohol at a given time can impair reactions, depth perception, and personal judgment. Motor vehicle crashes are the leading cause of injury and the primary cause of death for those under age forty-five. In the 1990s, almost half of all traffic accidents in which a person was killed were alcohol-related.

The use of alcohol is very much a part of our society. But when alcohol interferes with performance on the job, affects relationships, or poses harm to self and others, it is a problem. Alcoholics and alcohol abusers represent approximately ten percent of the adult population. As with tobacco, studies indicate that adolescents are experimenting with alcohol at ever earlier ages.

American industry has become increasingly aware of the cost of alcohol abuse, and so employers often support care in a hospital or treatment center. Also successful is Alcoholics Anonymous, an organization that is totally operated by recovering alcoholics and is famous for starting the modern self-help movement and introducing the twelve-step program.

Illegal Drugs

Prescription medicines and over-the-counter medications can be useful for restoring health, but if they are misused, they can create more problems than they were intended to solve. When you use illegal drugs, risks

---

[1] Siegel, Mark; Alison Landes; and Nancy Jacobs, eds. *Illegal Drugs and Alcohol: America's Anguish.* Wylie, TX: Information Plus, 1995.

increase exponentially. First, the product has not been carefully created under standardized conditions, so unlike prescription drugs, you cannot really know the quality or strength of the product. Because of the illicit nature, you run the risk of arrest and spending time in jail. And, finally, long-term effects of some of the drugs such as crack and marijuana are still undetermined.

What is known is that drugs such as heroin and crack are highly addictive. Some experts believe that only one use of crack can begin to establish an addiction. Heroin, cocaine, crack, and marijuana all alter memory, coordination, and mood. An overdose of heroin or crack is deadly. Heroin addicts are at risk of becoming infected with AIDS from used needles.

Treatment for drug abuse includes use of medication, therapy, and support groups. The National Institute for Drug Abuse has a free hotine number: 1-800-662-HELP.

SEXUALITY

Sexuality is an important aspect of health. Our own sexuality is based on personal values and on values influenced by our family, culture, religion, and society. How we show affection and love, and how we bond with and befriend others, is a matter for personal choice. Because these issues involve emotions, we might not think of them as ideal topics for critical thinking. Yet our decisions about our sexual relations can have a huge impact on our lives. This section focuses on the health issues of birth control and sexually transmitted diseases.

Birth Control

Adolescents and young adults are at the time in their lives that they are deciding when to first become sexually intimate. It may come as a surprise to discover that later in life some adults are faced with the same decision, perhaps because of a divorce. Some of these adults find that times have really changed since last they dated and courted.

Regardless of your age, it is important to prevent unplanned pregnancies. No one wants to be in the difficult situation of deciding about adoption, abortion, or parenthood. Sexual abstinence is, of course, one hundred percent effective.

If you choose to engage in sexual intercourse, health professionals can help you decide which method of birth control meets your needs. Some are more effective than others. Effectiveness is judged by how many accidental pregnancies occur per one hundred women in one year. With that as the criteria, there would be pregnancies in three out of one hundred women using oral contraceptives, twelve out of one hundred using only a condom, and eighteen out of one hundred where withdrawal was the method of choice. If one hundred women gambled and used no contraceptive method, there would be eighty-five pregnancies.

Sexually Transmitted Diseases

Infections passed from person to person through sexual intercourse or genital contact are called **sexually transmitted diseases (STDs)** or **venereal disease (VD)**. The most common STDs are chlamydia, genital herpes, genital warts, gonorrhea, hepatitis B, and syphilis. AIDS (autoimmune deficiency syndrome), the most virulent and deadly of all

STDs, is caused by the human immunodeficiency virus (HIV). HIV is spread only when blood, semen, or vaginal fluid from an infected person enters someone else's body.

Although AIDS has grabbed the front-page headlines, it is genital herpes that seems to be the most prevalent. The Centers for Disease Control and Prevention reported that herpes has increased fivefold since the late 1970s. As of 1994, one in five Americans over the age of twelve had genital herpes, a total of forty-five million Americans.[2] Most people don't realize they have it because it often has no symptoms. However, there is concern, since those with herpes sores may be more vulnerable to HIV infection, and if a woman has herpes when pregnant, her newborn can die if infected.

Preventing an STD is easier than treating an infection once it occurs. Only monogamy between uninfected partners or sexual abstinence completely eliminates risk. It is important to know and believe that a person may have no symptoms of chlamydia, genital herpes, gonorrhea, hepatitis B, syphilis, or HIV and still be able to transmit the disease. Some of these diseases are easily treated, while others are life-threatening.

There are some actions you can take that will *reduce* your risk of contracting STDs. They begin with thinking and talking. If you are beginning a sexual relationship, take time before having sex to talk about HIV and other STDs with your partner. Find out if your partner has ever been exposed to or infected with a sexually transmitted disease. Use latex condoms with any new partner until you are certain that neither one of you has an STD. Do not rely on spermacides, the sponge, or the diaphragm to protect against STDs. They add some protection to condoms, but do not provide adequate protection when used alone, and they do not protect against HIV.

It can take a few days, weeks, or months before an STD can be detected, and up to six months before HIV can be detected in the blood. Again, keep in mind that a person may have no symptoms but still be able to transmit STDs.

INDIVIDUAL ACTIVITIES

1. Little by Little

Purpose: To identify small changes in your eating and fitness habits that you would be willing to make, and then to follow through on three or four of those changes.

Small, painless changes can make a big difference over the long haul on the state of our health. Make a list of at least ten food changes and five fitness changes that you would consider making. An example of a food change is to put sliced strawberries on your pancake instead of butter and syrup; another might be to use nonfat dressings on your salad. An example of a fitness change is that you would walk up three flights of stairs instead of taking the elevator. Write your ideas on Figure 6–1.

Now for the next week, concentrate on making one or two of these changes. Then the following week, make two more of the changes. Write about your experience in the space in Figure 6–2.

---

[2] "Herpes Cases Soar Amid Safe Sex Alerts, CDC Says," *Los Angeles Times,* 16 October 1997, p. A26.

Changes in eating	Changes in fitness

Figure 6–1 Possible little changes

Figure 6–2 How I felt about the little changes

2. Spiritual Renewal

Purpose: To set aside some time for a spiritual activity of your choice, and then to reflect on the results.

To be healthy, each one of us needs to pursue our spirituality. Each one of us has a spiritual side, whether it be expressed by adhering to an organized religion, or by living according to our ethical standards, or by searching for the meaning of life. What are you willing to do to renew your spiritual self? It might be regular attendance at church or synagogue, meditating, praying, reading inspirational literature, attending twelve-step meetings, participating in personal growth workshops, writing, or spending time alone.

Choose one of these activities, or something similar. Schedule time for this activity each week for a month.

I plan to: _____

_____

_____

I will do this (where and when): _____

_____

_____

After the month, write about your experience and what you learned in the space provided in Figure 6–3.

3. A Day Alone with Yourself

Purpose: To set aside a time to get to know yourself, and to reflect on your life's direction.

It is said that time is the most precious of gifts. With this task, you are going to give yourself a whole day to *do nothing*. You will not be shopping, running errands, or even going to the movies. You will do nothing—well, something, but not much.

Plan to spend the day at a place that you loved as a child. This might be the beach, mountains, park, school yard, or a garden. Take nothing to do—no radio or TV, no pager or cell phone. For the first two hours, all you need to do is *listen*. For the second two hours, all you need to do is *reflect*. In the last two hours, all you need to do is *conclude*.

Figure 6–3 My spiritual renewal

Figure 6–4 My reaction to a day alone with myself

What you learn about yourself can remain private, but be sure to write about your feelings and thoughts in regard to the process in the space provided in Figure 6–4.

4. Exploring the Twelve Steps

Purpose: To learn more about the twelve-step program, since it has been used as a model to change habits and behavior.

The twelve-step program was first introduced in 1935 as part of the formation of Alcoholics Anonymous. Today, it has many variations and is used by recovering alcoholics and their families, as well as by those who have changed their eating or drug abuse habits. Find an organization in your neighborhood that uses the twelve-step program, obtain information about it, and interview someone from the group if possible. Report on your research in the space provided in Figure 6–5.

5. Smoking: Why?

Purpose: To understand why a young person smokes and why an older adult smokes, and to compare and contrast your findings.

It appears that young people start smoking for social reasons and that eventually people continue to smoke because it becomes a physical and psychological addiction. This activity asks you to interview a young smoker, preferably someone under age eighteen (the legal age for smoking). Devise a series of questions that address when, why, and how they got started. Do the same for an adult, someone who has been smoking for at least twenty years.

Compare and contrast their stories in the space provided in Figure 6–6. What role do you think television advertising played in the smoking pattern of the older adult? Did the younger smoker mention advertising?

_____
_____
_____
_____
_____
_____
_____
_____
_____
_____

Figure 6–5 Twelve steps as used in a neighborhood program

_____
_____
_____
_____
_____
_____
_____
_____

Figure 6–6 Tale of two smokers

6. Evaluating a Gym or Fitness Center

Purpose: To apply understanding of fitness and weight loss principles to the selection of a safe and effective gym, health club, or fitness center.

There is a wide selection of places to exercise, including the YMCA, the YWCA, public membership clubs, private membership clubs, and school facilities. Begin this exercise by brainstorming features you would want in such a facility. Record them in the space provided in Figure 6–7.

Now, let's review your criteria. You probably thought about the cost and the convenience to home, work, or school, right? Did you consider

1. _____
2. _____
3. _____
4. _____
5. _____
6. _____
7. _____
8. _____

Figure 6–7 Criteria for evaluating gyms or fitness centers

whether the times for classes, sports courts, and so on would be convenient? How about the cleanliness of equipment, pool, and shower area? What kind of general atmosphere would you want? What about safety of equipment and workout floors? Did you include the qualifications and safety knowledge of instructors? How about the emergency medical equipment on hand? Other considerations might be whether the facility is affiliated with clubs in another city that you might visit regularly and whether the policy could be canceled if you were to move.

7. One Leisure a Day Keeps the Doctor Away

Purpose: To plan a leisure activity every day, rather than waiting for the weekend. The results will be decreased stress and more happiness.

Leisure activities are often saved for the weekend because we feel that we don't have time during the week. There is also a tendency to "professionalize" leisure activities, so that we expect a high degree of skill when we participate in them. The intent of this activity is to teach you to sprinkle leisure activities throughout the week. This will provide an opportunity to relax, enjoy a sense of enrichment, and have some fun.

In Figure 6–8, check some of the fun, relaxing activities that you enjoy. At the bottom of the table, personalize the list by adding activities that are not already mentioned.

Now, plan time for at least one item each day for the next two weeks. Perhaps you will spend only thirty minutes on this activity each day, but you will find that it makes life more fun and you will feel better.

At the end of two weeks, report to a friend what you did and how it went.

8. Campus Health Center as a Resource

Purpose: To discover what resources your campus health center provides in regard to family planning, birth control, and STDs.

The health center on your campus isn't there just for when you have a cold or the flu. Most campus health centers provide information on family planning and birth control, and some provide low-cost birth

listen to music	pursue a hobby	garden
study investments	draw or paint	read a book
create a meal	exercise	watch television
start a collection	do a puzzle	attend a sports event
join a club	create a craft	repair something

Figure 6–8 One leisure a day keeps the doctor away

control products such as condoms, the pill, and so on. Some even do low-cost tests for STDs and pap smears.

Interview someone at your campus health center regarding the services available, and then describe your results to other class members or to a friend.

9. Community Resources for Staying Healthy

Purpose: To discover what resources your community provides to help people with fitness, substance abuse, and STDs, and then to publicize this to someone else.

Pick one aspect of staying healthy that excites you. For example, let's say that you are strongly against underaged drinking. Let that be your issue. Then investigate what is happening in your community at the schools, churches, clubs, and organizations to encourage healthy habits.

Report what you have discovered to a friend, your class, or an organization that you attend. You can do this orally, by creating a flyer or handout for people to keep, or by writing an article for a newsletter or creating a poster. Choose whatever method seems suitable, or come up with your own idea of how you would like to communicate the information.

10. Competency Matrix

Purpose: To review the Competency Matrix in the Appendix and rate your current knowledge and skills in regard to life management.

Through your work with the last two chapters, you have further expanded your life management skills. Your ability to use decision making and to implement action plans is growing. Re-evaluate your current level of competency on the matrix found in the Appendix.

EXPAND YOUR LEARNING

The Complete Manual of Fitness and Well-Being. Pleasantville, NY: The Reader's Digest Association, Inc., 1984.

http://www.aegis.com. AIDS Education Global Information Service (AEGIS).

McGargh, Eileen. *How to Work for a Living and Still Be Free to Live.* Dana Point, CA: Loch Lomond Press, 1989.

Siegel, Mark; Alison Landes; and Nancy Jacobs, eds. *Illegal Drugs and Alcohol: America's Anguish.* Wylie, TX: Information Plus, 1995.

Waterman, Robert H. *The Renewal Factor: How the Best Get and Keep the Competitive Edge.* New York, NY: Bantam Books, Inc., 1987.

GROUP ACTIVITIES

1. The Mind and Body Connection

Purpose: To explore the role that visualization and positive attitude have in physical performance.

Each person in the class should stand up at their chairs. Everyone raises their right arm until it is out straight, parallel to the floor. Then, with arm outstretched and without moving their feet, everyone turns to the right as far as they can, and then turns back to face the front again.

Next, each person needs to visualize themselves repeating the exercise but turning farther around than before. Then, everyone does the exercise for a second time.

Form small groups to discuss the result of this exercise. Have each person describe a time that they exceeded their previous performance or expectations. What role can visualization and positive thinking have on physical performance? How can we incorporate this knowledge into our daily activities?

Changing Habits:
The Self-Change Model

A t this point in your life management studies, you have grasped the process of setting goals, and you have learned to break down large goals into smaller ones. You have learned about creating action plans for tasks in which each step is different and unique, and so you are able to confidently plan a vacation, a party, or the route to finishing your education.

THE SELF-CHANGE MODEL

Now it's time to learn about a different type of action plan, one that involves a **behavior goal**, a response or action that you want to exhibit more frequently or less frequently. We looked at behavior goals when we explored study skills, nutrition, and physical fitness. Perhaps, as a result, you have attempted to make some changes in those areas of your life. For example, you may have decreased the amount of sodas that you drink and increased the amount of water. Or, you may be spacing your study times over several days, rather than both reading and studying for a test during the same sitting.

Life goals and related outcome goals are reached only through behavior changes. The purpose of this Explorations is to provide you with an opportunity to follow the **self-change model.** In doing so, you will reach one of your goals and learn how to change other behaviors or habits that you wish to change.

Most of us have set behavior goals when we made a New Year's resolution. Common resolutions include to lose weight, quit smoking, and save more money. However, within a month, commitment wanes, and the goal is often abandoned. It turns out that changing a habit is more difficult than expected. In *Manage Your Life,* Williams and Long describe an effective process for changing habits. They call it the self-change model and identify its five basic steps:[1]

1. Select a goal and do a cost/benefit analysis.
2. Assess your current behavior or situation.
3. Develop a supportive environment.
4. Use supportive affirmations.
5. Monitor your progress.

---

[1] Robert Williams and James D. Long, *Manage Your Life,* 4th ed. (Boston, MA: Houghton Mifflin Co., 1991).

Select a Goal and Do a Cost/Benefit Analysis

Do you recall how to write a SMART goal? That skill will be very important now, as your behavior goal needs to be specific and measurable. It needs to be feasible and realistic as well. It makes no sense to set your goal to drink sixty-four ounces of water each day if you are currently accustomed to drinking ten ounces. Setting a goal that is attainable now is very important to maintain motivation.

A **cost/benefit analysis** asks you to consider the costs and benefits of making a change. It also asks you to identify the costs and benefits of *not* making the change. It is essential that this part of the process include emotion and passion. You will find this easier if you exaggerate somewhat. A cost/benefit analysis that engages your emotions inspires motivation. Research on changing behaviors indicates that when the emotions are tied to an internal desire for change, people are suddenly able to stick with their resolve.

Let's look at an example. The costs of more exercise might be time, sore muscles, and sweating. The benefits might be a more toned body, improved health, and more energy. When you add some passion, the benefits might include a better love life, a promotion at work, and a lot more fun. The costs of *not* exercising might be weight gain, poor appearance, and less energy. When you insert emotion, the costs might also include social stigma and shortened lifespan. The benefits of *not* exercising might be more time to watch television and no sweating.

Any behavior change will have costs and benefits. The costs often tend to be in the present and the benefits in the future. By identifying the long-term benefits and focusing on them, you are more likely to stay committed to your goal. Writing all of this down serves as a visual reminder and can increase your probability of success. You can look back to this cost/benefit analysis to identify rewards as you work on other steps of your action plan.

Assess Your Current Behavior or Situation

Having selected a goal, the next step is to determine where you presently stand in relation to that goal. This is called a **baseline assessment.** For example, if you wish to exercise more, how much exercise are you getting now? Most people do some sort of assessment before going on a diet, such as weighing themselves, measuring their waist or hips, or trying on a particular pair of pants. All of these are assessment tools to identify your current situation.

Most behavior changes that are permanent and successful occur gradually. By having a baseline assessment, you can measure the small increments of change that might go unnoticed. There are two basic types of behavior assessment records: a frequency count and time duration. A frequency count is a tabulation of the number of times a behavior occurs. A time duration is a record of the amount of time spent doing a certain behavior. Choose one or both of these methods, depending upon your goal.

The assessment tool itself might be a graph or chart. It may also be helpful to record events that precede or follow the behavior that you want to eliminate or diminish. For most situations, data should be collected for a week so that the typical pattern can be determined.

Keep in mind that the data you collect might indicate that you engage in the undesirable behavior less often than you believe. Certainly this would be a pleasant surprise, making your change of behavior easier.

Develop a Supportive Environment

Now it's time to analyze the environment in which the undesirable behavior occurs, so that you can develop an external support system for the desired behavior. You probably need to eliminate something and add something, and then create a reward for doing the new, desired behavior.

For example, let's say that you have decided to stop snacking on ice cream every night. The first step to making the environment supportive of that goal would be to eliminate ice cream from the freezer. The addition might be a substitute food, such as a frozen juice bar or sherbet. Or it might be to plan an activity other than eating, such as taking a walk. Your reward for following your behavior change would be highly personal, so an example is a bit difficult. But it might be having an ice cream cone after six days of no ice cream, or it could be treating yourself to a movie or some small item that you want.

Rewards keep us interested and motivated and, therefore, need to pay off in the short term. They can be activities, or they can be material in nature. It's best if they follow each time you do the new behavior. Soaking in a hot tub after each exercise session is such an example.

Use Supportive Affirmations

By this point in your studies of life management, you have experienced using positive self-talk, or affirmations. Using affirmations to support your behavior change can be very powerful. Plan to write at least eight statements, two for each of the following categories: personal responsibility, long-term benefits of the change, supportive environmental cues, and self-confidence. Keep in mind that the statements usually begin with "I," are positive in nature, and speak as if the new behavior is already a habit.

Affirmations help you stay focused on the positive action you are taking. As you will recall, you need to say these statements several times a day. Some people like to make an audio recording as well, so that they can hear themselves more easily.

Monitor Your Progress

Growth does not happen at a steady pace. There will be plateaus, where it seems that there is no progress. We need to recognize that plateaus are normal yet temporary. It is important to have a plan for these times, and for the times that are real setbacks or reversals. Affirmations are very useful, but what may really be called for is a supportive, empathetic friend. Identify someone who has had a similar experience, who will encourage you and reaffirm your worth.

The self-change model will be implemented with variations each time you use it. It can be perfectly suited to many situations. Just follow the five steps, using your creativity, and your skills will develop and expand each time.

YOUR TURN TO USE THE SELF-CHANGE MODEL

Now you have a chance to change a habit by using the self-change model. Consider what habit you would like to influence. It might be health-related, such as a change in eating habits or exercise routines. Some people decide to reduce or give up smoking. Or maybe you want to begin using a time management technique more regularly, such as a "To Do" list. Or you may have decided to become more assertive. The list of behaviors are unlimited. Just be sure to choose only one, so that you can concentrate. Remember you are both changing a habit and learning a new process.

So, you've selected a behavior. It's time to start thinking and planning. You will spend about a week following steps 1 and 2 of the self-change model in preparation for the new behavior. Then, because research suggests that it takes at least twenty-one days to establish a new habit, you will spend three weeks following your plan.

Step 1—Selecting a Goal and Rewards

a. Describe in one sentence the behavior goal to which you will devote energy and time in the next month. The behavior/habit I am going to eliminate is: _____

_____

_____

What I am going to replace it with is: _____

_____

_____

_____

b. Do a cost/benefit analysis of your behavior change or habit. This will provide you with ways to motivate yourself. Be sure to get *emotional* here, since feelings (passion) are essential to make a change. Record your thoughts in Figure Explorations 3–1.

Step 2—Assessing Current Behavior

a. Before you begin any changes, create or choose some comprehensive method of assessing your *current behavior*. Keep records, make a chart or graph, or use some other evaluation device to identify and measure your current situation. Describe your assessment tool here: _____

_____

_____

_____

_____

_____

b. Use your assessment tool for a week.

Benefits of the new habit or behavior:

_____

_____

_____

_____

Costs of the new habit or behavior:

_____

_____

_____

_____

Benefits of *not* doing the new habit or behavior:

_____

_____

_____

_____

Costs of *not* doing the new habit or behavior:

_____

_____

_____

_____

Figure Explorations 3–1 Cost/benefit analysis

c. Now, what did you discover during assessment? Write a few sentences about your conclusions here: _____

_____

_____

_____

_____

d. What could stand in the way of your reaching the goal?

Shortcomings/obstacles: _____

_____

_____

_____

_____

What you can do about it: _____

_____

_____

_____

_____

_____

e. If your experiences in self-assessment allowed you to refine your goal and make it more specific or measurable, restate it here: _____

_____

_____

_____

_____

BEGIN YOUR NEW BEHAVIOR NOW. Do it for three weeks. Proceed to Step 3 as you begin your new habit.

Step 3—Developing a Supportive Environment

a. Your next step is to identify changes in your situation that will encourage the behavior that you want and diminish the "old" behavior. Identify what you will *eliminate* in your environment:

_____

_____

_____

_____

_____

_____

b. Identify positive changes in, and what you will add to, your environment: _____

_____

_____

_____

c. How will you reward yourself for following your plan? (Keep in mind that this is a short-term, immediate sort of reward.)

_____

_____

_____

_____

d. Who can help you achieve your behavior change, and what will you ask of them? _____

_____

_____

_____

Step 4—Using Supportive Affirmations

Behavior change is an ongoing process, and therefore, so is assessment. One way we access ourselves is through self-talk. What can be useful is to be sure that this naturally occurring process is a positive one.

a. What positive self-talk have you been using recently related to your behavior goal? Write those statements here:

_____

_____

_____

_____

b. What additional affirmations could you use? Write at least two for each of the following categories:

1. *Personal responsibility:*

_____

_____

2. *Long-term benefits:*

_____

_____

3. *Supportive environmental cues:*

_____

_____

4. *Self-confidence:*

_____

_____

c. Write your positive self-talk statements on a file card, and repeat these phrases several times a day. In a few days, you will have memorized the affirmations.

Step 5—Monitoring Your Progress

a. After three weeks of implementation, write a paragraph about your progress toward your behavior goal: _____

_____

_____

_____

_____

b. How do you *feel* about this experience? _____

_____

_____

_____

_____

c. Have any other people noticed a change in your behavior? If so, what were their reactions? _____

_____

_____

_____

_____

d. Depending upon the behavior goal, there is a chance of a recurrence of the "old" behavior. Reaching a plateau is also typical. Therefore, it is smart to be prepared with a plan. What will you do to keep the environment supportive? _____

_____

_____

_____

_____

e. What will you do if regression occurs? _____

_____

_____

_____

_____

PRACTICE, PRACTICE

One use of the self-change model will not make you an expert. You will find it a slightly different experience each time you use it. As with most things, the more you use it, the better you will get at it. So, one behavior change will not turn your life around, but as you experience success at effective self-management, you will feel encouraged. Hopefully this will contribute to continued use of the self-change model, making it easier to influence and sustain the changes that you desire.

Goal Management

Over the last few weeks you have had many opportunities to set short-term and long-term goals. And now you have begun to acquire the skill of reaching behavior goals by changing habits. With the latter, it is particularly important not to work on too many behavior goals at one time. It can be stressful and overwhelming. So take it gradually. Remember to use affirmations, keep the environment supportive, and be patient.

Personal Goals Book[2]

One way to bring all your plans for changing habits and achieving goals together is to create a visualization tool that includes pictures and affirmations to focus your thoughts. People from all walks of life from athletes to pilots to successful business leaders use visualization to achieve goals. They know that whatever a person can imagine and vividly picture will become reality and fact.

Visualization can be applied to the creation of a Personal Goals Book. Using pictures that you draw yourself, computer clip art, or pictures cut from magazines, you will create images of the things and

---

[2] Adapted from Bonnie Rader, "Personal Treasure Book," *Teaching Life Management in California Community Colleges* (Sacramento, CA: Chancellor's Office, California Community Colleges, June 1996).

events you want to occur in your life. You will be like a movie director and scriptwriter rolled into one.

Select specific pictures that are colorful and as clear as possible. If you select a small, dull, black-and-white photograph of a house, you are likely to end up with a small, dull, colorless house! *Put yourself in* your Personal Goals Book. Use a photograph or caricature of yourself and add it to the story. For example, put a picture of yourself at the front door of that beautiful, colorful house that you have selected. *Use art materials* such as colored paper, colored pencils, and a sturdy notebook. This will increase the attractiveness as well as the durability of your Personal Goals Book. *Include your affirmations* that connect to the pictures. For example, near the picture of the make and model of car you want, you could write, "I love driving my new (type of car), and I paid for it easily." Do this with each picture.

Your Personal Goals Book is a very powerful tool that can mobilize your thoughts and creative energy towards achieving your desires. But you must *use it daily*. Always look at it first thing in the morning and last thing before you go to sleep. Take it with you whenever possible during the day. It won't work if it's hidden away on a bookshelf. Many people like to *keep it confidential*. This way they feel more free to tell the story as they want, to include pictures, words, and affirmations without feeling they will be judged by others. *Keep adding pictures* for whatever you want to accomplish or obtain. Add affirmations such as "This is mine NOW!" Finally, *remain trusting and confident.* Thoughts precede action. What you thought about yesterday is what you have today. What you think about today is what you will have in the future. Don't give up! You can never know what forces may already be at work on your behalf.

EXPAND YOUR LEARNING

Seligman, Martin. *What You Can Change and What You Can't*. New York, NY: Fawcett Columbine, 1993.

Williams, Robert L., and James D. Long. *Manage Your Life*. 4th ed. Boston, MA: Houghton Mifflin Co., 1991.

UNIT FOUR
Developing Your Social Potential

Chapter 7
Communicating Effectively

Chapter 8
Effective Listening

Chapter 9
Effective Speaking

Chapter 10
Getting Along with Others

Chapter 11
Functioning in Groups

Explorations
How to Delegate

Chapter 7

Communicating Effectively

Since your first day of life you have tried to communicate with others. Although you don't remember it, your first actions after birth undoubtedly included a stretch, a wiggle, and a cry. Your facial expression showed your surprise and displeasure at the change of environment. As time moved on, you learned to charm people with your smile, gestures, and words. Sometimes you were effective, sometimes not.

We know that clear communication is essential to achieving goals such as successful interpersonal relationships and a rich and rewarding life. So we want to be as effective as possible with our friends and family and in our careers. Yet it is evident from personal experience and research that effective communication does not take place nearly as much as we would like. Therefore, this topic deserves our attention, so that we can increase our skill levels, feel better about ourselves, and reach our potential.

This chapter discusses the communication process. You may have already learned something about it in a speech or business class, and certainly you have personal experience with it. Chapter 8 will focus on the art of listening. Then, Chapter 9 will become more personal and invite you to think more about your own conversation style and its effectiveness.

THE COMMUNICATION PROCESS

Clear communication is the basis for harmonious living and cooperative actions. We fill our lives with communication. Some communication is one-way, that is, a message is sent but no apparent feedback is given. This happens when your boss sends you a memo or announcement. It also happens when you retrieve your phone messages from your answering machine or service.

In conversations, when one person sends a message to another, and that other person then responds, two-way communication has taken place. In this process, symbols such as words or gestures comprise the message. If both people recognize and attach at least a similar meaning to the symbols, they reach understanding. This process might be represented by a circle as shown in Figure 7–1.

Using a circle to represent the communication process is appropriate because effective communication is a continuous two-way process. When two people communicate orally, at a given time, one person functions primarily as a **sender.** The sender puts his or her thoughts into words and actions, a process that is called **encoding.** The thoughts and actions are the **message.** They include spoken words, the verbal part of the message, as well as gestures and facial expressions that are part of the nonverbal message.

This circle shows that communication is a continuous two-way process.

Figure 7–1 The communication process

If all goes well, the second person in this process, the **receiver**, begins interpreting, or **decoding**, the message. Decoding is dependent upon the receiver speaking the same language as the sender. The term *language* is used here in a broad sense. Therefore, this might mean that they both speak Spanish, or it might mean they both understand the language of the computer industry. So, how much vocabulary a person can use to put the message together and how skillfully that can be accomplished is of utmost importance.

The level of accuracy or effectiveness of the decoding can be measured by the particular words and actions that the receiver chooses, which is called **feedback**. If there is **interference** with this process, the level of effectiveness will diminish. Examples of interference include noise in the environment, a receiver's inability to decode and lack of trust or rapport in the relationship, or preoccupation on the receiver's part.

A Closer Look at the Message

The verbal or linguistic skills of the sender and the receiver are of primary importance to the effectiveness of communication. If each of them has an extensive vocabulary in the same language and is familiar with the nuances of the language, their ability to encode and decode will be greater.

Nonverbal messages are sent with facial expressions, tone of voice, eye contact, body language, and posture as well as the amount of physical space allowed or created between sender and receiver. For example, a pleasant smile, a calm well-modulated tone, and an open body posture signals a desire for rapport. When evaluating or "reading" these signals, it is important to look for a cumulative message. It may be that a person who is making eye contact, has an attentive facial expression, and is standing close to you, but with arms crossed, is receptive to your ideas. The person may just be feeling physically cold.

Encoding entails choosing words and actions that the receiver will understand. For effective communication, the two parties should attach the same meaning to the verbal and nonverbal message. This can happen if they share a common language and culture. It should be noted that speakers from different parts of the country or different social or economic groups are not likely to attach identical meaning to a word or action, even if they share the same language. The disparity is even greater when the sender and receiver are from different countries.

The nonverbal aspects of communication, in particular, are affected by our cultural backgrounds. A *culture* is a set of traditional beliefs, values, and paradigms that are shared in a given group. Businesses often speak about the culture of a particular company, such as the beliefs and values of IBM compared to Apple Computers, for example. Cultures can exist within a country and can be based on the group members' age, occupations or income, sexual orientation, ethnic or racial heritage, or religious beliefs. There can be other differences, for example, between people from two-parent families and people from single-parent families, and between people who are able-bodied and those with disabilities.

Nonverbal aspects of communication have different behavior patterns and can be interpreted differently from culture to culture. In some cultures, for example, gestures are kept to a minimum, while in others they tend to be sweeping and expansive. And the popular assumption that facial expressions are a universal language turns out to be inaccurate. In a recent experiment, photographs that were recognized in the same way by Americans were shown to medical students in Japan. Many, sometimes most, of those students interpreted the emotions behind the expressions differently.[1]

Our preferred space bubble or distance from other people is another nonverbal communicator affected by culture. In the dominant culture in the United States, close family members or intimate friends might stand about a foot apart, or even close enough to touch. Acquaintances usually stand four feet apart, and strangers are expected to stand six to twelve feet away. People from other cultures and countries may choose to narrow the space.

Because the United States houses many cultures, good communicators are on the alert for differences and seek opportunities to learn new ways of doing things from other groups. Chapter 9 presents more information on this topic.

---

[1] Steve Emmons, "Emotions at Face Value," *Los Angeles Times*, Orange County ed., 5 December 1997, p. E1.

Decreasing Interference in the Communication Process

If the receiver cannot hear the message due to noise in the environment, two-way communication cannot take place. Anyone who has tried to talk to a person who is concentrating on a television program can appreciate this concept. It is the sender's responsibility to analyze the environment for noise or other distractions that might interfere with decoding. Then these barriers to communication must be eliminated or the conversation postponed.

Besides noise, there may be other factors affecting the ability to decode, such as the emotional state of the receiver. The receiver might be too tired or hungry, or might be focusing on a problem or worry. A good habit for a sender to have is to ask the receiver if "now is a good time" to talk. If not, the sender can select a more appropriate time.

Sometimes the issue is that the sender or receiver has long-held feelings and attitudes of a negative nature toward a person because of their apparent membership in a group. The group might be people of a certain age, occupation, race, or those who dress in a certain way or listen to certain music. This attitude is called *prejudice,* and it interferes with people communicating effectively as individuals.

Finally, lack of trust or rapport in a relationship interferes with communication. Every relationship has a characterizing tone or level of connectedness. It might be a level of synchronicity and harmony, indifference and neutrality, or one of distrust. When we are in harmony with another, we experience *rapport* with them. Clear communication involves the interchange of ideas and feelings and an opening up of one person to another. This will not occur unless the environment is secure and intimate and rapport has been established.

If people exchange messages in an environment of acceptance, they feel valued, and a degree of trust emerges. They feel comfortable and willing to take a risk to reveal their true feelings. With each risk, a little more trust develops until people are willing to take greater risks. The level of rapport increases, as does the openness, freedom, and spontaneity within the relationship.

DEVELOPING MORE EFFECTIVE COMMUNICATION SKILLS

All of us have had communication successes. Perhaps you have been able to explain your feelings or thoughts to a parent or spouse to the extent that they really understood you. Or maybe you made a persuasive speech at work or school, and others told you later that your comments had caused them to change their minds.

It is also a certainty that each of us has had communication mishaps. We've had times when people misunderstood our thoughts and motives, causing angry encounters. These occasions are not failures unless we miss the opportunity to learn from them. By knowing more about your communication style and by being assertive, you can be a more successful communicator.

Our Personal Communication Style

Each of us approaches communication in a particular way. If we take the time to identify our communication strengths and weaknesses, and to change our weak points, we will have more successes and fewer mishaps.

At this point, we will focus on the role of the sender. In the next chapter, the role of the receiver will be given more attention.

There are many styles or approaches to communication. Some of us make sense of the world by seeing and others by hearing. This is reflected in our verbal messages. Do you recall this idea from Chapter 3? Individual Activity 3 especially provided a chance to analyze language for a preference for auditory, visual, or kinesthetic input. Our preferences are reflected in our choice of words.

Some people begin a conversation with small talk before approaching the topic of discussion. Others want to get right to the point and exit when a decision is made or an answer provided. Remember that some of us have more highly developed interpersonal skills and are more sensitive to the responses of others.

All of these factors affect our personal communication style. Differences in styles are normal. A heightened awareness of styles allows us to identify successful communication strategies. Then we can incorporate these strategies into our own styles. It also allows us to recognize that the styles used by others are habitual. They are not aimed at us particularly, and therefore, we should not feel hurt or slighted by approaches that might be different. Rather, we should strive to be flexible and feel comfortable with the differences.

Regardless of our personal style, we want to enter conversations with a supportive attitude. Sincere empathy can be conveyed by direct eye contact and our full attention. We need to project feelings of equality, indicating a willingness to listen and intention to value the thoughts and feelings of the receiver. The focus should be on the needs and desires of the receiver, not just on our own desires.

We also want to become aware of personal prejudices. All of us developed beliefs and attitudes in childhood that from a rational perspective we might not accept today, but which still affect our emotions and reactions. Being on the alert to these feelings and learning to moderate them will allow us to personally grow and improve our relationships.

In effective communication, we want an atmosphere that is open and trusting. One way to achieve that is for the sender to use "I" statements rather than "you" statements. "You" statements tend to blame and judge, and to assume things that may or may not be true. An "I" message focuses on what the sender really knows about: personal feelings, motives, and actions. For example, "You make me so angry" becomes "I feel so upset." With "I" statements, the speaker takes ownership for his or her feelings.

Three-Step Assertion Model

Part of good communication is being open about personal feelings and desires. Many people find this difficult, especially when dealing with issues that they would rather avoid, ignore, or deny. Sometimes we might need to ask for help or for a favor, or we might need to admit a mistake. Perhaps we want our housemate to be more helpful in keeping the house clean, or as a host of a party we need to ask a guest not to have any more to drink, or we wish our boss would plan ahead better when it comes to deadlines and not operate in a crisis mode.

These are particular opportunities for using "I" statements and the three-step **assertion model:** I feel . . ., I want . . ., and I vow. . . . Begin by identifying the situation using facts only, such as "The house is very dirty. The kitchen counters are covered in crumbs and dishes are piled high in the sink." Do not place blame or judge, just describe the situation. Focus on the action or behavior, not the person. Then move into the assertion model:

1. *I feel*—How you feel cannot be challenged by others, since you are the expert and authority. Informing others of your feelings can be very valuable feedback for them. Reminder: Use "I" statements. For example, "I really feel uncomfortable when the kitchen is dirty" or "I really like carpooling with you, but I feel really frustrated when I'm late for work."

2. *I want*—People are not mind readers, and so it is unfair to assume they know what you want or need. It is your responsibility to tell them. For example, "I want the dishes to be rinsed off and put in the dishwasher right after a meal" or "I want to be in the parking lot at work by 7:45. This way I will be able to get to my desk before 8:00 A.M."

3. *I vow*—This is a statement of what you want to do. It needs to be a plan independent from another person. It also needs to avoid a threat or judgment, since that would not meet the criteria for creating a trusting environment. For example, "I am willing to do all of my own dishes, but not yours" or "I am willing to be at your house at 7:15 A.M. to pick you up, but we must drive away by 7:20 at the latest."

Like any new behavior, being assertive may feel awkward at first. But people who have made being assertive a habit are easier to be around, less stressed, and happier.

INDIVIDUAL ACTIVITIES

1. Effective Communication at Work

Purpose: To determine the criteria or standard that is used on the job for judging effective communication.

Regardless of the field or type of work (called *function* in the Explorations section at the end of Unit 2), employers from around the world indicate that effective communication skills are an essential part of job preparation. In most settings, these skills are a requirement for advancement. Your task is to interview an employer, preferably *your* employer, to identify what effective communication means for a particular job.

In Figure 7–2, write about the qualities you feel you consistently practice and the ones you want to improve upon.

Now, ask your classmates who did this exercise to share what their employers said. In what areas did the employers agree?

2. Same Word, Different Meaning

Purpose: To explore how vocabulary can affect whether a message is properly and clearly decoded.

Figure 7–2 Analyzing my communication at work

If you overheard a conversation about "making out," what would you say was the major topic? Perhaps you would say the topic was about success or progress, or maybe you would say it was about necking, smooching, or kissing. Effective communication requires that the sender and receiver attach the *same* meaning to words and actions.

Over the next week or so, ask people over the age of thirty-five to identify slang or fashionable words from the time when they were adolescents. Then ask young people to identify words they are using today. Create a list with definitions, and identify the time period in which each term was used.

What can you conclude about the need for attaching identical meaning to a word if the goal is clear communication? Why do some people use words that might be unclear to others?

3. My Journal

Purpose: To recall a recent conversation that went particularly well. Reflect on the impact this success has had on the time period since then.

It is said that one success leads to another. With this in mind, recall a recent conversation that worked well, where you expressed an opinion or feelings and were clearly understood.

Write about the strategies that worked. Maybe you carefully chose vocabulary, or consciously controlled the nonverbal message or the space around you and the other person. Record these observations in Figure 7–3 or in your private journal.

4. Space as a Communicator

Purpose: To become more aware of the amount of space that people put between themselves and others according to the relationship and setting.

Spend some time observing people talking and walking together, in restaurants, at work, in elevators, everywhere. Notice who is allowed to enter personal space (four feet from an individual) and intimate space (one foot from an individual).

Write about your conclusions in Figure 7–4.

Figure 7–3 My journal—A conversation worked well

Figure 7–4 Space as a communicator—My observations

5. Cultural Differences

Purpose: To become more aware of nonverbal messages and cultural differences as expressed in communication.

Much has been written over the last decade about the different meanings behind certain gestures, eye contact, and phrases by peoples of various cultures. Make a picture collection of nonverbal messages using pictures gathered from magazines, clipart, or the World Wide Web. Then survey people of various cultures to identify what the gestures mean to them.

Make a record of your findings and share it with other class members.

6. Establishing Trust

Purpose: To review relationships to determine how trust has been established, since it promotes honest and effective communication.

Establishing trust in a relationship is essential for honest and open communication. Describe how you did this in one of your friendships and how you did it in one of your business relationships. Write your response in Figure 7–5.

7. Practicing the Assertion Model

Purpose: To provide an opportunity to apply the three-step assertion model to a current problem or irritation.

Consider something small that has been irritating you. Imagine how you might normally handle that problem. Now, using the three-step assertion model, write out the script of what you might say in Figure 7–6.

In a friendship

_____

_____

_____

_____

In a business relationship

_____

_____

_____

_____

Figure 7–5 Establishing trust

_____

_____

_____

_____

_____

_____

_____

_____

Figure 7–6 Practicing the assertion model

Wait a day or two and re-read the script, making improvements where possible. Now, use this script to assertively discuss the irritation or problem with the other person involved. Write about your experience in Figure 7–7. Include the results, your feelings, and what you wish you had done differently.

8. Communications Timeline

Purpose: To expand understanding of the changes that have occurred in the speed of communication over the last one hundred and fifty years.

Historians tell us that it took three months before everyone in America knew the Civil War was over. The speed of communication and the frequency of contact have changed drastically since the 1860s. Innovations such as the telephone, television, e-mail, and the Internet have changed how fast we can get information as well as the quantity of information available.

Make a communications timeline, marking significant innovations and events. Feel free to include pictures of the people or products involved. What did you learn about the speed of communication today? How do you feel about the universal need for communication skills in the workforce? Share your results and your timeline with class or family members.

EXPAND YOUR LEARNING

Dresser, Norine. *Multicultural Manners: New Rules of Etiquette for a Changing Society.* New York, NY: Wiley, 1996.
Dyer, William. *Pull Your Own Strings.* New York, NY: Harper Books, 1994.

GROUP ACTIVITIES

1. Assertive Requests

Purpose: To practice being assertive in a nonthreatening environment.

Form groups of three people. Each person will get to play each of three roles: the sender, the receiver, the observer. Each sender is to imagine a request—perhaps for assistance, for a change in a situation, or a change in another person's behavior. The sender first needs to describe the facts, using nonjudgmental language, and then express feelings and

---

Figure 7–7 My assertion experience

wants using "I" statements. Finally, the sender will state his or her vow—what consequences or events are likely to happen if there is not a remedy to the situation.

After each role play, the participants should discuss what they might have done differently in making and responding to the requests. Observers can comment on nonverbal communication and offer suggestions on how the requests and responses might have been different and more useful.

2. My Pet Peeve

Purpose: To be able to share with other people what stereotypes you think are commonly held by cultures of which you are a member.

Many of us are tired of hearing commonly stated generalizations about a culture to which we belong. This culture might be based on but not limited to the following: age, gender, sexual orientation, religion, occupation, racial or ethnic background, and so forth.

Form groups of four or five people. Individually, each person should identify at least two cultures in which they are a member. Then, on a piece of paper, each person should answer the following question: "What would you like to *never* hear again about the (fill in the blank) culture?" For example, the author of this book would like to never again hear that because her education is in Home Economics, she must be a good cook.

Going around the group, one person at a time, share your answers for one culture. Then, go around the group again for the second culture you selected.

Did any of you have similar examples? If some of you selected the same culture, did you have the same pet peeve? What general insights about stereotypes did you gain by doing this exercise? Write your answers in Figure 7–8.

Now, share your insights with Norine Dresser, author of *Multicultural Manners*. You can reach her by e-mail at norined@earthlink.net.

Figure 7–8 Pet peeves and cultural diversity

Chapter 8

Effective Listening

Much of our time each day is spent communicating: reading, writing, speaking, listening. Many careers are centered on these activities in fields such as journalism, advertising, and sales. You may remember early experiences in school where you were organized into a reading group, taught to use cursive writing and proper grammar, and taught proper pronunciation. Do you remember the training that you received in listening? No? You don't remember being in a listening group?

Most experts find that listening skills of adults are poorly developed because there is little formal training in this skill. A large part of our early education focuses on reading, writing, and speaking. But what we learn about listening is only the technical aspect: identification of sounds (dog, cow, and so on), listening for directions ("Stay in your seat until the bell rings"), and distinguishing significant ideas in stories that we read or that are read to us. What we are *not* taught is to listen for the emotion and feelings attached to the words in the message.

Listening fully and actively takes energy and commitment. Done properly, the listener can re-create for the speaker the intent, the meaning, and the emotion behind what was said, not just the words. Because we have been inadequately trained to hear the whole message, our personal relationships suffer, as does the effectiveness of business and government.

Good listeners are popular, and usually successful. They are appreciated by friends, family, and business colleagues. Good listening skills can make learning easier and faster and, so, are an asset to a student. Obtaining these skills takes commitment to understanding the communication process and a willingness to use more effective listening strategies.

THE PROCESS OF LISTENING

Hearing is a physiological activity, one that most of us take for granted. What are you listening to right now? As you thought about your answer, did your mind switch focus? Did you become alert to sounds that you hadn't noticed before? We hear a lot of things that we edit out: the droning of airplanes, the whizzing of cars, the hum of heaters and air conditioners. In our lifetimes, we have become very adept at editing environmental sounds out of our consciousness.

Editing of sound is imperative for survival and to avoid overload, but this necessary skill can be a bad habit if we edit at inappropriate times. We can overcome this if we recognize that listening is really an interactive process. **Active listening** is an emotional and intellectual activity that takes concentration and energy. The listening process is composed of five steps that occur in rapid succession: hearing, selecting, assimilating, organizing, and responding.

The first step in listening is *hearing.* It is important that the receiver can physically hear or in some other way perceive the message. For example, hearing-impaired individuals might perceive the message by seeing it in the form of sign language. Next the receiver *selects* the particular message to which he or she will attend, ignoring other competing messages. So a driver momentarily tunes out the radio and focuses attention on the passenger of a car. As the driver mentally processes the sounds of the passenger, he or she *assimilates,* or begins to assign meaning to the sounds. The sounds are *organized* in the brain, which searches memory for similar sounds, attaches meaning to the sounds, and then evaluates them for similarities and differences from previous conversations. In *response,* a thought forms in the brain, which may or may not stimulate a sound from the listener.

WHY IS LISTENING SO HARD?

The brain is incredibly powerful. It allows us to do many tasks simultaneously. For example, do you ever drive down the street, eating, listening to the radio, and conversing with the passengers? Because hearing does not take all of our brain power, we can do many other tasks and still hear sounds. Unless we are engaged in active listening, really concentrating, and asking questions of the speaker, our brain does not have enough to keep it busy. In that situation, our focus blurs and our mind tends to daydream.

Distractions frequently interfere with effective listening. As a receiver, you might be too hot, too cold, or too tired. You might be worried about the parking ticket you just got or the fight you had with a loved one. Or maybe there is something else within sight or hearing that interests you. When this happens, good listeners stop the conversation and admit that they weren't concentrating. They ask the speaker to begin again, now that their attention is refocused and they are prepared to assimilate, organize, and respond.

Preconceptions and prejudice against the speaker or the topic also can be barriers to effective listening. In these situations, we shut our brain down, hence the term *close-mindedness.* Refusing to listen because you don't like the message is a missed opportunity to learn. Try to focus on the emotional content behind the message. Pay attention to the pitch, tone, speed, and body language. Keep in mind that a speaker who feels that you have genuinely listened to them is more inclined to listen to you when it's your turn to talk.

ACTIVE LISTENING IS EFFECTIVE LISTENING

To reach our potential and have the most satisfaction from life, it is essential to have highly developed listening skills. An active listener concentrates on the speaker and is mentally and emotionally engaged in the message. We can learn to be good active listeners if we are willing to break the old habit of never getting beyond just hearing a message.

Eliminate Distractions

In order to hear, select, assimilate, organize, and respond, we must be able to focus on the speaker and hear and see all the verbal and nonverbal information encoded in the message. You can increase your ability to hear by eliminating noise and other interference in the environment. Create a setting where you can see the speaker, make eye contact, and where you won't be distracted. If this is not a good time for you to listen, perhaps because you have a deadline to meet, be honest and say so. Explain the situation and ask to set aside a different time when you can give the person your full attention.

Be Open

Effective listening entails having empathy for the speaker. This means you strive to really understand their thoughts and feelings, although you do not need to agree with them. You acknowledge the speaker's right to personal expression, and you willingly listen so that trust is established and honest exchange can occur.

Active listening is a little like brainstorming. You want to gather the information, that is, listen to the whole story, before judging. This requires a willingness to accept that people have different values, styles, and opinions. It requires that you react to the ideas, not to the person.

Concentrate

In order to assimilate and organize information, we probably will need to ask questions of the speaker. Generally the most effective questions are open-ended, ones that cannot be answered with a "yes" or "no." Open-ended questions yield more information, clarify intent or feelings, and expand the content of the message.

When listening, limit your own talking. Focus your mind on what the speaker is saying, not on what you want to say next. Make occasional interjections such as "yes" or "I hear you" so that the speaker knows you are concentrating. If possible and appropriate, take notes. This will help you remember important points that might be relevant later.

Finally, be very attentive to nonverbal messages. See if the verbal part of the message seems to match the nonverbal. For example, if a person says something is "no problem" but seems to have an angry facial expression and a closed off body posture, it is possible that person is not being totally honest.

Listen for the True Meaning

Often people are not assertive because they fear hurting the feelings of others or they do not want to be rude. As a result, they may not be as clear or direct in their comments as they should be. An active listener is sensitive to questions or complaints that actually are requests. For example, a wife who asks her husband if he would like to go out to dinner may, in fact, be expressing her own preference.

One way to know if you really understood the message is to paraphrase, which is summarizing what you heard in your own words. You might start out by saying, "What I hear you saying is . . ." or "Let me see if I understand. . . ." This is a feedback strategy that can be very effective.

INDIVIDUAL ACTIVITIES

1. Practice, Practice

Purpose: To prepare for an important conversation or discussion by planning what you want to say, how you want to say it, and how you will listen to your partner.

Sometimes in our lives we can anticipate an important conversation. If we think about it beforehand, select particular verbal and nonverbal messages to use, and anticipate the feelings and needs of the receiver, we can be more effective. We can anticipate how we will actively listen to the other person.

Select a conversation that you know is coming up. Think about your role as a sender and a receiver. Plan to use particular strategies that you think will be effective. Write about your plan in Figure 8–1.

Now spend a little time rehearsing. Modify your words and actions until you feel comfortable. Then, proceed to actually have this conversation.

In Figure 8–2, write about the effect or benefits of planning ahead and practicing for an important conversation.

2. An Appointment to Listen

Purpose: To practice creating a positive and supportive way of telling a person that you cannot listen to them right now, but want to establish another time to talk.

Our lives are hectic and filled with the needs and problems of ourselves, our family members, and those at work. To be effective listeners,

Figure 8–1 My conversation plan

Figure 8–2 The effect of practice

1. _____
   _____
   _____
   _____
2. _____
   _____
   _____
   _____
3. _____
   _____
   _____
   _____
   _____

Figure 8–3 Let's make an appointment

we must be free from distractions. So to be fair to ourselves and others, sometimes we need to be honest and say that it is not a good time for us to listen. Your task is to create two or three ways to say this in a positive and supportive fashion. Write your answers in Figure 8–3.

Now find a friend who will let you practice your scripts. In your friend's opinion, which one seemed to work the best? Why?

3. Paraphrasing

Purpose: To provide an opportunity to practice paraphrasing in order to be a more effective listener.

There is no need to plan for this exercise. Just be on the lookout for a time this week when someone shares an opinion or feelings. Pause for a moment, use an introductory comment such as "Let me check if I heard what you said . . .," and practice paraphrasing.

Do this at least twice this week. Then write a short paragraph about your experience, including how it went and what you still need to know about this process, in Figure 8–4.

4. Listening to a Loved One

Purpose: To provide an opportunity for students to practice active listening with a close friend, spouse, or child.

_____
_____
_____
_____
_____

Figure 8–4 Paraphrasing practice

Select a person who is very close to you, such as a spouse, child, or significant friend. You will listen to them for twenty minutes. Do nothing else but listen. In preparation, you will eliminate distractions. You will show openness with your body language and eye contact. You will concentrate on what they say, and listen for the true meaning.

Write what you discovered in Figure 8–5, or report the results to a group of classmates, friends, or colleagues.

Figure 8–5 Listening to a loved one

5. Two Ears and One Mouth

Purpose: To become aware of how much time in a conversation we devote to talking and how much time to listening.

Although we have two ears and one mouth, it is a fair bet that most of us don't spend two-thirds of a conversation listening and one-third talking. This is your opportunity to determine your typical ratio.

Over the next few days, perhaps for as long as a week, keep track in two-person conversations, as best you can, how much time you talk. Do it informally but as accurately as possible. Having a clock or watch with a second hand might be very useful.

Now, what did you discover?

6. Notes as Memory Joggers

Purpose: To establish a new policy of taking notes when it will be useful for business or personal conversations.

Have you ever forgotten some important information that you know a friend told you? Not just an appointment, but maybe his birthday, or the name of a newborn child. Or maybe you made a promise and then forgot about it. If so, read on.

Obtain a small notebook where you can make informal notes. Keep the notebook handy so that you can regularly record information from significant conversations. You will know which conversations are significant based on previous forgotten information. Write the date of the conversation, the commitments or agreements reached, and who is responsible for what. You might also make note if you shared a message with someone. This way, it won't nag you, nor will you end up repeating yourself to them.

After three weeks evaluate the use of this system. In Figure 8–6, write the advantages, the disadvantages, and your decision about whether or not to continue using a notebook.

7. Story Time

Purpose: To evaluate your current abilities in technical and active listening.

Listen to a book on tape. Stop the tape periodically to record the facts and events of the story. At the same time, record the motives, feelings, and emotions of the story's characters. Which was easiest for you to identify? What helped you with determining the motives, feelings, and emotions in the story? What hindered you? What listening skills do you want to improve upon? How will you do that? Write your answers in Figure 8–7.

8. A Double Challenge

Purpose: To learn more about how a hearing-impaired individual becomes aware of the total message.

Figure 8–6 Using a notebook as a memory jogger

Figure 8–7 Analyzing my listening skills

It has already been noted that hearing is an important part of listening and that although listening is key to interpersonal relationships, most of us aren't very good at it. Imagine the double challenge of someone who cannot hear well to begin with.

Interview someone who is hearing-impaired or who knows a hearing-impaired individual well. Try to uncover what they substitute for the hearing step of listening. Report your findings to the class or record them in Figure 8–8.

Figure 8–8 The double challenge

EXPAND YOUR LEARNING

Carnegie, Dale. *How to Win Friends and Influence People.* New York, NY: Simon and Schuster, 1991.

Smith, Manual J. *When I Say No, I Feel Guilty.* New York, NY: Bantam Books, 1985.

GROUP ACTIVITIES

1. The Greeting

Purpose: To evaluate the message behind a handshake, and to determine whether yours is as effective as it might be.

A handshake tells a lot about a person and is as much a part of conversation as our facial expressions. It can convey confidence and enthusiasm, aloofness, or indifference.

The rules pertaining to shaking hands have changed in the past two decades as our society has become more casual and as more women have entered the workforce. People of all ages and both genders need to be comfortable with shaking hands, since it is an important step to establishing rapport. Formal receiving lines may have vanished, but the need to know how to properly shake hands remains.

Divide the group exactly in half. Form two circles, one within the other. Members of the inner circle will offer a handshake and an introduction to a group member standing opposite them in the outer circle. Then the inner circle will keep moving one position to the left and repeating the process until the round is complete.

Take a few minutes for feedback. What felt good? What worked? What were the problems? Typical answers to the question on problems include too tight a grip, too weak a grip, or jewelry in the way.

This latter problem can be avoided if the thumb is held at a ninety-degree angle to the fingers as the hand is offered for the handshake.

2. Listening and Paraphrasing

Purpose: To give each student an opportunity to practice and evaluate paraphrasing.

Divide into groups of three people. One person will be the sender, one the receiver, and one an observer. Then the roles will rotate until everyone has played each role.

The sender should pick one topic and make brief comments on it, pausing after each comment to allow the receiver to clarify what has been said or to paraphrase the comment. A topic might be an enjoyable vacation, a consumer problem or complaint, or some current event.

When clarifying a point, the receiver should summarize the other's idea in his or her own words or give an example that shows the perceived thoughts or feelings. For example, "As I understand it . . ." or "Would this be an example of the point you made?" (then stating the specific example). When paraphrasing, the listener should try to make the paraphrase more specific than the original statement. The observer can make suggestions if the receiver and sender feel they need help.

After everyone has had a turn at all three roles, the three people in each group can discuss how they felt about the experience and what they might do differently to improve their communication.

The entire group can comment on the process and generate a list of questions and statements that would be useful in clarifying a speaker's message. These might include "What do you mean by . . .?" and "I'm not sure I understand."

Chapter 9 _____
Effective Speaking

onversations are a little like dancing. They require the skills and cooperation of both participants. We can analyze the parts to a dance, as we did the parts of the communication process in Chapter 7. And we can talk about the steps that both partners need to take, as we did in Chapters 7 and 8. But it is not really a dance until the two participants come together and step out on the dance floor in time with the music.

In this chapter, we will look at the performance of communication, the personal aspects of conversation. These include making a first impression, modifying speech qualities, and applying effective strategies in person-to-person conversation, on the telephone, and in speaking to groups.

When we communicate, we are usually trying to inform, persuade, or convince people. This occurs by applying all we know about the communication process, including listening and speaking. Along the way, remember that a powerful tool of communication is your personality. Learning to let it shine is part of effective communication.

FIRST IMPRESSION IS A LASTING ONE

It is said that we never have another chance to make a first impression. This is so true, and a bit scary, if you realize that a **first impression** is created in ten to fifteen seconds of meeting. We "read" people's clothing choices, hairstyles, posture, facial expressions, and handshake. We look to see if the clothes are clean and appropriate, if the individual is well-groomed, if they stand tall and confident, if they smile and look us in the eye as we shake hands. It isn't until then that we begin to hear what they say.

If our first impression is a negative one, what we say may never be heard, let alone organized and assimilated. If we really want successful communication, we need to rid our appearance of negative aspects that would cause us to be prejudged, however unfair that might be.

Perhaps the first impression is positive, but there is still something in a person's appearance that is so distracting the listener may not be able to focus on the message. For example, one person might fidget in a chair, while another might be wearing noisy jewelry. Try to screen your actions to avoid these distractions.

SPEECH QUALITIES

As you know, we communicate without words as well as with them. In fact, nonverbal communication is the biggest part of the message. Our words may convey facts and information, but the tone of voice and pace of our speech reveal our feelings. By consciously selecting and altering the nonverbal aspects of our speech we can be more precise and clear with our message.

Pronunciation

If you turn on the national news, you will discover that most broadcasters pronounce English in a similar manner. They are using standardized English. Regional variations or accents, such as southern, midwestern, or Bostonian, are understood by most people. However, because of the influence of television, standardized English is the norm against which people's speech is judged. It can provide a standard for you to work toward as well.

Volume, Rate, Pitch, and Tone

The boring speaker drones on and on in a monotonous voice, and you wish you could get up and run away. Instead, you fall asleep. Clearly, the speaker needs to know more about volume, rate, pitch, and tone. We can convey feelings, moods, and attitudes with these voice qualities. When carefully controlled, they can create drama and excitement and inspire people to action.

You can raise the *volume* of your voice and speed the *rate* to generate excitement, and you can lower your voice to a whisper to heighten drama. Volume should always be loud enough for your whole audience to hear you clearly. In face-to-face conversations, this usually isn't a problem, but when speaking to a group, don't hesitate to request and use a microphone. This way you won't strain your voice, nor will you sound too shrill.

Pitch, or intonation, refers to the level of sound on a musical scale. When pitch is too high, the voice sounds shrill and unpleasant. In the 1988 presidential campaign, George Bush hired a voice coach to help him lower his voice an octave. Even though he had a distinguished military career in World War II as a Navy pilot, his high-pitched voice was contributing to his image as a "wimp." He recognized that a lower-pitched voice conveys strength and confidence.

Of all the voice qualities, it is **tone** that can most dramatically convey our feelings. Tone reveals whether we are happy or sad about our message. It reveals our mood. It can help us establish rapport and trust. Gaining more control over tone allows us to control our message more effectively. It even allows us to keep feelings a secret if necessary. After all, there may be times when we would rather not reveal that we are very angry. It may be better to show a more moderate temper.

Grammar and Vocabulary

When you talk with a friend, write a report, draft a business letter, or make an oral presentation, words can be your friend or foe. Carefully selected, they can lead you up the road of success; poorly chosen, they can lead down the path of self-destruction. The way you use words has an impact on how you are viewed in the business and academic worlds. If you use correct grammar and vocabulary, you will be perceived as knowledgeable, intelligent, and competent. The ability to write and speak concisely and accurately is highly valued in the marketplace and the classroom, and it yields substantial rewards.

Like anything else, using words effectively takes learning and practice. Selecting the proper vocabulary is not as easy as it first seems.

Consider this: Let's say that you get up in the morning and *run* a hot shower, then you *run* out the door to get the newspaper. After eating breakfast, you *run* a comb through your hair. As you are about to leave the house, you discover that you have *run* out of money, so on your way to work you *run* to an ATM. As soon as you get to work, you *run* off some copies of a report for the 8:15 meeting. The meeting *runs* longer than you expected because someone from another department couldn't resist *running* off at the mouth.

This simple, and perhaps silly, story illustrates that the English language is complex. There are many words like *run* that have multiple meanings. Some sounds have multiple spellings (*red, read*), and some spellings have multiple pronunciations (for example, *wind,* as in "listen to the wind," or "please wind the clock"). Linguists say that it takes ten years of daily use to gain command of a second language, but a lifetime to study and perfect the first. Can you see their point?

EFFECTIVE COMMUNICATION STRATEGIES MADE PERSONAL

As you have seen in Chapters 7 and 8, effective communication involves the use of critical thinking skills to carefully encode and decode a message. It requires planning and commitment to quality. It includes being assertive. It requires that we analyze our personal styles so that we can best fit them to a particular situation. The way we do all of this may be a result of our cultural background.

Cultural Diversity

Culture provides just one way of doing something. Since the human race is composed of billions of people, influenced by their cultures and personal experiences, no one way of communicating will be effective with all people. As the many cultures mix, we begin to see other ways of solving problems and making decisions. This has a synergistic effect, like the uniting of the members of a basketball team. By themselves, players have certain skills, but together they are much more than just a good defensive player or a great shooter.

Since the beginning, North America has had cultural diversity. However, due in part to the lack of mobility and the slower pace of change, the impact of that diversity was not felt as much on a personal level until recently. The fact that today many cultures meet face-to-face each day is a very great change from the past. Our neighborhoods, workplaces, and classrooms have begun to look like a little United Nations. Our ability to work and play is dependent upon our ability to accept diversity now and to see it as a value. By looking at communication patterns from a global perspective, we will discover approaches that are different and perhaps more effective.

There is a wealth of information on the specific communication behaviors of various cultures. For example, it has been noted that many Asians who wait on a customer in a store will not make eye contact, in order to show respect to the customer. Many Japanese are uncomfortable with direct language and will use the term *maybe* rather than *no,* because the latter would be considered rude. Many people from Mediterranean and Middle Eastern cultures are comfortable with a small space bubble around them. Thus, for them, talking face-to-face may involve only a six-inch distance.

The point of these examples is not to single out particular groups but to encourage people to look at communication with fresh and nonjudgmental eyes. This is more important now than ever as the world economy grows and, with the assistance of electronics, we become a global village. It takes spirit and daring to look at the world from another person's eyes. But the effort will make your life more interesting and stimulating, and you will be rewarded both personally and financially.

Men and Women Communicate Differently

Over the last twenty-five years, there has been much research to indicate that there are differences between the way men and women communicate. Since some of our most intimate and significant relationships are with persons of the opposite sex, it behooves us to learn about these differences. In this section, we will view communication styles of specific genders from a cultural perspective.

Most people accept that our conversations are shaped by many factors such as age, ethnicity, religion, geography, and social class. If we ignore that our conversational styles are also shaped by gender, we hurt both men and women, because we miss an opportunity to understand our dissatisfactions with certain conversations, and we cannot learn how to communicate more effectively.

Understanding the conversational styles of men and women is essential now, since more women have entered the workplace and are progressing to supervisory positions. Correct behavior and effective communication depend on understanding the culture of your gender and that of the opposite sex as well. If disagreements and misunderstandings about communication styles occur, they can affect careers, salaries, and promotions. We need to recognize that a culture works fine internally; it is only when two different cultures come together that there are misunderstandings.

From the first moment of birth, boys and girls are treated differently. In effect, they come from different cultures. Boys are handled in a more rough-and-tumble manner. They are allowed to play games that deal with conflict and competition. Girls, on the other hand, are treated more gently and play games that teach them how to negotiate and build interpersonal relationships. As a result, men tend to perpetuate hierarchical structures reinforced by sports and the military, while women tend to support a networking or connecting structure based on understanding and friendship.

This translates into a pattern of framing conversations in a particular way. Men set up and recognize hierarchies and authority, and they often speak as if they are giving orders. Women often begin conversations with words that will build the relationship and allow for the preferences of the other person. For example, a man who needs a report finished by the end of the day might say to a subordinate, "Please have this report on my desk by 3:30 this afternoon." A woman in the same situation might say, "Hi, how are you? . . . Great! . . . Well, I need this report finished soon. Do you think you could possibly finish it this afternoon? . . . Yes? Could you possibly finish it around 3:30? . . . Okay, great."

There is a tendency for men to be more goal-focused in conversation than women. Men seem to prefer to give the answer, and they will supply the information about the process that led to the choice only if they are asked to do so. Women, on the other hand, want to include a description of the process in the conversation before expressing their choice or decision. This is one reason that women are labeled talkative and indecisive. Some people who tend to be more goal-focused might tune out before they even hear the decision.

Person-to-Person Conversations

To be a good conversationalist, you need to borrow the Boy Scout motto: "be prepared." When conversations are important, review the environment to eliminate distractions and interference. In crucial conversations, like job interviews or negotiating with others, plan ahead and decide what you want to say.

To be a good sender of a message, carefully select your words so that they have meaning to your listener. Use body language, facial expressions, and gestures that show openness. Be alert to nonverbal feedback from the receiver, mirroring the facial expressions and posture, and be sensitive to the preferred space bubble of the receiver.

To be a good receiver, engage in active listening. Lean forward, make eye contact, concentrate. Listen for the meaning behind the message. Let the other person talk without interrupting. Mirror their communication style to help them relax and be open with you.

Speaking on the Phone

The telephone often replaces face-to-face communication. It is used increasingly by business to sell products through telemarketing. Teleconferences are used by corporations, government agencies, and even clubs and organizations to "gather" people from across a region, a country, or the globe into one "location." Telephones can save the costs of travel and time, but their effective use requires special concentration, since the nonverbal components of communication are missing.

When using the telephone, it is very important to identify yourself. This will avoid confusion and wasting of time. Be courteous and respectful. Experts who train customer sales representatives tell them to smile as they talk. Even though this cannot be seen by the receiver, the smile affects speech qualities in a positive way. And let the speaker know you are there by making interjections periodically, since nodding will not work here.

Speaking to Groups

Most jobs today require people to be a part of a team or committee. Most educational programs include assignments and projects that are presented orally. And so, it is likely that you will need to occasionally give a report or presentation before a group.

Surveys of the general public repeatedly show that the number one fear that people have is public speaking. It is not uncommon for college students to postpone enrolling in a speech class that might be required for graduation until their last semester. Don't let this be true of you. Many of today's speech teachers make this course fun and painless, so ask other students to recommend such an instructor. Then you can have more opportunity for practicing and increasing these skills. Who knows, they could lead to higher grades or a job promotion. Why postpone benefits like those?

The first guideline for public speaking is to *be prepared*. Know your audience so that you can select appropriate vocabulary, degree of formality, examples and stories, facts and information. Plan to involve them by asking questions, using a volunteer from the audience, and engaging them mentally and emotionally in the content of your presentation.

Remember that the first step of communication is hearing. *Be sure that everyone can hear you* and that all are prepared to listen. Announce that you are starting and have some sort of introductory comments to help listeners make the transition from their previous thoughts and conversations to concentrating on your message. Be sure you really have their attention before you move forward to the heart of your message.

It often helps at the very beginning to *state your premise* or the few key points that you want to make. Then, speak with confidence and present your ideas using supportive data, as well as visuals wherever possible and appropriate. Visuals might include pictures or charts on overhead transparencies, videos, or a demonstration.

Look for feedback from your audience. Modify what you say to make the message as meaningful as possible. There are often questions from an audience, particularly small audiences in informal settings. Use all your listening skills to undercover the true meaning of the question. Respect the rights of the individuals in the audience—always remain courteous and tactful. Most of all, be yourself. Let your personality shine and your enthusiasm show.

INDIVIDUAL ACTIVITIES

1. First Impressions

Purpose: To analyze your current appearance so that you can identify characteristics that might associate you with a certain group and to determine what message you are sending to others with your appearance.

Clothing, hairstyles, accessories, and other forms of embellishment are ways to communicate to others the fact that we want to be identified with a certain group. But what does membership in that group communicate to others? Are you happy with that message?

Identify five or six characteristics of your current appearance. Think in terms of your hairstyle, the kind of clothes you commonly wear, and the colors and patterns of those clothes. Include accessories such as shoes and jewelry, and embellishments such as tattoos or body piercing.

Then search for pictures of people who have selected a similar style and use them to make a collage. Show these pictures to people who do not dress in your chosen style, and ask them to describe the personalities, interests, career goals, lifestyle, and personal qualities of the people in the pictures.

Do the responses sound like you? Were you surprised at the responses? Are you satisfied or happy with the responses? Do you think your appearance advances your message or distracts from it with most groups of people? Write your analysis in Figure 9–1.

2. Candid Tape Recorder: Analyzing Your Speaking Voice

Purpose: To provide an opportunity to tape and replay a conversation so that it might be evaluated for volume, pitch, rate, tone, and enunciation.

The goal of this exercise is to hear yourself as others hear you. Then you can assess your speech qualities and plan to make improvements.

_____

Figure 9–1 An analysis of my first impression

With the permission of all parties involved, you are to tape-record an ordinary conversation. This might be upon arriving at home at dinner time, or it might be the dinner table conversation. You may decide to do this a few times so that the conversation becomes more natural.

Later, with all participants present, play the conversation back. How does your speech compare to standardized English? This experience can provide valuable feedback regarding speech quality and uncover conversational styles.

Write about your conclusions, indicating any changes you plan to make, in Figure 9–2.

3. Candid Camera

Purpose: To provide an opportunity to see how you look to others when you are engaged in conversation. Provides feedback regarding your nonverbal skills.

_____

Figure 9–2 Candid tape recorder: The analysis

It is said that we frequently are not as kind to our loved ones as to strangers. As we have seen, our conversations convey more than just words. The goal of this exercise is to determine if we are really conveying our true feelings and emotions.

With the permission of all parties involved, you are to videotape-record an ordinary conversation. This might be at the dinner table or while sitting around the house. If possible, set the camera on a tripod so that no one needs to hold it. You may decide to do this a few times so people become more comfortable and the conversation more natural.

Later, with all participants present, play the video back. Anyone can ask to stop the tape periodically to comment on their feelings or reactions to the verbal and nonverbal messages. This experience can provide valuable feedback because it can uncover conversational styles and personal habits.

Write about your conclusions, indicating any changes you plan to make, in Figure 9–3.

4. Copy the Experts

Purpose: To provide a model for improving pronunciation, enunciation, volume, pitch, and tone, and an opportunity to make some changes in your speech qualities.

Actors, broadcasters, and public speakers of all types have taken the time and effort to improve their speech qualities. It makes sense for all of us to do this.

Your task is to obtain an audiotape that can illustrate good speaking qualities and that can serve as a model for improvements you wish to make. You might find this tape at a library or media resource center, or at a book or music store. The content is not important. Your intent is to just emulate the speech patterns that you hear. Therefore, you can actually use a variety of tapes, such as motivational tapes, a book on tape, and so forth.

Listen to the tapes daily in a setting that allows you to repeat what you hear. You might do this while driving in your car or when exercising. As an assessment tool, tape-record your voice on the first day of your practice and again after three weeks of practice. During this time, be more conscious about your own speech qualities and pronunciations. For example, do you say "worsh" for "wash"?

Figure 9–3 Candid camera: The analysis

In Figure 9–4, record the changes you have made in your speech and the ones you still plan to make.

5. Body Language

Purpose: To become more aware of nonverbal messages and more adept at reading body language.

Find pictures of people exhibiting various body postures, for example, arms crossed, arms open and at the side, leaning forward and maintaining eye contact, and so forth. Now, research what interpretations a psychologist might put on these postures.

Make a chart with your pictures and the results of your research. Share it with the class or your family. Describe what conclusions you think you can draw about body language in Figure 9–5.

6. Prejudice and Appearance

Purpose: To identify stereotypes or prejudices that you have, to evaluate them for truth, and to develop empathy for and insight into the appearance and actions of someone different from you so that clear communication can be achieved.

Figure 9–4 My plan for copying the experts

Figure 9–5 Body language

We all have prejudices. All of us, at some point, prejudge another. Sometimes we are not conscious of our stereotypes or prejudices. Your task is to examine one of your prejudices. Select someone unlike yourself and your friends. This might be someone from another generation or another lifestyle. Make a tentative list of characteristics that you think distinguish this group of people.

Now, find three or four members of this group and interview them. Act as an objective reporter. Do they all exhibit the characteristics on your list? How were they unique? Did they all have the same personal qualities? How do you feel now about prejudging people? Write your responses in Figure 9–6.

7. Word Wizard

Purpose: To begin a new habit of learning one new word a day and incorporating it into daily conversation.

Each of us could benefit from expanding our vocabulary. Make a vow to learn a new word every day and to incorporate it in conversation. There are books and calendars that choose the word for you, or you can select a word each day at random from the dictionary.

Keep a list of the words, and review them each day so that you continually incorporate them in conversation. After three weeks, write about your experience in Figure 9–7. Describe how you selected the words, how many you continue to use, and whether you plan to continue with this activity, and why or why not.

8. Day Tripping to Another Culture

Purpose: To explore another culture's foods, architecture, dress, and customs in order to discover another way of doing something.

In most communities, there is an opportunity to explore another culture without the costs of flying overseas or getting a passport and inoculations. Your task is to discover what might be available for a one-day excursion to another culture. You could do this by attending

Figure 9–6 Prejudice and appearance

Figure 9–7 Word wizard

a special public festival or by attending an event in a neighborhood community where people of a particular culture have established themselves. It is often fun to take a friend with you.

Sit down ahead of time and make a list of what you think you will see, hear, taste, and smell. Then, go off and have fun!

While you are on your excursion, act as a reporter or correspondent and take some notes. If you wish, take a camera. You might record what you see and do, and the names of particular items that you eat. If you see a ceremony or a procedure that is new to you, ask questions. What are people doing? Why? What similarities do you see in this culture to your own? What might you consider adopting from this culture?

Upon your return, write a story or make a photo essay about your experience. Share your report with the class or a member of your family.

9. Cultural Connection

Purpose: To learn about another culture via the media to discover a new way of doing something.

Over the last decade, many popular books and films have presented a glimpse at another culture, for example, *The Joy Luck Club, How to Make an American Quilt,* and *Soul Food.* Although it is impossible to learn everything about a culture from one book or film, we can develop empathy from this exposure. We also might learn a new way of doing something.

Your task is to find a book to read or a film to see that will teach you about another culture. The format can be fiction or nonfiction, documentary or popular. If you select a film, you might want to watch it with a friend and discuss it afterward.

Reflect on what you learned about the culture you selected. What similarities do you see in this culture to your own? What might you consider adopting from this culture? Write your comments in Figure 9–8.

Figure 9–8 Cultural connections

10. Search the Web for Communication Tips

Purpose: To utilize the Internet to learn more about speaking and listening.

You have been focusing on your own communication. Now, take a few minutes to explore what communication means to others and how some have used it as the basis of a career.

To do your research, use the latest form of communication, the Internet. You might search the *Wall Street Journal* (http://www.wsj.com), the *New York Times* (http://www.nytimes.com), or CyberWireDispatch (http://www.cyberwerks.com/cyberwire). Find at least one example where communication skills are the basis for someone's occupational success.

Share your results with classmates.

EXPAND YOUR LEARNING

Farrell, Warren. *Why Men Are the Way They Are*. New York, NY: Berkley Publishing, 1988.

Goldberg, Herb. *What Men Really Want*. New York, NY: NAL Dutton, 1991.

Qubein, Nido R. *How to Be a Great Communicator: In Person, on Paper and on the Podium*. New York, NY: John Wiley & Sons, Inc. 1997.

Tannen, Deborah. *You Just Don't Understand: Women and Men in Conversation*. New York, NY: Ballantine Books. 1990.

GROUP ACTIVITIES

1. Women and Men in Conversation

Purpose: To identify the common characteristics of one's own gender and then those of the opposite sex, and to reframe the behavior of the opposite sex into a more neutral perception.

Divide the group by gender, and form one or more groups with men only or women only. On a flip chart, have participants identify and list the common characteristics of their own gender. On a second list, have them identify characteristics common to the other gender.

Bring all the groups back together. Post the lists on the wall, with all the men's lists together and all the women's lists together. Have a spokesperson from each group report on their results.

Next, ask the participants to compare the way women see themselves with the way men see women. What are the parallels? For example, if men say women are slow to make decisions, do women say they are careful and deliberate decision makers? Do women think men are arrogant when men think they are confident?

Now, how would these divergent perceptions affect people in the workplace, say a man who has a woman for a boss? One way to help people look at situations in a neutral fashion is to ask, "What if the sexes were reversed?" This helps people begin to see that women often judge male communication by female criteria, and vice versa.

2. Putting It All Together

Purpose: To mobilize everything you know about effective communication and use these strategies in a conversation about a controversial topic.

After three chapters of discussion on effective communication, it is assumed that you have learned something new and have begun to apply it in conversations. So, let's see if that is true.

As a group, compile a list of controversial topics. Issues might include legalization of drugs, a total ban on smoking, prayer in schools, free trade, curfew for underage drivers, managed health care, making Social Security contributions voluntary, gays in the military, same-sex marriages, and assisted suicide. Feel free to add to this list.

Pair up with another person and choose a topic on which you *disagree*. Everyone has two minutes to plan a persuasive argument and explanation of his or her position. Then, in three minutes, one person explains their position to the other person, with the receiver listening to the sender in a polite manner. When three minutes are up, the roles are reversed, and the other side of the issue is presented.

Next, take a one-minute pause to gather your thoughts, and then switch positions, that is, each person adopts the arguments of the other. The sender now needs to describe the opposite position to the receiver in an objective way with at least a modicum of enthusiasm. Then the receiver becomes the sender and describes the opposite position with equal enthusiasm.

When all teams conclude, the group reassembles to discuss the experience. Issues to consider include how individuals felt when expressing opinions opposite from their own, what communication skills were used, and what was learned from this exercise.

Chapter 10
Getting Along with Others

Everything is connected to everything else. As you have seen, we live in a huge system, in which every action has a reaction, and what happens to others makes a difference in your life. Life is about these relationships, these connections among other people, animals, plants, and other aspects of the environment.

Even before you were born, you were connected to your mother and the environment. Since birth, the quantity and sophistication of those connections have changed and increased. Gradually your realm expanded as you moved from the primary grades to middle school, and then to high school. You met more people, perhaps people a little different from others than you knew previously.

You may have come to college right from high school, or perhaps are returning to school after years spent in the workforce, the military, or as a full-time parent. Whatever your circumstance, you are the sum total of your experiences and relationships.

Humans develop physical and emotional connections to others in order to thrive and be happy. But not all relationships are happy and successful ones. What makes the difference?

BEGIN WITH YOURSELF

Successful relationships are based on beliefs and values that support a positive self-belief. People with good self-belief are convinced of their own worth. They think they can effect change in a positive way. They have self-confidence in their abilities to solve problems and handle stress. They also think the best about others.

Chances are this description sounds at least a little like you. You decided to learn more about life management because you believe that you can personally develop and grow, and that you can get better at what you do and who you are each and every day.

So, you have been increasing your self-awareness, and you have identified your highest values. Three values that contribute to good relationships are trust, respect, and empathy. As Throop and Castellucci explain it:

> Trust means that you can rely on someone else, and he or she can rely on you. Respect means that you value the other person, and he or she values you. And empathy means you can experience another person's feelings or ideas as if they were your own.[1]

---

[1] Robert Throop and Marion Castellucci, *Reaching Your Potential*, 2nd. ed. (Albany, NY: Delmar Publishers, 1998).

Conflicts and Your Values

As you have learned, people have different value hierarchies. Since we base our beliefs and actions on these values, we learn early in life that people do not agree on what is right and what is wrong. When it comes to ethical issues, you can pretty much behave according to your values if the situation involves only yourself. For example, let's say that it is after midnight and you are driving on a deserted street. You arrive at an intersection that has a red traffic signal in your direction. You stop, see no one, and decide to drive right through. By some people's standards, not only did you do something illegal, since it was wrong, it was also unethical.

Most people don't give much thought to questions of right and wrong until there is a conflict of values between themselves and another person. Your value clarification skills can help with these issues. Keep in mind that the laws and rules of society usually set a minimum standard and that an ethical standard might be higher. When faced with an ethical problem, always take time to clarify your values and to determine how you feel about the situation and what effect the questionable behavior has on others.

Besides your skills with value clarification and setting standards, you have also been increasing your communication skills. Chances are you are using active listening techniques more often than before, and you are learning to express your thoughts and feelings in an assertive manner. All of these skills will make your interpersonal relations run more smoothly. Interpersonal skills are among the most sought after by employers as well as in a friend.

NURTURING GOOD RELATIONSHIPS

With some attention to the needs of others, most of our relationships can be successful ones. This means that we need to really listen for the underlying meaning when others talk. Even though you are busy, it is important to take the time to notice people's moods and body language. Even if you can't give more than a minute or two, your full attention during that time will be appreciated.

Building a relationship requires both individuals to focus on their own behavior, intentions, and expectations. People who focus on personal growth can handle negative feedback constructively.

Although receiving negative feedback is rarely fun, learning from it can strengthen you as an individual as well as strengthen the relationship.

First, realize that *you don't have to agree* with the criticism to listen to it calmly. Then, *consider the source.* Is this person upset about something else and you just got in the way? Is this person in a position to know about the situation? If not, the criticism may not be valid. If so, listen to learn more. *Ask for specific information.* Focus on the behavior that upset the other person. This will allow you gain the most from this experience. *Think about it.* Take time to react, and consider what behavior change you would be willing to make.

In each relationship, it is also important to set clear boundaries. **Boundaries** are the lines we draw, or the standards we set, to help us preserve our self-respect and sense of control. Each person in the relationship has certain personal rights that are established by these boundaries:

> *Physical boundaries:* The right to control your body and your possessions

Emotional boundaries: The right to respectful treatment from others
Intellectual boundaries: The right to express your ideas and opinions
Spiritual boundaries: The right to stand up for your values and
   beliefs

We may allow our personal boundaries to be invaded because we want to feel liked or loved. This behavior pattern may be rooted in our childhood experiences. It is important to understand that we all have the right to set boundaries, and now that we are adults, we can be assertive and see that the boundaries are enforced.

CONFLICT IS NORMAL

It is normal and predictable that once two people have spent some time together, they will disagree about something. It escalates to a conflict when the parties involved perceive incompatible goals, values, or standards. If each person digs in their heels, the disagreement can escalate to shouting, and maybe even to body blows. Everyone loses in a power struggle, as the ante is constantly raised and the struggle consumes all the creative energy. On the other hand, if handled in a fair and assertive manner, using negotiation skills, conflict can have healthy and productive results.

Four Aspects of Successful Negotiation

When a conflict arises, it is extremely important to remember good communication skills and the ways to nurture relationships, particularly applying our knowledge about boundaries. More often than not the conflict is with someone we really care about. Beginning a serious conflict by reaffirming your commitment to the relationship can go a long way to reducing tension and resolving the problem.

Fisher and Ury, in their best-selling book, *Getting to Yes: Negotiating Agreement Without Giving In,* recommend that we focus on aspects other than our position, or what we want. They point out that the more you clarify your position and defend against it, the more committed you become to it. This makes the disagreement more and more difficult to resolve.

This first step is to *separate the people from the problem.* We should try to see ourselves on the same side, attacking the problem, rather than having our egos identified with our position. Next, *focus on interests,* not positions. Fisher and Ury point out that a negotiating position often clouds what people really want and need. Focusing on interests allows you to find areas of common agreement and similar needs and desires. Third, *invent options for mutual gain,* which means brainstorming for alternatives that allow each side to get what they need most. Finally, base the results on *objective criteria.* Such criteria would be agreed upon by all parties and might include expert opinion, custom, or law.

So, how might all this work? Let's say that the owner of the Driggers Widget Company accepted an order for five thousand widgets, knowing that this was beyond the company's capacity to produce on time unless some changes were made in the work schedule. Boss Driggers also agreed that if the widgets were late, they would not be accepted, but if the widgets were delivered early, there would be a substantial bonus. To meet this order, Boss Driggers could demand that all employees cancel any upcoming vacations and work longer hours, including Saturdays, or Boss Driggers could sit down with a representative group of workers and focus on the four aspects of successful negotiating.

"Separate the people from the issues" would require that no blame or negativity be attributed to those who do not want to work more hours or who do not want to cancel vacations. Also no blame would be assigned to Boss Driggers for taking on a task beyond the usual workload. Some of the "interests" that all parties have in common is that the Driggers Widget Company meet its commitments in a profitable way, that workers have a right to earned vacations, that everyone receives a fair wage for their work, and that workers are happy and in good spirits, since that affects productivity.

Certainly some of the options available are limited by labor laws. Yet "options" could include hiring more workers, adding another shift of workers, offering ten-hour days with overtime, making overtime and the postponment of vacations optional, making Saturday and Sunday schedules optional, offering a bonus for workers who take on extra hours, or any combination of these. "Objective criteria" could be expert opinion on labor laws, a survey of workers' desires, and an estimate of how many worker hours are needed to complete this job on time.

As you think about the Driggers Widget Company, you may see other ways of looking at the four aspects of successful negotiating. The point is to be thinking holistically, with what is called a win-win attitude. The goal is that you are looking at this as if everyone is on the same team, and that you are trying to solve everyone's problem, not just your own.

Conflict Resolution Options

Sometimes differences aren't very dramatic or even important, and so you may not feel that the negotiation process is necessary. Or you may suggest that the easiest thing to do is compromise. Before you get too enamored with compromise, let's take a look at six basic conflict resolution options. As you discover each one, ask yourself if you have selected it as a solution to conflict in the past and, if so, why.

A commonly selected option is **dominance**. This occurs when one side has its own way. The implication is that submission is not voluntary, but that it is established through the use of fear, threat, or abuse. A second option is **voluntary submission**, which occurs when one side voluntarily gives in to the other. This might occur because the issue is deemed unimportant or because the submitter believes they would lose in the end anyway. They may even prefer to view themselves as a victim and passively withdraw. In both of these scenarios, there is a winner and a loser.

Conversion happens when one side is so persuasive that he or she convinces the other, and both parties are satisfied. **Accepting differences** is a fourth option. This does not result in joint action like the first three. Both sides accept the right of the other to choose and make an independent decision. No attempt is made to convert the other party at a later date. **Compromise** occurs when people choose a solution that is acceptable to both sides, but it is *not the first choice* of either party. Each has given up something of importance to arrive at this solution. Finally, the sixth option is **integration**. This occurs when all parties strive to find mutual gains and arrive at a new, even better solution to the problem. While each party might give up something, it is something of lesser importance. All participants feel that the solution respects the rights and needs of all.

The next time you are faced with a conflict over what to have for dinner or what movie to see, or perhaps something more critical like the price of a car or a raise in pay, think about nurturing relationships, conflict resolution, and the six available conflict resolution options.

INDIVIDUAL ACTIVITIES

1. Setting Boundaries

Purpose: To expand your understanding of boundaries in interpersonal relationships.

Being alert to personal rights and boundaries is a fundamental part of getting along with others. This task asks you to find either news articles or pictures, or both, that will illustrate your understanding of the four personal boundaries. Create a poster or collage with your collection. Then write at least a half page about what boundaries now mean to you. Finally, find a friend, family member, or classmates and show them your collage, explaining it to them.

2. Conflict at the Movies

Purpose: To gain a better understanding of how a conflict develops, and how different options can be utilized to resolve conflict.

A standard plot for movies is to introduce a conflict between two or more people, and then show how the conflict is resolved. Your task is to select any movie you wish and chart the conflicts. Depending on the film and your perception, you can do this in a linear fashion or use a mind map or storyboard. Regardless of your presentation format, identify the conflict and state any relevant known facts or information. Then, as the story unfolds, identify which of the six options the people attempt to use and the result of *each* such attempt. Conclude with a description of the final choice and its result.

What did you learn about conflict from studying it at the movies?

Are there particular options that you might like to try as a result of this exercise? If so, which ones and why?

	Situation 1	Situation 2	Situation 3	Situation 4	Situation 5	Situation 6
Utilized active listening						
Attended to the needs of others						
Focused on my own behavior						
Tried to learn from feedback						
Showed respect for boundaries						
Didn't listen						
Thought only about my needs						
Blamed and faulted the other's actions						
Shut out feedback						
Invaded the boundaries of others						

Figure 10–1 Assessing my nurturing behavior

Figure 10–2 Nurturing a relationship: Feedback to myself

3. Nurturing a Relationship

Purpose: To perform a personal assessment to determine if you are consistently nurturing a significant relationship, and to identify areas for improvement.

Even though you may feel that you treat others well, until you actually make a structured assessment, you won't have the whole story. This exercise provides you with such a tool.

From among your committed relationships (friend, spouse, parent, child), select one to analyze. Over a number of days, use Figure 10–1 to chart the times when you exhibit nurturing and supportive behavior, and the time when you do not. Feel free to personalize the chart to reflect your behavior.

In Figure 10–2, write about your discoveries and your recommendations for yourself. Be sure to include specific behaviors that you want to continue or increase, and those you want to diminish or eliminate. The next step would be to follow the Self-Change Model found in the Explorations section at the end of Unit 3.

4. Picture the Options

Purpose: To provide an opportunity to imagine options and choices so that you are better able to apply this information when conflicts arise.

In this activity, the beginning of a story is presented. Your task is to complete the story in six different ways to illustrate the six conflict resolution options. The story is completed for the first option as an example and to get you started, so actually you only have five more versions to imagine. Write your stories in the space provided in Figure 10–3. Then discuss them with another person *or* find a partner and role play each scenario. The following is the story you are to complete:

> Scott and Kiesha have been married for one year. They both have worked very hard, saved money, and are ready for a vacation. Kiesha wants to go skiing because the snowfall has been fabulous

Options

Dominance: Kiesha totally ignores what Scott says he wants. She calls the travel agent, makes the reservations, and buys two nonrefundable plane tickets. Then she buys a new ski outfit. Afterward, she brags to their friends about her new clothes and their plans for the trip.

Voluntary submission:

_____

_____

_____

_____

_____

Conversion:

_____

_____

_____

_____

Accepting differences:

_____

_____

_____

_____

Compromise:

_____

_____

_____

_____

Integration:

_____

_____

_____

_____

_____

Figure 10–3 Picture the options

and she has not had a chance to ski for some time. Scott wants to go to a sunny beach where he can be warm and enjoy a good book.

To conclude your picture of the options, identify which conflict resolution options you prefer and why.

5. Constructive Feedback: Build the Relationship

Purpose: To provide an opportunity to practice constructive feedback both as a sender and as a receiver.

Constructive feedback can help build solid relationships. It is a way to express feelings and reactions in a positive way, so that the receiver can be aware of these reactions. It also provides the receiver with the opportunity to evaluate the feedback and choose whether to modify future behavior.

Your task is twofold: to find an opportunity to *give* constructive feedback and to observe your own behavior when you *receive* feedback. (There's no guarantee it will be constructive.)

Now, write about this experience. What seems to work and what doesn't? How did you feel when you gave feedback? How did you feel when you received it? What can you do differently as a sender of feedback to make the experience more constructive? What can you do as a receiver to make the experience more useful to you? Write your answers in Figure 10–4.

6. Consumer Complaint: Enforcing Your Rights

Purpose: To utilize decision making and communication skills plus knowledge of interpersonal relations to solve a consumer problem.

My experiences as a sender:

_____

_____

_____

_____

My experiences as a receiver:

_____

_____

_____

_____

Figure 10–4 My experiences with constructive feedback

Because we consume so many goods and services, eventually each one of us is involved in a consumer dispute. Even with government regulation, quality control, and personal responsibility, a toy might break on the first use, a shirt might have a sleeve set in backward, or a CD player might conk out before its time. When you face such a situation, before you do anything else, find out whether the problem is a simple one. For example, check to see that the item is plugged into the wall socket or that the "on" switch is really on. (A high percentage of "repairs" involve only these basics.)

If you have determined that you really have a problem, use a combination of the decision-making process and assertive communication techniques to solve the problem.

1. Identify the problem.
2. Explain what you expect the firm to do about it.
3. Support your request with copies of proof of purchase, receipts, warranties, or hang tags.

Start your complaint at the local level, beginning with the business that sold the service or product. A telephone call or a visit may solve the problem. If not, you may need to type a letter in a concise business format. Using a computer makes this easy. Leet and Driggers recommend that you include the following information:[2]

1. Your name, address, and home and work phone numbers
2. The name of the product with style and serial number, or identification of the unsatisfactory service that was performed
3. The date and location of purchase
4. The reason for the complaint
5. What you have already done
6. A request for action within a reasonable time
7. Copies of all documents to support your request

Keep a copy of your letter in case further action is needed. If the problem is not adequately resolved, research the availability of industry mediation panels, gather more information from the company's Web site, and plan your next action.

7. Becoming a Mediator

Purpose: To practice the negotiation guidelines and use the best communication and interpersonal skills to help mediate a problem.

Everyone negotiates something every day. It might be a deadline for a project at work, or it might be a "lights out" rule or curfew for a younger member of the family. Negotiation is a basic means of getting what you want from others. This activity asks you to serve as a mediator for two people or two groups of people who want to resolve a conflict. This will help you learn the process and help others to see a different way to resolve conflict.

---

[2] Don R. Leet and Joann Driggers, *Economic Decisions for Consumers,* 2nd ed. (New York, NY: Macmillan Publishing Co., 1990).

Review the process described in this chapter. If you still want more guidance, visit your library or bookstore and review the Fisher and Ury book, *Getting to Yes.* Then meet with each individual or group to get their perception of the situation and to explain the process, or four aspects, of negotiation. Make notes about interests and brainstorm options for mutual gain.

When everyone has had some time to think, come together to resolve the conflict. Then write about what you learned from this experience in Figure 10–5, report your results in class, or both.

8. My Journal

Purpose: To give you an opportunity to reflect on your experiences with past relationships both when they were nurturing and when they were nonsupportive.

We learn how to handle relationships in our families. Then we carry these patterns of behavior into adulthood, where they become part of our daily experiences with family, colleagues, and strangers.

Write about your positive and negative attitudes and behavior patterns related to building relationships. Write about how these attitudes and behaviors are similar to and different from those of your parents. Write about any behavior changes you want to implement now so that you can continue to nurture current and future relationships.

9. Dealing with Anger in Others

Purpose: To expand your understanding of anger and how to deal with it in others.

Anger is the result of unresolved conflict. It might be expressed directly to an individual involved with the conflict, so that the involved parties can work together to resolve the problem. On the other hand, the

Figure 10–5 My experience as a mediator

anger might be expressed indirectly and aimed at a third party not involved in the conflict, such as an innocent bystander. Or the anger might be internalized, to come out later as hurt, fear, or rage.

Your task is to improve the way you deal with angry people. Perhaps you have a friend or coworker who uses you as a "dumping ground" for anger. If this is the case, your task is to anticipate the situation and rehearse what you want to say. This will help you to feel more confident and in control. Or perhaps you want to rehearse in anticipation of an unexpected conflict. That's fine, too.

Communicating with angry individuals can be very difficult. Although neither of you may totally understand the anger at the time, remember that everyone has reasons for what they do. So, the first guideline is to be *empathetic*. The second guideline is to *underreact*. Be as calm as you can. Remember that anger is an emotion and a result of childhood training, not logic. Maintaining an even tone of voice and low-key body language will help the angry person calm down.

The third guideline is *stabilize*. Do not attempt to present facts or contradict the angry person, as that will just escalate the situation. One way to help stabilize the situation is the *feel-felt-found* approach:

> *I know how you feel about* . . . not getting the work schedule that you wanted.
> *I felt that way when* . . . I wasn't able to get my vacation when I wanted it last summer.
> *I found that* . . . I needed to apply earlier, so that I would be the first one to request a specific time.

If you remain calm and poised while allowing the angry person to vent some emotions, the energy usually dissipates. Then you can talk about the *causes* of the anger rather than the anger itself. This puts you in the position of focusing on issues, not people. At that point, you can *negotiate a solution*.

After your experience with an angry person, reflect on the results. You might informally seek feedback from that person, as well as others. Then, in Figure 10–6, write about what you learned and what you will do next time. Use either a narrative or outline format.

Figure 10–6 My experience with handling anger in others

Figure 10–7 Analyzing my music

10. Music: Nurturing or Hostile?

Purpose: To listen to contemporary music and evaluate its degree of nurturing and support compared to its degree of hostility.

Certain contemporary music is nurturing and supportive in nature. The lyric topics are life-affirming, encouraging, and hopeful. On the other hand, some lyrics depict the world as filled with anger, hate, and greed and show no concern for the needs of others. Most music is probably somewhere in between.

Your task is to select a tape or CD that you listen to often. It could be a collection from a particular artist or a sequence that features several artists. Listen for the tone and spirit of the music, and then focus on the lyrics. What are the primary topics? What emotions are presented? How do *you* feel after listening to this music? These questions can be answered in Figure 10–7, or you can create a collage that visually represents what you heard. If you create a collage, your choices of color, shape, images, and texture should reflect your conclusions.

11. Conflict and Violence

Purpose: To establish the connection between how individuals handle conflict and anger, and the violence in our communities.

Community authorities such as police departments, women's shelters, and crisis hot lines report that abuse and violence are often endured by people who know their abuser. Your task is to investigate any part of this issue that interests you.

Topics that are part of this issue include gangs, date rape, spousal abuse, and child abuse. You may want to focus on the abuser, the abused, or the help available in your community for either group. You may want to explore the pattern of behavior of the abuser or the abused. Your research may be through a search of periodicals, books, and journals, or you may want to conduct interviews with community workers or view videotapes on the subject.

So, what did you learn? Who else could benefit from what you learned? Your task now is to share your results with at least one other person, or possibly a whole group of people. Examples of people with whom you could share your information include your family, extended family, classmates, younger students at your alma mater, and members of your church or temple. How could you best present this information? Do it!

EXPAND YOUR LEARNING

Fisher, Roger, and William Ury. *Getting to Yes: Negotiating Agreement Without Giving In.* New York, NY: Penguin Books, 1983.

Throop, Robert, and Marion Castellucci. *Reaching Your Potential,* 2nd ed. Albany, NY: Delmar Publishers, 1998.

GROUP ACTIVITIES

1. What Would You Do?

Purpose: To review a current event, identify the problem, and analyze how others dealt with a conflict.

Conflicts are not always black-and-white. Sometimes the issue becomes one of ethics, that is, what is right or wrong. Your sense of right and wrong might be determined by what is legal, or what is the rule, or what matches your values.

For this exercise, you need to form groups of four. Each person will play a role to resolve this conflict.

Bus driver: You are a bus driver for a national bus company. You like your job, and you are good at it. You realize that safety is important, and you follow all the rules of the road and your company.

Bus company manager: You are proud of the reputation of your company. Your Human Resources office has worked hard to create fair rules that will ensure the safety and comfort of all passengers.

Elderly woman: You turned eighty years old yesterday. Last week you took the bus to visit your daughters, who live over three hundred and fifty miles from your home. Now you are returning by bus to your home. The trip is almost complete, with about eighty more miles to go. It is 3:00 A.M.

Reporter: You work for a major newspaper. You love human interest stories and prefer to report on the good deeds in which people regularly engage, rather than crime and natural disasters.

The situation: Elderly Woman is carrying a very small dog on the bus. It was given to her by her daughters as a birthday present. The Bus Company has a regulation that prohibits animals on the bus. The Bus Driver has just discovered the little dog. The Reporter is aboard the bus gathering information for a future story. No one knows the Reporter's occupation.

Your task: Based on this information, imagine what each person would do. Role play this story based on your projected outcome. Then choose another solution and role play that one. Feel free to add people to either story, to assume the availability of other resources, and to take the story into the future.

When you are finished, develop, as a team, a statement of the conflict and how you think it could be best resolved. Share your choices with other class teams.

2. Anger in Families

Purpose: To use an affinity diagramming process to gather information about the source of conflict in families as well as how anger is handled.

Although this may be a sensitive topic, it is well worth a group discussion. If individuals receive general feedback from others about this typically private topic, they may more easily be able to establish boundaries and successful conflict resolution strategies.

Supplies: Blackboard space, or five big pieces of paper, and many sticky notes.

An affinity or mountains diagram allows groups to collect a lot of information quickly, in a nonjudgmental way. Five questions will be considered. One question should be posted at the top of each piece of paper. While *silent*, participants individually respond by writing their answers to each question on individual sticky notes. Answers should be kept brief, to just a few words. Sometimes there might be more than one answer. Then participants randomly stick their answers on the appropriate paper. When done quickly, this allows for anonymity. The following are the five questions to consider:

1. On a scale of 1 to 5, describe the amount of arguing/fighting that took place in your home as you were growing up. Choose 1 for rarely, 2 for less than average, 3 for average, 4 for more than average, and 5 for a lot, daily.

2. What were the common topics that you and at least one of your parents fought about?

3. From your perspective now, what topics should never have been fought over in the first place?

4. How did most of these arguments end? In other words, which conflict resolution options were usually used?

5. What do you recommend to families to better manage family arguments?

To tabulate the results, several participants should be grouped at each big sheet of paper. Then they rearrange the sticky notes into like categories. The notes can be moved more than once, until the major ideas emerge. A header card can then be placed at the top of each category of responses in order to label the category.

When results are tabulated, they can be discussed by the group as a whole. The role of boundaries should be included in the discussion.

Chapter 11 _____

Functioning in Groups

Sometimes it was thrust upon you, and sometimes you volunteered. Some lasted for only minutes and others will last a lifetime. The first group you belonged to was your family. Since your birth, there have been hundreds of groups in your life, from informal groups such as your early neighborhood playmates, to clubs and community organizations, which usually have a more formal structure. The focus of this chapter is the structure of groups. Understanding how they work can help you be an effective group member and expand your leadership skills—something that is viewed as an essential workplace competency, as well as highly useful.

You might think that this topic was covered in the previous chapter, since we looked at getting along with other people and resolving conflicts. But there is another perspective that is necessary, since at the end of the twentieth century, you can observe a paradigm shift in the United States regarding organizational structure.

GROUPS: AN OVERVIEW

Group dynamics is the study of how people interact in groups. A group is more than just a collection of people. *Groups* consist of two or more people that consciously interact with the intent of working to achieve a goal. Groups have roles for their members, norms and standards of behavior, communication patterns and a degree of cohesiveness. The more explicitly defined the roles, norms, and communication patterns are, the more formal the group. Examples of informal groups include members of a movie audience or friends at a party. More formal groups include families, businesses, schools, and community organizations.

Until the latter part of the twentieth century, in the United States and Western Europe, the most common organizational structure for a group was the hierarchy. In this structure, there is one person at the top who is responsible for decision making. In other words, that person's role is to see that the group's goals are met and that the norms or standards are maintained. The communication pattern typically used is the chain of command: the orders are passed from the highest to the lowest person in the hierarchy. An obvious example of this structure is the military, but until recently, many businesses, schools, and families operated this way as well.

We must realize that organizational structure and communication patterns of groups reflect their historical time. In the twentieth century, an authoritarian hierarchical style prevailed over a populace characterized by limited economic and educational resources, constrained by lack of a common language, and isolated by geography and restricted by lack of communication. As these limitations have been reduced, and economic resources and education increased, the hierarchy has begun to flatten, bringing more people into the decision making.

Today communication can be instantaneous, almost eliminating geography as a factor. With a move in many businesses to systems thinking, and a recognition of the interdependency and complexity of our world, there has been a shift to a flatter structure emphasizing cooperation and teamwork to solve problems. Knowing how to work in and organize a team is essential for the twenty-first century.

PARTICIPATING IN GROUPS

Think about the last group you joined. No doubt the first few minutes, and maybe even first couple of days, felt a bit awkward. You were, consciously or not, probably observing the group dynamics and analyzing the roles and norms in order to fit in better.

Roles, Norms, and Goals

As you may have realized, a **role** is a set of expected behaviors for a particular position. The range of behavior accepted for a student is different from that accepted for a teacher, which is different than that accepted for a college president. **Norms** are the standards or rules that measure that behavior. You will be more comfortable and fit into a group better if you choose behaviors that suit both the group and your role within the group.

Besides roles and norms, all groups have goals, even if they are unstated. This workbook has discussed goals extensively, and up to now, most of your thinking about the topic has probably been of a personal nature. In a group, sometimes the goals are *cooperative* and intend that people in the group work together to achieve a common objective. This happens when a booster club plans a car wash or a candy sale. When group goals are *competitive,* people in the group work against one another to be the winner and gain the reward.

In many groups, you will encounter a goal that is both cooperative and competitive. For example, in the classroom, you may be encouraged to study in teams and learn in groups, yet the same instructor might grade "on a curve," allowing a fixed portion of As, Bs, and so forth. At work, your company may have instituted a team approach to cooperatively design and produce a product, yet team members may need to compete with each other for promotions, raises, and recognition.

Cohesiveness is the emotional bonding that exists between members of the group. Cohesiveness is in the middle of a continuum, with connectedness at one end and separateness at the other. If someone is too connected to group members, they can become enmeshed in the relationship, decreasing objectivity and losing sight of the goal. Drifting too far toward separateness can indicate a lack of commitment and interest. A balanced middle position is optimal.

Analyzing Group Structure and Behavior

By analyzing group structure and behavior, you can improve the way you interact with others. How are the goals established? Are they cooperative, competitive, or do they have both aspects? Knowing which goals are cooperative and which are competitive allows you to maintain appropriate communication patterns and interpersonal relations.

Consider what roles the organization seems to have. Who is the leader? Is there a dominant, controlling person? A dependent worker? A facilitator? A few who seem to run the whole show? A supportive leader who shares authority? And determine the norms, or rules, of the group. Some of them may be in writing, for example, in a company manual or a club constitution, but some will be unwritten. Observe carefully, and make a friend in the group who can clue you in to the norms.

One way to understand a group's structure is to look at its communication pattern. Is a message passed down the chain of command, from the higher to the lower ranks? Is the communication pattern more like a wheel, with one person communicating with each group member, but with no communication between members? Or does each group member communicate with every other group member freely? In this latter model, there is likely to be more cooperation and sharing of decision making.

LEADING IN GROUPS

President, captain, manager, director, chair—all of these are names for people who have formal authority. But are they all leaders? Not necessarily. A leader has more than a title. In fact, one of the greatest leaders in recent times, Gandhi, had no formal position.

Although our influence on the world will most likely not be as dramatic as Gandhi's, each of us influences and leads people around us through our words and actions. A leader has a vision and is able to communicate and share it with others. This vision is sustained by a set of values that inspires others. Hence, **leadership** is a set of behaviors, beliefs, and values that enable one person to persuade others to act.

To be effective as a leader, a person needs *good interpersonal skills*. Since you began your life management education, you have been expanding these skills. You have learned about respect and trust, assertiveness and conflict resolution. Second, leaders are *goal-oriented* and *motivated*. They can communicate a consistency of purpose to others. They persist in the face of setbacks and can inspire others to continue working toward the goal. They have strong self-belief and a positive outlook on life. They use this positive attitude to create strategic alliances and partnerships with others, creating synergy.

Leaders will look and act in individual ways. Leaders do not all act alike. After all, there are many variations of personalities. However, successful leaders of the future will all need an appreciation of how systems function and be able to inspire a spirit of cooperation.

FAMILY COMPARED TO OTHER GROUPS

It has been mentioned that a family is the first group to which we belong. It is also a unique group, in that membership is not voluntary, and it continues for the lifetime of the members, and beyond.

The roles and norms in a family change and evolve as the age and needs of the members change. Babies are born dependent upon parents for all their needs. Then they gradually grow into adults, and may become responsible for all the needs of the parents, who are now aged and infirm.

Unlike a business, the goal of a family is not profit—it is quality of life. As a result, decisions in a family about resource allocation are based on different goals and values than are those in business. For example, the family may choose to reduce its income in order to increase time spent together.

There are multiple structures and communication patterns exhibited by families. Each has its strengths and weakness, but they all have something in common: the group operates twenty-four hours a day, seven days a week, fifty-two weeks a year—much more than any other group.

The family is the most cohesive group to which you will belong. Even after divorce and remarriage, many people are still connected to a former spouse because of their loyalty or respect, because they share children, and because of love for other family members.

The challenge for the twenty-first century is to adequately meet the needs of our multiple roles, of all the roles that we have as a result of belonging to multiple groups.

INDIVIDUAL ACTIVITIES

1. Leaders in My Life

Purpose: To identify people who have positively influenced your life through their leadership, and to provide you with an opportunity to thank them.

Each of us has learned from others and has been inspired to action as a result of the leadership of other people. Take a few minutes to list four or five people who have influenced your life in a positive manner. They might be friends, relatives, teachers, coworkers, or even someone you have never met.

Have you expressed your thanks to these individuals? Choose one or two of them and write a letter, telling them how grateful you are to them for being a part of your life. Tell them what they have done, how meaningful it is to you, and how it has made your life better. Thank them for the positive effect they have had in your life.

2. Roles, Roles, Roles

Purpose: To identify the multiple roles that you currently possess, and to consider the demands that you feel as a result of the norms or standards that go with these roles.

Each of us has multiple roles in our lives. For example, the author of this book is a consumer-purchaser, a homeowner, a teacher, a counselor, a friend, an aunt, a great-aunt, a cousin, a gardener, a citizen, a dog owner-lover, the younger child, a writer, and . . . well, that should give you the idea.

Each role comes with its group, whose members have certain expectations and norms. Your task is to use Figure 11–1 to identify a minimum of a dozen, but more probably two dozen, roles that you play. Then match each role to a group, and identify at least one expectation or norm that goes with each role. Two examples have been provided to get you started.

	Role	Group	Expectation
1.	Friend	Several	Take time to listen
2.	Dog owner	Family	Feed, water, play, love
3.			
4.			
5.			
6.			
7.			
8.			
9.			
10.			
11.			
12.			
13.			
14.			
15.			
16.			
17.			
18.			

Figure 11–1 Roles, roles, roles

3. Analyzing Group Structure and Behavior[1]

Purpose: To help you sharpen your ability to analyze group dynamics so that you can better understand groups.

We belong to an array of groups at work, at school, and in the community. Your task is to select and analyze the next group that you join. It might be a committee, a new organization, or a team at school. Complete the questionnaire in Figure 11–2. If this project interests you and you do not foresee a new group in your future, you may analyze a group to which you already belong. However, you probably will need to work harder at being an objective observer.

What conclusions can you draw as a result of this exercise?

[1] Robert Throop and Marion Castellucci, *Reaching Your Potential,* 2nd. ed. (Albany, NY: Delmar Publishers, 1998).

What group are you analyzing?

Is this a formal or informal group?

What are the goals of the group?

Are the goals cooperative or competitive?

Does the group have a leader? Who?

How was the leader selected?

Does the group function as a team or are there rivalries among members?

What other roles are apparent in the group?

What are the norms of the group?

What communication patterns are being used?

Throop, Robert and Marion Castellucci, *Reaching Your Potential*, 2nd. ed. (Albany, NY: Delmar Publishers, 1998).

Figure 11–2 Group structure and behavior questionnaire

4. My Journal

Purpose: To provide an opportunity to personally reflect on your own style of leadership.

Even though you may not be the president of an organization or a manager at work, you do have situations in which you are a leader. Remember, a leader has an idea or vision and is persuasive, inspiring others to action. The last time you took a position and others followed you, you were a leader.

So, think about the last few times you exhibited leadership. Write about those experiences, commenting on your personal style of leadership. Include specific ideas about how you might expand your leadership skills.

5. Getting Help from Consumer Groups

Purpose: To take the initiative and utilize groups that are prepared to provide you with consumer information and assistance.

There is a collection of more than eleven hundred consumer resources available from Consumer's World on the Internet. You can get help filing a consumer complaint with a state agency, research a law, or find a Better Business Bureau or Consumer Credit Counselors. There is also product information ranging from wholesale car prices to air fares.

Decide what you need to know, or just visit the site and explore: http://www.consumerworld.org. Then describe what you discovered to a friend. Offer to help them find information that they need.

6. Competency Matrix

Purpose: To review the Competency Matrix in the Appendix and rate your expanding knowledge and skills in regard to life management.

This unit has been a long one, so it's definitely time to revisit your Competency Matrix if you haven't done so lately. Re-evaluate your current level of competency on the matrix found in the Appendix. Think about how you know that you can apply the information and concepts. Are there more skills that you need to achieve? Or do you need to reach higher levels of competency with specific skills? How can you accomplish that?

EXPAND YOUR LEARNING

Bennis, Warren, and Patricia Ward Biederman. *Organizing Genius: The Secrets of Creative Collaboration.* Reading, MA: Addison Wesley, 1997.

DuBrin, Andrew J. *The Complete Idiot's Guide to Leadership.* New York, NY: Macmillan Publishing Co., 1998.

Willingham, Ron. *The People Principle: A Revolutionary Redefinition of Leadership.* New York, NY: St. Martin's Press, 1997.

GROUP ACTIVITIES

1. Roles and Norms in the Classroom

Purpose: To help establish a clearer concept of the roles and norms expected of student and instructor in a shared learning environment.

Although this task is best accomplished at the formation of a group, if it was not done then, it will still be educational to do it now. The task is to create an affinity or mountains diagram that allows groups to collect a lot of information quickly, in a nonjudgmental way.

Supplies: Blackboard space, or two big pieces of paper, and many sticky notes.

Post each of these topics at the top of a separate piece of paper: Instructor Norms and Student Norms. While *silent,* and sitting in their own chairs, participants individually respond by writing their thoughts on each topic on individual sticky notes. Answers should be kept brief, to just a few words.

In this exercise, many responses are expected from each participant. When finished writing, each participant randomly sticks their answers on the appropriate paper. When done quickly, this allows for anonymity. Responses might include some of the following: the right to expect respect from others and the need to show respect for others; focusing on the issues not the people; staying on schedule and being on time with attendance and class projects; resolving conflicts constructively in a win-win manner.

To tabulate the results, divide participants in half, and position each group in front of one sheet of paper. Then each group rearranges the sticky notes into like categories. The notes can be moved more than once, until the major ideas emerge. A header card can then be placed at the top of each category of responses in order to label the category.

When results are tabulated, they can be discussed by the group as a whole. This list then becomes the norms, or code of cooperation, for the class group.

If you are doing this partway into the term, discuss how the students and the instructor have met the norms up to this point. How will following these norms affect reaching goals?

If you did this exercise at the beginning of the term, discuss how the norms you established have helped you meet your goals. Re-evaluate the norms, and make appropriate changes.

2. Teams Evaluating Organizational Styles

Purpose: To practice researching and reaching a consensus in teams, and to learn more about effective organizational styles.

There are several organizational styles, such as the chain of command, as exemplified by the military; the hub of a wheel, where a chair or director communicates to each individual but where there is no cross-communication; and an all-channel pattern where everyone talks with everyone else.

As a team, research the characteristics of these styles, and find newspaper or magazine articles about companies or organizations that use each style effectively. Then reach consensus about when each style might be appropriate. Prepare a report in any format you wish, and share it with the whole class.

3. Teams Evaluating Leadership Styles

Purpose: To practice researching and reaching a consensus in teams, and to learn more about effective leadership styles.

Some leaders focus on the result—on getting the job done. Some focus on the members in the group—on relationships and people. Other leaders focus on the process.

As a team, research the characteristics of these styles, and find newspaper or magazine articles about companies or organizations that use each style effectively. Then reach consensus about when each style might be appropriate. Prepare a report in any format you wish, and share it with the whole class.

4. Shifting Toward Cooperation

Purpose: To analyze the paradigm shift from competition to cooperation that is occurring in groups in schools, businesses, and communities.

Form teams of people with various ages and backgrounds. Then using a force-field analysis, think about the forces that are driving groups to using the cooperation model and the forces that are preventing change, and causing the retention of the competition model.

Supplies: Blackboard space or large flip chart for each group. If you plan to have all groups work on the same topic and to reach a consensus, you might prefer to have some sticky notes available to facilitate the merging of group ideas by creating an affinity or mountains diagram (see Chapter 11, Group Activity 1).

Procedure: On the writing surface, draw one line down the center. Then draw another line across the top (two inches from the top) to create a space for a header. Title the left column "driving forces" and the right column "preventing forces."

Take five to ten minutes for each column to brainstorm as many ideas as possible from the group. Don't evaluate or discuss them at this point. Once ideas are merged, discussion can begin. Focus first on the forces that are preventing change, and then focus on those that are advancing change.

5. Working Creatively with Others

Purpose: To determine on a personal level who would be the best people for your team, and to meet in a group with people who need your strengths.

Each reader has looked at their own strengths and determined their best learning styles, personal temperaments, and brain dominance preferences. Your task is to identify the styles of people you need on your team.

The best people to have on your team are those who are different or opposite from you, because they will interpret situations differently than you will. They will have different perspectives and solutions. They will probably also like to do certain aspects of the job that you don't particularly like.

After identifying the different modes or styles, find members of the group that fit. In other words, if you are linguistic, match up with a spatial and a logical. If your True Color was blue, match up with an orange, a gold, and a green.

As a team, solve a problem or resolve a conflict. Then discuss how combining your styles affected creativity and group productivity.

6. Conflict Resolution at Work

Purpose: To work in a team to propose methods to resolve conflicts in the workplace that will lead to improved communication, understanding, morale, and productivity.

Although there is a shift to cooperation in the workplace, many companies still use a hierarchical structure, and many bosses still use a domineering style. With that in mind, discuss in your group how to establish a procedure or system to handle conflict at work.

Your team may need to research specific examples of employer-employee relations, labor laws, and arbitration policies. Then, discuss what you have learned and propose solution strategies.

How to Delegate

onald Reagan and Bill Clinton excelled at it, while Jimmy Carter struggled with it. Henry Ford never learned how, and almost bankrupted his company as a result. It is vital to successful management, but it is not universally practiced. The *it* is delegation—an essential but elusive management skill. Without it, managers can sabotage their careers and those of their subordinates, and jeopardize the fate of the whole organization as well.

Effective delegation is assigning additional duties and authority to another person in a manner that ensures that the expected results are mutually understood and that the person feels that his or her talents are being used wisely. This may sound complicated, but it really isn't. It's just a matter of emphasizing results while enhancing motivation.

Some readers may be thinking that they have no situation in which to delegate. In fact, you might be wishing for an opportunity to delegate. If that is the case, for the time being, view this information from the position of a delegatee. Has someone assigned a task to you that you completed in good faith, only to discover that you did it "all wrong"? The results can vary from creating an uncomfortable situation to a disaster. Wouldn't you like to avoid such a situation in the future? Understanding the process of delegation will make that possible.

WHY DELEGATE?

As a manager of a household or a business or as a chair of a committee, it is your responsibility to see that goals are met. Delegating allows you to *use time effectively*. It frees you to handle the important tasks of planning and controlling, while increasing productivity. Delegating allows you to *use people effectively*. Those you manage have special skills and talents and are capable of learning more. In a family or community/club setting, delegating multiplies your productivity, saving your energy for other activities. In a business setting, every task you delegate to a subordinate saves money for the company. In both settings, *subordinates experience personal growth* and become more productive.

This latter point cannot be emphasized enough. Managers should strive to delegate half of their tasks to others, while accepting tasks from their own supervisors. This way everyone is learning and growing and preparing for their next position or promotion. If a subordinate is not being trained, the supervisor is cheating the organization, the subordinate, and himself or herself.

WHAT TO DELEGATE

When practicing effective delegation, the starting point is to consider what to delegate. The first category of tasks is *anything routine,* anything

227

that occurs on a frequent or regular basis. This might include completing routine paperwork, filing, checking inventory, ordering supplies, and responding to routine correspondence. Managers should know that delegation is an opportunity to train others, not to rid themselves of unpleasant or meaningless tasks. The importance of these routine tasks needs to be clear to everyone. If they are not important, they should be totally eliminated.

A second category of tasks to delegate is *detailed and technical matters*. In an office or factory setting, this could include machine settings or procedural steps. Let the most appropriate person become a specialist in such detailed matters.

Finally, delegate *tasks with developmental potential*. These tasks include any assignments that would enable a person to learn new things, acquire new skills, or exercise creativity in the solution of a problem. Subordinates will be challenged and motivated and, therefore, enjoy their jobs more.

HOW TO DELEGATE

Successful delegation involves selecting the right person, creating a thorough action plan, granting sufficient authority to the delegatee to implement the plan, and maintaining feedback. Can you see that you are creating a system?

Select the Right Person

A supervisor needs to carefully match a task to the talents of the subordinates. Not everyone can be trained to do all jobs. Plan to invest time and effort in this training, and select someone who wants the task and challenge. Select a person you can trust, someone who will follow the action plan that you mutually create and who will give you feedback.

Create a Thorough Action Plan

Effective delegation always includes setting SMART goals. The manager and subordinate should create an action plan that provides information on what, where, when, why, and how. To complete the task, a subordinate must clearly understand *what* results are expected using measurable standards and *what* the limits of authority are, *why* the task needs doing, *where* the work is to be performed, *who* else is involved in the task, and *how* the task is to be performed if a prescribed procedure is important.

If the task is complicated, some or all of the action plan should be written down. Taking time to do so demonstrates the importance of the project and shows that the manager is willing to be held to his or her word. It also provides a timeline for feedback and a future checkpoint to clarify details that might have been forgotten.

Training the worker is part of the action plan. What steps will need to be taken so that the person understands this new task? When will the worker first be observed? How can you motivate and encourage the worker?

Grant Sufficient Authority

When we delegate, we must give up authority and keep responsibility. This is the reverse of what we would like, and may be the hardest part of delegating. However, **authority** must be clearly spelled out and granted to the delegatee. This can include the right to obtain materials, use equipment, instruct others, and make decisions about procedures.

The action plan sets standards for the result and a completion deadline as well. Having set these parameters, it is often possible to leave the procedures, and possibly the format, up to the delegatee. This is where they can use their special skills and creativity, and practice decision making and scheduling.

Maintain Feedback

In the original action plan, a manager needs to establish a time for feedback as soon after the project is begun as is feasible. This can act as an early warning device to ensure that the project is on track and to head off problems as soon as possible. Failure to communicate thoroughly at this point can result in lost time, ruined materials, missed schedules, frustration, and bruised egos.

The time for feedback is also a time to answer questions and note progress. It is the manager's job not to solve the delegatee's problems, but to provide guidance and to ensure that the delegatee has access to all needed resources. The role of the supervisor is to explain and encourage. If criticism is necessary, the errors in the performance should be the focus, not the individual. Criticism should be done privately and as soon as the error becomes apparent. If the project warrants, future reporting times should be set at the first point of feedback.

As the plan is implemented, control is always necessary to ensure that the assignment is done properly and on time. But it is important that the supervisor not "hover" over and spy on the delegatee. It is also important to keep in mind that when mistakes are made, the supervisor should not take back the assignment or undercut the authority of the delegatee.

A supervisor's trust and confidence in a subordinate is critical to effective delegation. A key principle of delegating is that if someone else does the job, it won't get done exactly the way you would have done it, and that's okay. It is the result that counts. As you can see, delegation is a learning experience for the manager as well as for the subordinate.

Reward Performance

A supervisor should always recognize a good job and call it to the attention of the person who did it. Praise in public proves to an employee that a manager will not steal credit for the subordinate's accomplishments. This builds further trust and confidence, and a willingness on the part of subordinates to take on additional assignments.

Extrinsic rewards such as promotions, merit pay increases, and bonuses can also be used as rewards for an employee who consistently demonstrates the willingness to learn more and to increase productivity.

SO, WHY DON'T PEOPLE DELEGATE MORE?

By now, hopefully, you are convinced of the value of delegation to the supervisor, the subordinate, and the organization as a whole. You might be wondering why more people don't delegate more tasks. Your thought is an important one. There are critical barriers to effective delegation, and they must be understood in order to overcome them.

The strongest barrier to delegating is a manager's negative attitudes and self-belief and his or her lack of skills. There will be little delegating if the manager is a perfectionist who must overcontrol the situation and who allows no mistakes. These attitudes are often a result of insecurity and low self-belief. As a result, the manager has limited skill in delegating. When delegating does occur, it is often less than successful, reinforcing the barrier.

Sometimes the negative attitudes and self-belief and the lack of skills of the delegatee are the barriers to delegation. The subordinate may have grown overly dependent upon the manager and, as a result, may not believe himself or herself capable. This is a waste of human resources and needs to be remedied to the benefit of all.

All of us find opportunities to be a delegator, and we all have experienced being a delegatee. Positive delegation increases motivation and enhances personal satisfaction because it fulfills the intrinsic needs of people to learn, to grow, and to be recognized as contributing members of a group.

INDIVIDUAL ACTIVITIES

1. Search Out Sacred Cows

Purpose: To analyze tasks to determine their relevance and to eliminate them if possible, and if not, to delegate them to someone else.

Kriegel and Brandt, authors of *Sacred Cows Make the Best Burgers,* suggest making a game out of hunting for time- and resource-wasting work activities. They believe every organization has some outdated beliefs and practices that remain unexamined and unquestioned, things which they call *sacred cows.* They recommend a periodic review to eliminate sacred cows. For example, in households, a commonly believed food storage rule is not to put a pan of hot food such as soup or chili in the refrigerator until it has cooled down. Where does that advice come from? From the 1930s, when food was stored in *ice boxes,* and the goal was to keep the ice from melting. Time and energy are wasted when you keep checking back to see if the pot is cool. Eliminate this sacred cow.

"Searching for sacred cows" is a challenge to you to evaluate every task that you do in a certain area of your life for a minimum of four days. You can choose tasks on the job, at home, related to education, or related to a particular work or family annual event or holiday. You judge each task based on five questions. On a scale of 1 to 5, you award each of the five questions the appropriate points, with 1 being a definite no to 5 being a definite yes.

1. *Does this improve the system or add value to the product?* Does it improve the quality? Improve communication? Increase motivation or morale? Encourage innovation? Speed up decision making? Add value to the product or customer?

2. *Is this worth the cost of continuing?* What if this task didn't exist? What would be the consequences if you stopped this activity?

3. *Are you unnecessarily duplicating effort?* Is this task already being done by someone else?

4. *Does the original rationale for this activity still hold true?* How and when did this practice come into being?

5. *Can you do it faster, better, cheaper than anyone else?*

Kriegel and Brandt encourage a team approach to this activity, so try to include other groups members if possible. Maintain an attitude of irreverence as you hunt down the sacred cows and challenge their existence. The key is not which cows you put out to pasture or how you set up the hunt—the point is that you develop a hunting and questioning mentality in order to eliminate time- and resource-wasters. Use Figure Explorations 4–1 (on page 232) to record your results.

What did you learn as a result of your hunt for sacred cows?

2. Personal Attitudes and Delegation

Purpose: To examine your attitudes and behaviors in order to evaluate your potential as an effective delegator.

Delegating is a management skill that all people can develop if they choose. The assessment tool found in Figure Explorations 4–2 (on page 233) will help you uncover attitudes that might be barriers to delegation. Respond thoughtfully to each statement by awarding it a score on a scale of 1 to 5, with 1 being "exactly like me" to 5 being "nothing like me."

Total your score. If you scored 40 or above, you have attitudes and behaviors that allow for effective delegating to take place. If you scored 30–39, you are on your way to having the necessary attitudes and behaviors. If you scored 20–29, you have some improvement to make. If you scored less than 20, you are sabotaging yourself and your organization due to overprotectiveness and perfectionism.

So, now what? Review your low scores, noticing what attitudes you have that create a barrier to delegating. As you know, attitudes are just habits of thought, and habits can be changed. Make a plan for yourself. Jump in, review your standards and attitudes, and give up some control. In Figure Explorations 4–3 (on page 233), describe your plan for reducing barriers to delegating.

3. Delegating Checklist: Do It!

Purpose: To provide a structure and an opportunity to practice delegating.

Most of us can learn how to be more effective when delegating. By now, you probably have discovered the weakest part of your delegation skills. Maybe it is that you don't analyze the task at the beginning, or maybe you forget about feedback. This activity gives you a checklist to follow and provides you with a chance to hone your delegating skills. Follow the outline presented in Figure Explorations 4–4 (on page 234), and then evaluate your results.

When you have practiced delegating following this format, write about your results, or share the results with others in a class or organization.

4. Delegating at Home: Role Sharing

Purpose: To analyze the differences between delegating to a subordinate and delegating to a partner, and to effectively implement role sharing.

	Task 1	Task 2	Task 3	Task 4	Task 5	Task 6	Task 7
1. Why are you doing this?							
2. What if it didn't exist?							
3. Is someone else already doing it?							
4. How did this come into being?							
5. Can someone else do it faster, better, cheaper?							

Explorations Figure 4–1 Hunting down sacred cows

_____ 1. I must be in control of my work and myself at all times.

_____ 2. I usually delegate tasks that I don't like or want to do.

_____ 3. I check every step of the work done by my subordinates.

_____ 4. I expect perfection in everything I do.

_____ 5. I work harder than anyone else in my group.

_____ 6. No one else can do the job as well as I can.

_____ 7. When I am gone, my subordinates are unable to finish routine work.

_____ 8. I can't take time off because my department would fall apart without me.

_____ 9. My job has a lot of day-to-day detail, leaving little time for goal setting and planning.

_____ 10. My subordinates don't know how to do any of the tasks that are my responsibility.

_____ Total Score

Figure Explorations 4–2 How well do I delegate?

Figure Explorations 4–3 My plan for reducing barriers to delegating

Select the task

Is this task really necessary or is it a sacred cow?

Is this a routine or technical task?

Does this task have developmental potential?

Select the right person

What skills or talents are needed for this job and who has them?

Who might be willing and able to learn this job?

Who can I trust to do this job?

Who will I ask to do this job?

Create a thorough action plan

SMART goal: Describe the job.

Action plan: What? Where? When? Why? How?

Teach the work: Train and motivate.

Set dates/time for feedback.

Grant sufficient authority

Provide materials and equipment.

Instruct others.

Make decisions about procedures.

Maintain feedback

Set time for feedback.

Answer questions.

Note progress.

Provide guidance and assurance.

Reward performance

Praise and thank.

Figure Explorations 4–4 Checklist for delegating

One area that is ripe for delegation is the typical family. Although not as prevalent today, there is the image of the superwoman who is trying to balance the demands of work and family with personal needs. Even though in the last decade there has been an increase in sharing of household tasks between spouses, for some, delegating and role sharing is still a matter of contention.

Historic Review. Let's lay some groundwork for this topic. In the early twentieth century, for numerous reasons, the responsibility for the care of the family and home shifted to women. Despite social changes in the last thirty-five years reversing that short trend, many people still have the view that home and family are primarily the woman's responsibility. This can create conflict if one partner, particularly the wife, adds additional responsibilities. This happens when a person returns to full-time work, takes on a second job, begins educational training, or has a baby. The new responsibilities are cumbersome without a compensatory reduction in the obligations of the previously existing roles.

In America, there is a big variation in who does which household tasks. As two-worker families have become the norm, men have taken an increasingly larger role in child care, meal preparation, laundry, and household cleaning. In some families, all members of the household have responsibilities, even the toddlers.

At this point, it is important to distinguish between taking responsibility and "helping out." Someone who is responsible for a task has a sense of ownership and has the decision-making authority. They are the "primary worrier" in regard to that task and must see that it is completed on schedule and up to par. Someone who provides help is assisting with the task, a much lesser commitment, and does not bear the emotional burden of the task.

Sharing and Delegating. All the basic principles of delegating apply in a household. The goal is to have a productive lifestyle that meets the needs of the family members by wisely allocating family resources. If husbands and wives see themselves as partners in managing this lifestyle, the role sharing will go more smoothly, as will the marital relationship.

Parents have a supervisory and teaching role to play with their children. They can help children develop valuable skills and show them how to accept responsibility for their own upkeep—the maintenance of their possessions and bedroom or play area. It will increase their independence and self-confidence, besides contributing to the family as a whole.

When reviewing tasks for possible delegation, the person with the current responsibility for the task needs to be identified. This person is the expert and understands the job best. They can describe the task, identify current standards, and identify the characteristics of an appropriate person. This may mean selecting a husband, wife, or young family member, or it may mean hiring someone outside the family to do the work.

Keep in mind that people often question change when new things are being asked of them. This is the perfect time to use all your communication and interpersonal relation skills to show the positive benefits of the mutually agreed-upon changes.

Make A Plan Together. Now, let's get to the plan. Remember that a household is a system. What you are doing in this activity is identifying the part of the system that isn't working as well as you would like. If there is more than one part, select one area at a time.

As a whole family, use systems thinking to set goals, clarify values, select priorities, and set standards. Consider the relationships and household needs. Some standards may need to be raised and others lowered. Some tasks may need to be eliminated. Reach a consensus regarding who has responsibility for what. Write down your plan. Be prepared to train, encourage, and support. Provide for feedback and rewards.

Implement your plan for two weeks. Then convene the family to check the plan and gather feedback. Adjust the plan if necessary. Write a one-page paper about your experience, or describe it to the class.

EXPAND YOUR LEARNING

Blanchard, Kenneth, and Robert Lorber. *Putting the One Minute Manager to Work*. New York, NY: Berkley Books, 1984.

Kriegel, Robert, and David Brandt. *Sacred Cows Make the Best Burgers: Developing Change-Ready People and Organizations*. New York, NY: Warner Books, 1997.

UNIT FIVE
Developing Your Action Plan

Chapter 12
Handling Change and Stress

Chapter 13
Managing Time

Chapter 14
Managing Money

Chapter 15
Preparing for Your Career

Explorations
Bring It All Together

Chapter 12 _____

Handling Change and Stress

One day to another, flip the page of the calendar—and on to another month, this one a little different than the one before. In a system, change is constant. Some of the time change presents new and exciting opportunities, stimulation, and adventure. But some of the time it brings disappointment, frustration, and sadness. This chapter is about dealing with change and managing the stress that often accompanies it.

Perhaps you've seen a stress rating scale that lists a series of events, each of which is assigned a rating, depending upon the amount of change or readjustment it requires. At the top of a typical scale is the death of a spouse. Usually a little further down is divorce or separation, death of a close family member, marriage, pregnancy, and adding a member to the family. Less significant is a change in work responsibilities or in living conditions. Toward the bottom of the scale is taking a vacation or a minor violation of the law.

Notice that some of these events might be judged "good news" and others "bad news." The changes that cause stress for you may be a routine event for someone else. And the impact of a specific event on your mood can even vary from day to day. Generally, though, an event that you view as negative will be more stressful than one you view as positive. And unpredictable events are more stressful than predictable events.

STRESS: SYMPTOMS AND TRIGGERS

So, what is stress anyway? **Stress** is a physical and psychological reaction to events, people, and our environment. Notice that the definition tells us that the cause of stress is not the event, such as a divorce, but our *response to the event*. Knowing this, we can find ways to understand the event and change our response to it.

A certain amount of stress is normal and actually necessary for growth and development. However, too much stress can be harmful. It is a major cause of illness, low productivity, accidents, and poor decisions. If we recognize these symptoms, or signals, of stress, we will be more prepared to reduce stress in our lives. So, let's take a closer look at typical physical and psychological reactions.

Symptoms

The physical signs of stress can vary from one person to another. Common symptoms include headache, neck or back pain, shortness of breath, increased pulse rate, nausea, insomnia, and fatigue. The psychological symptoms include inability to concentrate, irritability, hostility, or display of anger. Often people experience moods swings, including feeling sad and overwhelmed, resulting in a loss of perspective and an increase in negative thinking.

Related to stress is **anxiety**. Feeling worried, anxious, or nervous is a normal part of life, and symptoms usually disappear when the situation that triggers them disappears. Many of the same strategies for dealing with stress can diminish or reduce anxiety as well.

Sometimes prolonged or severe stress may cause **depression**, a disorder characterized by sadness and difficulties with eating, sleeping, and concentrating. Unlike normal sadness or grief, depression lasts for a long time and interferes with your ability to go about your daily business.[1] Most serious depressions involve an imbalance of neurotransmitters to the brain. This might be triggered by the loss of a loved one, a very stressful event, chronic stress, or illness. Anyone who experiences prolonged depression should seek the advice of a health professional, who can provide treatment for full recovery.

What Triggers Stress?

There are really two categories of events that can trigger the physical and psychological reactions that generate stress symptoms. The first is *major life changes,* including marriage, parenthood, new job responsibilities, moving, and taking a vacation. Even if you are happy and excited about such a change, it causes stress because it takes thought, concentration, changed behavior, and energy to readjust to the change. If many life changes occur at once, your stress level is likely to increase. Since life events are often scheduled by you, keep this in mind.

The second category of change, and source of stress, is daily irritations. This might include losing something, being late, getting cut off by an inconsiderate driver, catching a cold, or having a check bounce. Note that many of these events are unpredictable, leaving us with a feeling that we lack control. They may generate feelings of anger and hostility. **Anger** signals your body to prepare for a fight. **Hostility** is being ready for a fight all the time, a situation that makes a person especially prone to heart attacks and high blood pressure.

COPING WITH STRESS

Like any problem, it is best to acknowledge and deal with stress before the situation grows to enormous proportions. It is like the old proverb, "a stitch in time saves nine." Take care of the problem when it is small, when it only takes one stitch to fix it. Some ineffective ways of dealing with stress include ignoring it, dulling it with alcohol and drugs, and overeating. Luckily, there are three *effective* approaches to coping with stress that you can use independently or in any combination: dealing with the cause of stress, reframing your thoughts, and relieving the symptoms of stress. These approaches are discussed in detail in the following text.

Deal with the Cause

One way to decrease your stress level is to eliminate the event or person that triggers the stress. If driving in rush hour traffic elicits symptoms of

---

[1] Robert Throop and Marion Castellucci. *Reaching Your Potential,* 2nd ed. (Albany, NY: Delmar Publishers, 1998).

stress, can you change the time of day that you commute? Can you car pool? Can you work at home? By looking at the event that triggers our stress symptoms, we take control and reduce stress.

As noted, the more life events you experience over a given time, the larger your stress load. To prevent overload, forecast future commitments and anticipate life events, so that you don't schedule too many at one time. Chapter 13 will help you with that.

Reframe Your Thoughts

By changing how you think about a person or situation you can reduce stress. You have experience with reframing, since that's what you did when you changed a negative thought to a positive affirmation.

In this case, you focus on what you can control in the situation. For example, you may have a difficult coworker. You can control your thoughts, and rather than focus on the irritating qualities, you can look for the skills that person has that complement yours. And you can notice that what irritates *you* bothers other people as well, and not take the objectionable behavior personally. You can also seek to spend as little time with that person as possible.

Relieve the Symptoms of Stress

It is said that without stress in our lives, we would die. The point is that we need to accept a certain level of stress in our lives, but plan to control it. We can relieve the physical and psychological symptoms through rest and leisure, exercise and recreation, using relaxation techniques, and seeking support from others.

Rest, adequate sleep, and leisure give your body a chance to restore your ability to handle stress. You will not be of much use to others if you are irritable or sick. Do everyone a favor, and take a break when you begin to feel stress. You will then be able to return to your usual productive self.

Exercise and recreation reduce stress and increase the body's ability to handle stress. It makes you feel better both psychologically and physically, because it can bring fun and joy into your life as well as cardiovascular benefits. Include activities that provide a change of pace from your usual routine and that have meaning for you.

Relaxation techniques abound and should be a regular part of your life. Some examples include deep breathing, yoga, tai chi, meditation, listening to relaxation tapes, and hot bubble baths (yes, even for men). Several activities in this chapter include more direction.

Seeking support from others is an example of using your resources wisely. The value of support from others should not be underestimated. Friends and family members may be able to take on a few of your responsibilities or brainstorm with you on ways to solve a problem. Or they may provide emotional encouragement and a listening ear. Others in your community, such as your physician, clergy, and professional counselors, can provide a fresh perspective on your situation and recommend alternative actions. Take advantage of these resources.

BEYOND A FAST-TRACK MENTALITY

So, we have looked at ways to deal with stress and examined the things that trigger stress, and we have begun to develop an understanding that the real cause of stress is our *reaction* to people, events, and the environment. It bears repeating that we bring some stress on ourselves by filling our schedules too full and making too many commitments. We also create stress by excessively accumulating material possessions, and then needing to work extra hours to pay off credit cards and loans.

It may, then, be time to review priorities, clarify values, and establish goals that allow more time for friends, family, and meaningful endeavors. Chapter 13 will discuss time management, and Chapter 14 money management. Both chapters will challenge you to truly live your values.

Ultimately, the ball is in your court. You can decide to feel helpless and vulnerable to stress, *or* you can decide that you must be in control at all times. *Or* you can choose to take the middle ground—to change what you can change, adapt to what cannot be changed, and learn to distinguish between the two.

INDIVIDUAL ACTIVITIES

1. My Journal

Purpose: To focus your writing on the changes that are happening in your life, and to consider what you can do to reduce stress.

Change comes to us daily. It can be a major life event or just a little problem. In your journal, write about the major life changes that have occurred for you in the last year or so. How stressful were they? If they were to happen again, what might you do differently? How can you reduce stress in your life?

2. Measure Your Stress

Purpose: To use an assessment tool to determine the stress level in your life now as a result of major life changes.

There are several assessment tools and rating scales that measure the amount of stress we are experiencing as a result of major life changes. You might find one in a psychology text, in a popular magazine, or on the Internet. Some are designed for young adults, while others are for those who have already established their careers and families.

Find two such assessment tools and answer the questions. Total your scores and compare them. Was your stress rate at about the same level with both assessments? Were there differences in the ranking that these two assessment tools gave a particular event? What can you conclude? Write your answers in Figure 12–1.

3. Are You a Perfectionist?

Purpose: to use an assessment tool to determine to what degree you "suffer" from perfectionism.

Nothing causes stress faster than being a perfectionist. It is great to be very good at one or two things, but perfectionists want to be good at everything, even on the first attempt. And they often expect the same from those around them. This behavior is almost guaranteed to trigger stress in someone!

To determine whether you tend toward perfectionism, review the five statements found in Figure 12–2. If a statement describes you and your

_____

_____

_____

_____

_____

_____

_____

_____

Figure 12–1 Measuring my stress level

_____ 1. I believe a job worth doing is a job worth doing *right*.

_____ 2. I should work at a project or job until it is the best it can be.

_____ 3. I set very high standards and refuse to change them.

_____ 4. I believe it is better to have nothing than to settle for less than your ultimate goal—it's all or nothing for me.

_____ 5. When I fail, I make sure that I criticize myself so that I won't make another mistake.

_____ Total score

Figure 12–2 Are you a perfectionist?

beliefs, give yourself 2 points; if it somewhat describes you, give yourself 1 point. If the statement does not describe you, do not give yourself any points.

Total your points. If you have zero to five points, you have a non-perfectionist mindset. If you scored nine or ten points, you probably lean toward frequent perfectionistic behavior. More than likely you would benefit from adjusting your attitudes and beliefs and reframing your thoughts. To do this, choose at least one of the options in Individual Activity 4.

4. Less Than Perfect Just This Once

Purpose: To find a situation where you can accept doing something well, without its being perfect, just this once.

It took a complex set of events that mixed with your temperament, plus a lot of practice, to make you a perfectionist. Therefore, it will take

Figure 12–3 Less than perfect just this once

practice to learn that under some circumstances, perfectionism is not necessary. Your task is to do one of the following:

1. Decide to do a task at a lesser quality, more realistic level, rather than at a level of perfection.
2. Discuss with someone in your support system the advantages of changing your perfectionist attitude. Identify specific gains that would come to your life as a result of this modification.

Then, in Figure 12–3, write about your experience at being less than perfect.

5. Snap Back to the Positive

Purpose: To become more aware of when negative thoughts about yourself are occurring, in order to reduce their occurrence and to reduce stress.

In several chapters in this workbook, the advantage of positive thinking has been emphasized. Research supports the idea that *what* you think has some influence on your level of stress as well as on your health and well-being. "Your immune system's ability to heal the body is linked to your state of mind and your state of mental wellness. Your level of optimism and your expectations of what could happen can affect what goes on inside your whole body."[2] Optimism and positive thinking are stress reducers and a resource for healing.

The purpose of this exercise is to make you more conscious of your negative thoughts about yourself, and to challenge you to replace the negative with the positive.

Whenever you catch yourself thinking a negative thought about yourself, immediately banish it from your mind and replace it with a positive thought. An effective strategy is to wear a rubber band around your wrist. Every time you think a negative thought, snap the rubber

---

[2] Donald W. Kemper, *Kaiser Permanente Healthwise Handbook: A Self-Care Guide for You and Your Family* (Boise, ID: Healthwise, Inc., 1995).

My experience

My conclusions

My plans for the future

Figure 12–4 Snap back to the positive

band and change your thoughts. Then think about your personal strengths, the things you can control in the situation, what you appreciate about today, or what has been successful in the day so far.

Follow this strategy for two weeks, then write about your experience in Figure 12–4, or share your story with another person.

Remember, you control your thoughts, and from your thoughts come actions. Gradually, thinking positive becomes a habit, a habit that supports your success, your goals, and a less stressful life. Plan to continue this activity for at least one more week—then positive thinking will be a habit.

6. Analyzing Your Support System

Purpose: To provide a framework for analyzing your support system with the intent of making it stronger, and more helpful.

None of us functions in a vacuum. Regardless of how independent we want to be, each of us will benefit by having a group of people who support us. Research shows that those who have a support group live healthier and happier lives. Unless you are a hermit, your support group already exists. The purpose of this activity is to take a critical look at the people who are currently in your life, with the intent of strengthening your support system.

Generally, you can classify people into four categories:

Positives: Your life is better because these people are in it. They are supportive, nurturing, encouraging, understanding, loving, and patient. They give some of their precious time and energy to you, and you are better for it. This group often includes a spouse, parents, children, friends, and even pets.

Neutrals: These people take up time in your life, and may be fun to be with. However, they do not enhance your life because they are focused on their own needs and activities. This group often includes friends, acquaintances, coworkers, and relatives.

Negatives: These people may profess their love for you, but they show it by being overly critical, protective, domineering, jealous, and possessive. They are negative and damage your self-esteem, and therefore, it would be wise to see them as little as possible. This group often includes friends, family, or even a spouse.

Possibles: These people are acquaintances who seem like they could be positives. They may deserve some of the time and energy you currently are sharing with Neutrals and Negatives.

Your task is to use Figure 12–5 to classify the people in your life. Consider the effect they have on your self-esteem and happiness, and then write each person's name in the appropriate section.

Are you happy with the results? Is your time and energy going to people who make your life better? Are you willing to sacrifice your happiness for the Negatives in your life? If not, what do you plan to do about it? Are there Possibles who could join your support system? Spend a few minutes to ponder these questions, and then write your thoughts and plans in Figure 12–6.

Positives	Neutrals
Negatives	**Possibles**

Figure 12–5 Analyzing my support system

_____
_____
_____
_____
_____
_____
_____
_____
_____

Figure 12–6 My thoughts about my support system

7. My Personal Stress Symptoms

Purpose: To become aware of the behavior patterns that indicate that you are beginning to experience stress, and to identify ways that you can decrease stress.

Recognizing that stress includes our physical and psychological response to events, people, and the environment, it is worth identifying our own personal response. This knowledge can serve as an early warning system, so that we can act to decrease stress sooner rather than later.

On the left side of Figure 12–7, list your personal symptoms of stress. On the righthand side of that figure, list two ways that you could diminish that symptom. For example, if you list "neck pain" on the left, you could list "do head rolls to stretch" and "deep breathing" on the right.

Review your two lists. More than likely the behaviors on the right side of Figure 12–7 can be used as stress preventatives. Make a short list of them on a file card and keep it handy, perhaps on your desk or in your car. Make a commitment to do something to reduce stress every day.

Symptom	Relief strategy

Figure 12–7 Ways to relieve my personal stress symptoms

8. Relaxation: Fives and Fifteens

Purpose: To learn more about relaxation techniques so that they can be incorporated into your life.

Relaxation is essential for stress reduction. Exercise and some form of physical activity is one of the best stress reducers. But many of us get stressed when we are overcommitted, right when we "have no time" for exercise. This activity presents you with two categories of stress reducers: the Fives and the Fifteens.

The Fives
- play with a pet.
- sit under a tree and watch the birds.
- stretch your neck, shoulders, and back.
- enjoy time with a child.
- breathe slowly and deeply.
- walk barefoot in the grass.
- watch a sunset.
- walk around the block.
- look at a picture book.
- laugh!

The Fifteens
- stretch your whole body, and then exercise.
- meditate.
- listen to quiet music.
- talk to a friend.
- read for pleasure.

Add to these lists ideas that interest you and fit your lifestyle. Then, at least once during the day, do a "five," and at least once do a "fifteen." After three days, write one sentence about your experience. Continue using the "fives" and "fifteens," and at the end of the week, write another sentence about your experience.

After three days of fives and fifteens: _____

_____

_____

After one week of fives and fifteens: _____

_____

_____

9. Progressive Muscle Relaxation

Purpose: To learn a way to relax that is easy and proven to be highly effective.

Just sitting is not necessarily relaxing. You may have noticed that after watching television, you still are not stress-free. In the 1930s, a relaxation technique was developed that is highly effective in controlling stress. It is easy to do and only takes about fifteen minutes. This technique consists of first tensing, then letting go, of each main muscle group in your body, and learning to associate the word *relax* with the feeling of letting go.

With practice, you will reach deeper levels of relaxation, and reach them faster. Eventually, it should become possible to feel relaxed even in a crisis by saying the word *relax* to yourself, and taking two or three deep breaths.

Follow the steps once a day for two weeks.

1. In a room by yourself, sit or lie comfortably with your eyes closed.
2. Breathe deeply. Hold your breath for a moment, and then release it. Do this two more times.
3. Breathe naturally, as you feel more and more relaxed.

In steps 4–11, you will tense each muscle group for five to ten seconds as directed. Then let your muscles go and focus on how relaxed they feel. The contrast allows you to recognize muscle tension, as well as enhances how relaxed you feel.

4. Clench your fists tightly, then let go.
5. Tense and relax your shoulders.
6. Roll your chin to your chest to tighten the neck, then let your neck go limp.
7. Clench your jaw, and then relax all your facial muscles.
8. Tighten and relax your stomach and chest.
9. Tighten and relax your thighs and buttocks.
10. Tighten and relax your calves and ankles.
11. Tense your feet, curl your toes, and then relax.
12. Breathe regularly, feeling your relaxation. Allow it to spread deeper and deeper.
13. Feel your easy breathing, in and out.
14. For the next minute or so, think the word *relax* each time you breathe out. Feel how relaxed you are.
15. Count slowly from one to ten, feeling refreshed and awake. Open your eyes. You will feel relaxed.

If you have ever listened to a relaxation tape, you probably can see the similarities in this technique to the directions on the tape. Use this process once a day. After two weeks, in Figure 12–8, evaluate how effective it was for you. Also discuss whether it got easier and better, and whether you used it as a stress reducer in a crisis.

10. Managing Anger

Purpose: To better understand the emotion of anger, and to learn ways to control it, in order to have reduced stress, better health, and better interpersonal relations.

Anger is a hot and quick emotion. It has three parts or stages: the thought, the feeling, and the behavior. The thought is usually based on a sense of threatened boundaries. There is the idea that someone is trespassing or encroaching on our rights. The feeling is fury, which causes adrenaline and other hormones to be released into the bloodstream,

Figure 12–8 Evaluation of progressive muscle relaxation

causing blood pressure to rise. The resulting behavior is an attack, either verbal or physical.

Anger and arguments are a normal part of a relationship. Anger can be an effective release and should not be suppressed. People who feel powerless, however, may not express anger *directly*. Instead, they become passively aggressive, showing anger by irritating or inconveniencing others. Forgetting, procrastinating, complaining, and being late are typical such behaviors. Those who express anger in a direct, positive way solve rather than ignore problems. They live healthier and longer lives.

Anger expressed in an inappropriate way can be destructive to the angry individual and to those around him or her. Those who are frequently angry are particularly prone to high blood pressure and heart attacks. Longitudinal studies show that people with high levels of hostility not only have a higher incidence of heart disease, but also are six times more likely to die by age fifty from all causes of disease.

Anger that leads to physical, verbal or sexual abuse is not an acceptable part of any relationship. This behavior has been learned, perhaps as a result of watching a parent. It is *not* a healthy solution to conflict, and *it can be unlearned.*

People can be trained to reframe their thoughts, which can alter feelings, and therefore change behavior and increase well-being. For example, rates of heart-attack recurrence fell in a group of people who were trained to practice patience in situations that previously made them angry. They tended to be intense, competitive, with a sense of time urgency, becoming angry over small daily irritations. People in the group were trained in relaxation techniques and learned to avoid frustration at daily irritations by reframing their thoughts.[3]

---

[3]Martin Hughes, ed., *Body Clock: The Effects of Time on Human Health* (New York, NY: Facts on File, 1989), p. 61.

This activity enables you to do the same thing. It has three steps that you will perform each time you get angry. Do this when you first notice the anger. This way, the anger will be more controllable, with less of a chance that it will get out of hand.

> *Step 1—Stop and Count from One to Ten:* Breathe deeply while you are counting, and think about what has just happened. Use empathy to imagine why the other person did what they did. Brainstorm all the possibilities. This will give time for your adrenaline level to go down.
>
> *Step 2—Identify Your Feelings:* Use "I" statements to explain them. Say "I feel angry when my possessions are used without permission" instead of "You make me mad when you are so inconsiderate."
>
> *Step 3—Resolve the Problem:* Use effective conflict resolution strategies and communication skills to resolve the problem.

Your task is to use this three-step model for two weeks. In Figure 12–9, keep a log of when you felt angry, and whether or not you used the three-step model. Make note of how you felt afterward.

Along with this, practice one relaxation technique each day. Choose to express your anger in healthy ways, such as through exercise or by taking a short walk. Reduce stress by talking with a friend or playing with your pet. Finding a private place to scream or yell can also be a good release.

Although it may seem difficult, if you can forgive and forget, you will feel better. Forgiving helps lower blood pressure and eases muscle tension. Thus, you feel more relaxed and are less prone to future stress and anger.

Date and time	What happened	What I did	How I felt

Figure 12–9 My anger log

Figure 12–10 My experience with anger management

After two weeks, write in Figure 12–10 about your experience, or describe it on an audiotape.

EXPAND YOUR LEARNING

Bridges, William. *Managing Transitions: Making the Most of Change.* Reading, MA: Addison Wesley, 1991.

Carlson, Richard. *Don't Sweat the Small Stuff, and It's All Small Stuff.* New York, NY: Hyperion, 1997.

Davis, Martha. *The Relaxation and Stress Reduction Workbook.* Oakland, CA: New Harbinger, 1994.

Seligman, Martin. *Learned Optimism.* New York, NY: Random House, 1991.

GROUP ACTIVITIES

1. What Can't Be Changed?

Purpose: To provide an opportunity to think about the kinds of things that can be changed and those that can't be changed, in order to be able to make the distinction in your own behavior and life.

Even the most positive thoughts will not cause an adult to grow taller. There are some things that just are, and we cannot change them. Often they are the result of nature, or government, or other people. It is important to recognize them, in order to not waste energy on such items.

Divide into groups of five or six people. Then, within the group, brainstorm specific examples of things that are beyond your individual control. Remember to accept every idea in the beginning. When you seem to have exhausted examples, review the list to be sure that there is consensus that all items are beyond control. Organize your responses into categories or chunks if appropriate.

Groups should share their lists with the whole class to identify similarities and differences.

2. Twenty-Five Years of Change

Purpose: To think about what life was like twenty-five years ago, and to identify the changes that have occurred. Then to use systems thinking, and to consider some of the results.

There have been many social, economic, political, and technological changes during the last twenty-five years. Your task is to work in groups to identify some of those changes and to consider the impact they have had on your lives.

Divide into groups of four or five people. Select a facilitator, recorder, timekeeper, and a reporter. Using sticky notes, each person should individually brainstorm as many changes as they can. Then, as a group, assemble all the notes and chunk them into like categories.

Now the recorder should take notes. Going around the group, each person identifies something that is possible in their life today as a result of these changes. If a person can't think of anything, they can "pass." Do this until you run out of ideas.

Discuss the results in terms of the positive and negative effects of change. The reporter should share the results with the class as a whole.

Chapter 13 _____

Managing Time

How you have chosen to spend your time in the past has resulted in where you are today. Is it to your liking? If so, you probably have a feeling of contentment. If you are like most people, there are some areas where you are satisfied, while others you find lacking. Although we cannot recapture the past, we can consciously decide to make the most of the present and future.

USE SYSTEMS THINKING TO MANAGE TIME

The goal of time management is to create more personal freedom. Planning frees up time to spend on the things that matter most to us, since it helps us anticipate or prevent problems. Time management is really self-management. It is knowing what you want, so that you can make the right decisions about what to do next. This chapter uses the systems model to help you create an integrated action plan. Then it introduces classic time management tools.

Time management, or self-management, is easy to understand and accomplish if you use your understanding of systems. You probably recall the four parts of a system: input, transformation, output, and feedback. Of course, **input** is **demands** (your goals, values, standards, and daily events) and **resources** that you have available to meet those demands. **Management** is the purposeful use of those resources to achieve our goals.

The **transformation** phase of a system is planning the allocation of our resources and implementing the plan. This chapter will expand your knowledge of the transformation phase, focusing on the resource of time. The **output**, or the end result, of effective time management is a less stressful life filled with accomplishments that you have chosen and, therefore, an increased level of happiness. As in any system, **feedback** is occurring all the time from the people and environment within and outside of the system.

How we organize our time is affected by our personal human resources and styles. This workbook has provided several ways for you to identify your resources and personal style, including a discussion of True Colors temperament, and left-brain and right-brain dominance characteristics, in Chapter 3. Of course, each style has its strengths and special talents when it comes to time management. Left-brain dominant people find traditional time management techniques relatively easy to follow because of their comfort with linear thinking. It is the left brain that is very conscious of time and is a good judge of how long it takes to do a task. Most left-brain dominant people find it comfortable to keep lists and schedules, and they are punctual more often than not. Like a camera with a macro lens, they usually find it easy to adjust to a narrow focus and to work on one problem at a time.

Right-brain dominant people view the world in a holistic manner, as if through a wide-angle lens. They are excellent at brainstorming possibilities and usually have well-developed interpersonal skills. They tend to think more globally and are likely to be comfortable working on many projects at one time. As a result, their work spaces tend to be more cluttered. As they work, it is common for them to lose track of time, and therefore, they may often be late to the next commitment.

This chapter presents strategies for both left- and right-brain dominant styles. It is important to remember that no particular style is best and that each person can learn to increase their skill level with a variety of strategies regardless of current strengths.

INPUT: BEGIN WITH GOALS AND PRIORITIES

In order to decide what to do with your time, you must have a vision or a plan of what you want out of life. Do you recall the process of setting SMART goals from Chapter 2? Hopefully the answer is a resounding YES!

If you are a little foggy on the notion of SMART goals, go back to Chapter 2 and review. Also, each one of you will benefit by looking through the goal-setting activities that you did to refresh your memory about some of *your* major goals and priorities.

Do these goals still strike you as being on target? Have you consistently been working to accomplish them? Are you directing your time to your highest priorities? An excellent way to assess this is to keep a time log. There are many formats that can be used, but basically a time log entails keeping a record for one week of how you spend your time. It is imperative to have the information you will gain from this exercise, so begin a time log *now*. Individual Activity 1 provides you with one model, but use any format you wish in order to keep track of your time for one week.

Once you have that information, you will need to evaluate the quantity of time you spent on various types of activities. Let's say that your record revealed that during the week you spent one hour exercising, five hours talking on the phone to friends, two hours reading for pleasure, and three hours volunteering in your community. Based on your values, goals, and priorities, you could determine whether your time was spent in a meaningful and wise fashion. How you spend your time is how you are spending your life. Does it please you as much as it could? Several activities in this chapter will help you to evaluate that issue.

TRANSFORMATION

Now that you have your goals in mind and have started your time log, you are ready to create an action plan and implement that plan. Thus, the transformation phase of a system has two parts—planning and implementation.

Planning

Planning is a process of deciding what to do and how and when to do it. It is said that goals are dreams with deadlines. Planning is the step that facilitates meeting those deadlines. You already have some experience with planning, since you created an action plan earlier this term to reach one specific goal. This time we will think about planning for several of your goals, and integrating all the activities that you have selected into one master action plan.

That might sound a little overwhelming to some of you. But it really is a simple process that anyone can learn. First you need to see the whole picture of your life as you want it to be, and then you break that picture down into sections or goals. You can breathe a sigh of relief now, because you have already done this in Chapter 2. Next, you break each goal down into activities or minigoals. This is the "swiss cheese" strategy described in Chapter 2. Again, you have already done this as well—the last time you created an action plan. Then, you set a time schedule, the backbone of all planning.

Set Standards. It is imperative to strive for excellence in the things that matter. Our priorities reflect what matters to each of us. They help us set standards and deadlines, and allocate resources in order to accomplish our goals. For example, sleeping on clean sheets may have some importance in your life, but how much? Do you change your bedsheets every day, just like a hotel does? Or is once a week enough? Or how about every ten days? Every two weeks? Every goal and activity needs a standard set for it before the task is begun.

Peter Drucker, perhaps the most respected management expert, points out that efficiency is concerned with doing things right, while *effectiveness* is concerned with doing the right things. By setting standards, you will make plans and allocate your time so that you are effective. Sometimes you will strive for excellence, and other times you will accept that "good enough is good enough."

Practice Planning. To be sure that the process of planning is clear, this chapter contains an activity on planning. It requires that you to look back at your goals and priorities, and then make a one-week plan based on your goals and current commitments. Then, after following that plan, you will evaluate the results.

To get started, gather several blank sheets of paper and, on the top of each, write goal categories such as career, education, family, personal, and financial. You set goals of this nature while completing some of the activities in Chapter 2.

Now, begin with one of the papers in front of you. Brainstorm a list of activities or minigoals that will allow you to complete that goal. You did this when you created other action plans. For example, your financial goal might be to be free from debt and have money in the bank. The financial activities you might brainstorm could include paying off your charge cards, saving one thousand dollars more this year than last, and going on a vacation.

As you brainstorm, remember to avoid judging; otherwise, you may miss a terrific activity. You might like to list each idea or activity on a sticky note. Then later they can be easily rearranged or thrown out.

After you have a list of activities, evaluate each idea based on your standards. Would the activity allow you to meet your goal at your desired standard of performance? For example, if two of your financial goals are to save one thousand dollars and pay off your charge cards, a vacation that consists of a world cruise might not work. But that's no reason to totally eliminate it. After all, maybe you could get a job on a cruise ship!

Select the activities that seem necessary or the most likely to lead you to your goal, and that you would be willing to do. Spend a few minutes to see if they generate even more specific and measurable tasks. Take your time in the planning stage. Remember the old maxim: measure twice and cut once. If you plan carefully, you will make fewer mistakes later, and spend less time completing your action plan.

Once you have selected activities or minigoals, you can use a mind map, an outline, or a list to organize them. Figure 13–1 presents a mind map illustrating activities that might generate one thousand dollars.

Prioritize Tasks. Part of planning is setting priorities. If you have completed a time log, were you satisfied that you were spending time on your priorities? Were there areas of your life, or certain goals, that were not well represented in the one week that you recorded and analyzed? Now is the time to make those goals a higher priority.

To practice prioritizing, think about next week. What tasks or activities do you want to do? Certainly other people's needs will affect your answer, so consider them as you make a list of possible tasks for next week. Have you covered your goals or just listed habitual tasks? Use your goal sheets as a source of ideas, as well as your memory.

Now assign a priority number from 1 to 4 for each task, according to these guidelines:

1—Highest priority, cannot be delayed
2—Important, should be done as soon as possible
3—Less important, can be done the following week if necessary
4—Least important, can be postponed more than a week or two if necessary

Now that you have set standards, broken big goals into smaller activities, and prioritized tasks, you are ready to schedule your time.

Sequence Tasks and Scheduling Time. For this step, you will need some type of calendar. If you don't usually use one, you might like to start with seven empty spaces on paper of your choice. After you see how this works and get a better sense of your preferences, you can create or buy one that suits your style. Pocket calendars and weekly planners are readily available at stationery and card stores and at department and discount stores.

People spend time in three types of activities: committed time, maintenance time, and discretionary time. Committed time includes the hours spent working at our jobs, going to school, and commuting. Maintenance time is spent taking care of daily needs such as sleeping, eating, cooking what we eat, and washing what we wear. Discretionary time is what is left over.

Start the scheduling process for the week by filling in your routine activities, including business, school, family, and social commitments. Next, schedule your discretionary time on your daily calendar, using the strategy of **backward planning.** For example, if you are going to a birthday party next Saturday and the sweater you want to wear needs cleaning, think backward and allow plenty of time for mistakes and emergencies. So, on the Friday box of your calendar, write "wrap birthday gift," on Thursday "sweater from cleaners," on Wednesday "buy gift and wrapping paper," and on Monday "take sweater to cleaners."

Follow this format, scheduling all your high priority activities for the rest of the week. Be sure not to put too much into each day, because you need time for maintenance activities, too. Be realistic

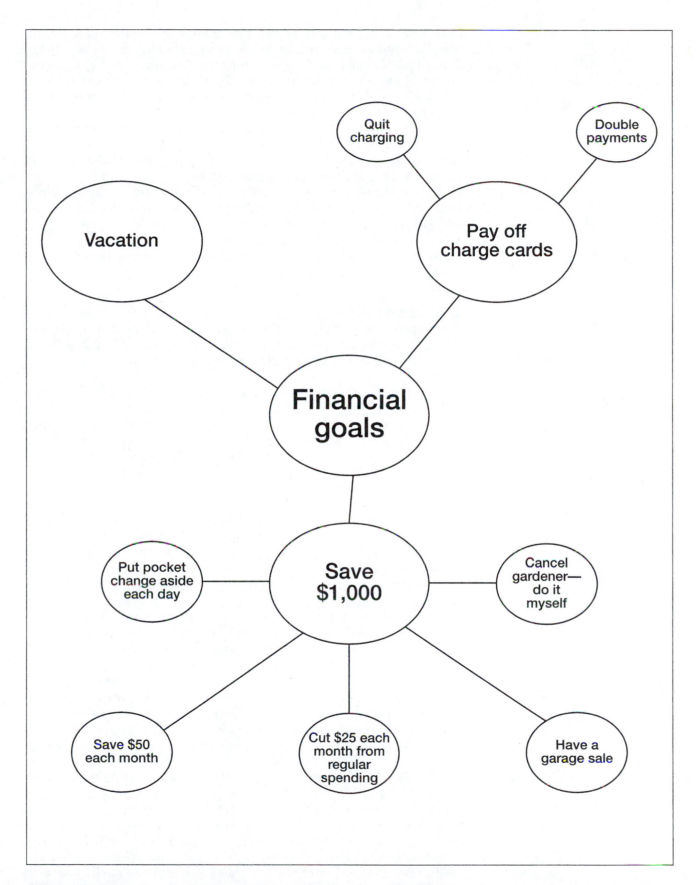

Figure 13–1 Mind map of financial action plan

about how long each task might take. A good guideline to follow is to leave twenty-five percent of your discretionary time unscheduled. This is called **buffer time**, and it allows for mistakes, emergencies, and spontaneity. Notice that buffer time was used in the previous birthday party example? The plan allowed for completion twenty-four hours before the party.

Finally, consider your **circadian rhythms** when planning a schedule. Try to schedule difficult or important tasks at your peak energy times when you are sharp and alert. Do easy tasks that require less thought during your low-productivity times.

Your calendar should now reflect all your goals: personal, family, work, school. It should include activities that are important to you and will lead you to desired results. You have now finished the planning step of transformation. Using demands and resources, you have set standards, prioritized, sequenced, and scheduled. Your action plan is set, and you are ready to implement it.

Implementation

At this point, you have an action plan. But your goal will remain a dream until you set your plan in motion. Implementation, the second half of the transformation phase, has two parts: *action* and *control*.

Take Action. Your calendar is your *action* plan, that is, it shows you what to do next and indicates reasonable completion deadlines. To actually get started and be effective with your plan, you may need to *motivate* yourself or others. Which motivational strategies have you discovered work best for you? Which are effective with those you often work with or delegate to? This is important to consider, since you will want to *delegate* wherever possible.

Maintain Control. Let's face it, even though we might have a great plan, with everyone motivated and delegation working great, life doesn't always go as planned. You may be terrific at scheduling and implementing, but more often than not, something unexpected occurs, a task takes longer than planned, or we can't find the materials or information that we need in a timely way.

This is when we need to stay on top of things and *control* the situation. Just be flexible, look for feedback, and adjust your plan. Move the due date of an activity, add a step that you overlooked, and learn from the experience. As long as you used backward planning and allowed buffer time in your schedule, you can still meet your ultimate goal.

If you get stuck on the project or feel that you are procrastinating on an activity, just stop for a minute. Reach into your bag of life management tricks and use a strategy that you learned previously to motivate yourself. If you find that time is short, ask others for help and delegate more.

Or maybe you discover in the middle of a task that you have become side-tracked and have begun an activity that is not on your calendar. Stop for a minute. If it is an activity that you want to pursue further, put it on the calendar for a future day, then get back to today's task and know that there is no greater feeling than putting a completed activity or project behind you.

To sum up the transformation phase, you want to "plan your work and work your plan."

OUTPUT: RESULTS AND EVALUATION

By now you have used your calendar for a week. You have also used up an important resource: one week of your life. It's time to check the results. Undoubtedly, you completed many, but maybe not all, of the activities. This means that you accomplished some of your goals and have moved closer to realizing others. Congratulations! Bask in the good feelings generated by your success.

Some of you may not be totally satisfied with your accomplishments or with this planning process. That is normal and to be expected. Time management is not a destination; it is a journey. What happens along the way is what is important. And along the way, some goals are met, lessons are learned, and skills are increased. For example, you may have found yourself at the mercy of **Parkinson's Law**, which says that a job will take as long as the time allotted to it. If you are too generous with the time you allow for a job, you may be less productive than you could be.

In this past week, your ability to follow a plan, honor your commitments to yourself, be flexible, handle interruptions, and deal with the demands of others may all have been tested. This will happen next week, too. How did your calendar help you in your time management? How could it be more effective for next week? Did you successfully integrate all of your plans? What could you do that would give you better results? Write your thoughts on these issues in Figure 13–2.

Please do not expect too much from yourself if you have not been a regular user of a calendar or planning book. If you tend to be right-brain dominant or are used to thinking only about this moment or this day, it is unrealistic to expect yourself to be totally organized in a week.

In other words, for some of you, using a calendar and an integrated action plan might have been routine, or a fun and easy exercise, while for others it might have been very challenging, and maybe even uncomfortable. When evaluating success, it is important to learn never to compare yourself with others. The intent is to get the results you want and to develop the skills you need to do that. You only need to live up to your own realistic expectations.

Figure 13–2 Evaluating my calendar

TIME MANAGEMENT TOOLS

Whether at work, school, or home, there are several basic time management tools and strategies besides an integrated action plan that can give you more control over your life as well as more freedom to spend your time as you wish.

Exploit Your Calendar

Your *calendar* is one of the best time management tools. It needs to be your single source of information about your schedule. Whatever format you select for it, make sure the planner is a convenient size to carry with you. You have already seen how to schedule one week's worth of activities, but that is just the beginning.

Using a pencil, since some things can change, schedule in all known events in which you, and your family if appropriate, are likely to attend or participate. Examples include:

Organizational events such as meetings, parties, practices
Special occasions such as birthdays, holidays, anniversaries
Work assignments or deadlines
Schools assignment deadlines
Goal activities that you have planned in the future

If this task seems daunting, just do a little at a time. For example, the next time you get a newsletter or flyer that includes a list of meetings or events, pencil the relevant ones onto your calendar. The next time you get a school assignment, plan backward and mark down the due date, as well as the date you will start on it. In time you may wonder how you got along without using a planning calendar.

People who routinely use a calendar or planner sometimes also make note of phone calls to be made, including the necessary phone numbers; addresses of a particular event; reminders of things to bring to a meeting or party; and similar information. The advantage of writing all of this in one place is that it unclutters your mind, reducing stress in your life.

Make Lists

A daily or weekly *"to-do"* list is often cited as the second most effective time management tool. A list frees you to do other things such as play, daydream, or listen to music. Lists are not just reminders, though—they are reinforcement. They help keep you on track and reduce procrastination.

You can decide on the format, but whatever you decide, be consistent. Don't use the backs of charge slips and old envelopes. Use the same paper, bulletin board, or erasable surface. Keep the list handy, in a prominent place, the same place every day. Cross off tasks when they are completed. Keep the list up-to-date.

Don't Do It

A third strategy is *don't do it.* Time and personal energy are limited resources, and so we need to be clear about our priorities and aware of previous commitments. First, this means that you need to learn to *say no* to yourself and others.

In regard to yourself, you always have a choice. Whenever you say, "I have to do that," ask yourself "Why?" Pause to consider what makes you think you must do that task. If you reply, "Well, I must do it to get the result I want," then you have totally changed the equation. Now you are saying, "If I want this, then I must do that." This is a more positive attitude and will probably give you more inner motivation to complete the task. If you would be just as happy with a different result, you have the freedom to not do the task.

Many people have trouble saying "no" to requests from others because they want to please family, friends, and acquaintances. They also may agree just out of habit. But if you constantly take on too much, you will sabotage your own life. So, when others ask you to do something, pause to see if it fits with *your* goals, values, and standards, and consider whether you really have the time to do it. Often, the truthful answer should be "no." Use your assertiveness to politely turn down such tasks.

Simplify Life

One of the basic assumptions about a system is that it gets increasingly complex. When it comes to *you* as a system, that means you increasingly know more people, have more stuff, and have more options. For example, just fifty years ago, it was common to have a "party line." This meant that your one telephone line into your house might be shared by another household, and you could only use it if they were not using it. Today, you have selected a phone company, which may have provided your household with more than one phone line and features such as call waiting, caller ID, and speed dialing. And there are even more options on the horizon.

What's the point? The more complex we allow our lives to be, the more decisions, commitments, and time we need to devote to maintaining it. It is just as important to get your *possessions* under control as it is to control your time, since it takes time to maintain all your stuff.

Pareto Principle. One way to help us simplify our lives is to remember the **Pareto principle**, which is also called the **80/20 rule.** This rule says that 80% of the results come from 20% of the effort. If you will take the time to think about this principle, you will be able to set priorities and make better decisions, while conserving your resources. Figure 13–3 illustrates the 80/20 rule.

Reduce Clutter. A fundamental law of nature is that all systems move toward decay, entropy, or disorganization. Being a saver is the largest cause of disorganization, and it can be a big time waster. It often leads to running out of storage space, to the point that people "buy" more storage by adding onto a house, moving to a bigger house, or paying for off-site storage.

There are many ways to determine if you have "too much" stuff, and there are many strategies that will help you reduce your possessions. Disorganization can be reversed by specific and frequent maintenance. Look in the activities section of this chapter for a couple of ideas, and in the "Expand Your Learning" section for excellent books on this topic.

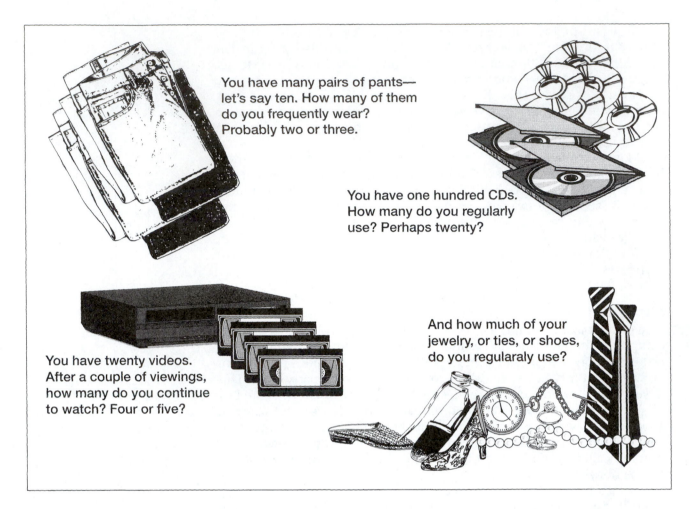

Figure 13–3 Pareto principle

INDIVIDUAL ACTIVITIES

1. 168-Hour Record—A Time Log

Purpose: To provide an idea of where your time goes and an opportunity to evaluate if your time management reflects your highest priorities.

Most books on time management feature a time log that resembles a spread sheet, with boxes for each fifteen minutes or so. The object is to record how you spend your time, minute by minute, in order to evaluate the result. This activity has the same goal, but approaches the task by listing types of activities in which you engage. In Figure 13–4, keep track for seven days, adding categories of activities if needed to suit your lifestyle.

After reviewing your results, answer the following questions:

What was the biggest surprise?

HOURS

	MONDAY	TUESDAY	WEDNESDAY	THURSDAY	FRIDAY	SATURDAY	SUNDAY
PERSONAL MAINTENANCE							
Sleeping							
Eating							
Grooming/hygiene							
Exercise							
HOME LIFE							
Meal preparation							
Laundry							
Cleaning/maintenance							
Mail/finances							
Time with family							
Errands/shopping							
SOCIAL LIFE							
Talking in person							
Talking on the phone							
Recreation/fun with others							
PERSONAL LIFE							
Hobbies, fun by yourself							
Reading, television							
Prayer/meditation							
EDUCATION							
Time in class							
Studying, homework							
EMPLOYMENT							
Commute							
Meetings							
Paperwork/computer							
Talking with coworkers							
Planning/production							

Figure 13–4 My record of 168 hours—A time log

Did you take any time out this week for yourself?

Did you have enough time for sleeping and eating?

How much of what you did was planned? Give examples.

How much of what you did was unplanned? Give examples.

What percentage of your time was spent on your top priority goal?

What percentage on your second and third priority goals?

How do you feel about these results?

2. Is It Urgent or Important?

Purpose: To learn to identify what is truly important, and to distinguish it from what is only urgent or even unimportant.

Because there are many possible activities that might lead to a particular goal, it is often difficult to set priorities for what to do. One way recommended by Stephen Covey[1] is to label a task as urgent or not, and

---

[1] Stephen R. Covey, *The Seven Habits of Highly Effective People* (New York, NY: Simon and Schuster, 1989).

as important or not. An urgent task demands your immediate attention. This might be a pot of water that is boiling over, a crying child, or an angry boss. Important tasks are those that will help you achieve your goals, such as regular exercise, monthly savings goals, and learning a new skill. Notice that these usually are not urgent and, therefore, are easy to neglect.

To see how this works, use Figure 13–5 to record some of the activities that you did in the last couple of days. List the activity under the heading that reflects your accurate feeling about it. For example, you might list "crying child" in the quadrant labeled urgent/important, while "reading junk mail" could fit in the not important/not urgent quadrant.

Where did most of your tasks fall? For many people, it is in the lower two squares. Urgent/not important activities include telephone calls, mail, and spontaneous ideas that are interesting to pursue but that contribute little to goals. This is the greatest time-consuming category for many people. Not important/not urgent includes busywork and time wasters such as perfectionist work, re-doing just for a minor appearance change, or doing an unnecessary task out of habit.

The urgent/important category needs to be our highest priority, since it represents emergencies, deadlines, and short-term goals. We should spend most of our time, however, on important/not urgent activities, something that is possible with better planning.

As you make your integrated action plan during the next few weeks, keep the result of this exercise in mind.

Urgent/important	Important/not urgent
Urgent/not important	Not important/not urgent

Figure 13–5 Prioritization matrix

3. My Journal—If I Had My Life to Live Over

Purpose: To provide an opportunity to consider your life so far and how you have spent your time, with the intent that you will be able to make more meaningful choices about time management in the future.

Consider how you have spent your life so far, including the highlights and disappointments. Most people are glad they took time for certain activities and regret that they did not include others. Reflect on this issue for a few moments. Then, in your journal or on a separate piece of paper, write at least a paragraph that completes this sentence: If I had my life to live over, I would. . . .

4. Charting Your Year

Purpose: To identify activities that occur *annually* that are important to complete in order to accomplish your most treasured goals, and to develop a scheduling format that prompts you to finish those activities.

There are certain activities that are important, but not urgent, that need to be completed in order to accomplish goals. For example, you may need to renew your automobile registration, visit the dentist for a checkup, send your Great Aunt Harriet a birthday card, and reserve the campsite for your annual family reunion. A calendar with all of these activities listed on it will free you from worry and the disappointment of missed deadlines.

Some people see the year in a linear fashion, month after month, calendar page after calendar page. Others see the year much like a huge pie, cut into twelve pieces. Others might imagine the months in another format. Which are you?

The first step of this activity is to find or create your own visual concept of a calendar that contains space for noting annual activities. Use any format that suits you—any format that is convenient and, hopefully, attractive. With some thought and imagination, this calendar can be used year after year.

Once you have your twelve-month calendar, you are ready to begin thinking about tasks that occur only once a year but that are important, and which you don't want to miss. One way to begin is with your list of goals. For example, let's say that you want to pay more attention to your home or apartment. Your plans might include painting, cleaning, and repairing. On your calendar, you would schedule those activities in a particular month. Figure 13–6 shows a calendar "under construction."

Don't make the calendar too full or complicated, because then you might get discouraged and not use it. The idea is to create a reminder tool for yourself. When it is finished, begin to use it immediately. Keep it visible in your home office, or handy with your bills.

5. Pick Your Principle

Purpose: To select one time management principle and practice it for two weeks, and then to evaluate the experience. (See also Activity 6.)

There are several classic time management principles and strategies that reap praises from the experts. But none are valuable to you until they become a part of your life. Choose one and use it for two weeks.

January	February	March
	Repair kitchen cabinet doors *Prepare taxes*	*Get new kitchen curtains*

April	May	June
Paint kitchen *Dentist checkups for* *everyone*	*Renew car registration*	*Paint living room and hall* *Reserve campground*

July	August	September
Clean carpet and sofa	*Physical checkups for* *everyone*	

October	November	December
	Plan for the holidays	

Figure 13–6 Charting your year

I selected:

First week:

_____

_____

_____

_____

Second week:

_____

_____

_____

_____

Conclusions:

_____

_____

_____

_____

Figure 13–7 Using a time management principle

Choices of principles might include: Parkinson's Law, the Pareto principle (the 80/20 rule), just say "no," or using a "to-do" list.

This activity asks you to use the time management principle or strategy of your choice for two weeks. At the end of the first week, write about your experience in Figure 13–7. At the end of the second week, use that figure to discuss how using this strategy helped you. Under "conclusions" in Figure 13–7, discuss whether you will you continue to use it, and why or why not.

6. Do It Now—Noted: Schedule for Later

Purpose: To learn to use each of these strategies to become a more effective time manager.

Many books on time management include "Do It Now" as a key time management suggestion. A parallel principle is "Handle It Once." The intent is that a task be completed or a paper be processed when it first appears. Under many conditions, this is good advice, but not always.

"Handle it once" works great when the mail arrives. Sort the junk mail from the real letters and bills. Toss out the junk mail, and put the bills in their designated space, such as a desk. But what about letters? Do you read them right now? If so, do you reply to them right now? Perhaps "Noted: Schedule for Later" is the approach to take. This means that you make note of the task and schedule it to do at a later time.

This approach will prevent you from getting away from whatever is scheduled for now. In the case of letters, it also might allow you to write a response at a later time that is more detailed and thoughtful than would be one written immediately.

Organizing experts Lehmkuhl and Lamping[2] suggest guidelines for making decisions like this:

Do it now if:
- it's an emergency.
- it finishes your present task.
- it can be done quickly.
- it will not interrupt or distract you from your present schedule.

Noted: Schedule for later if:
- it's not an emergency.
- it will interrupt what you are doing now.

This activity asks you to follow these guidelines for two weeks. At the end of the first week, write about your experience in Figure 13–8, making note of what you decided to "Do Now" and what you "Noted:

First week:

_____

_____

_____

_____

Second week:

_____

_____

_____

Conclusions:

_____

_____

_____

_____

Figure 13–8 Do it now or Noted: Schedule for later

[2] Dorothy Lehmkuhl and Dolores Cotter Lamping. *Organizing for the Creative Person: Right Brain Styles for Conquering Clutter, Mastering Time, and Reaching Your Goals* (New York, NY: Crown Trade Paperbacks, 1993).

Scheduled for Later." At the end of the second week, again list examples, in Figure 13–8, of tasks you placed in each of the two categories. Did this process get easier the second week? In the "Conclusions" section of the figure, discuss how using these strategies helped you. Did you schedule things for later or just ignore them? Did you follow through and complete those tasks? Will you continue to use this tool? Why or why not?

7. Easier Errands

Purpose: To apply time management strategies to taking care of lots of little trips and purchases.

Have you ever spent an hour going out to find one small, but strategic item when the day before you could have bought it while you were already out? For most of us the answer will be "Yes!" The intent of this activity is to reduce stress and frustration by reducing incidents like this.

The trick is to create a system for errands. This includes a plan for the environment, the procedures, and the people in your house.

Environment:
- Establish one place for a list of groceries, sundries, and errands that all household members will use.
- Establish a place for things you need to take someplace, such as dry cleaning and library books.

Procedures:
- Consolidate errands—do as many in one day as possible.
- Organize errands by geographical areas.
- Make a sequential list of the errands to avoid back-tracking.
- Save receipts in your wallet for dry cleaning, photos, and so on.
- Write on your calendar when items will be ready to be picked up.
- Use the phone to order or confirm availability.

People:
- Delegate errands to others who can run them on their way home.
- Train others so that more delegation is possible.

Based on these suggestions, identify how *you* will change your current system. For example, perhaps you will buy an erasable board and post it on the refrigerator to serve as your master shopping and errand list. Perhaps you have decided to train another member of the family to do the grocery shopping.

Describe your plan in Figure 13–9. Then after using it for three weeks, evaluate it, and make recommendations for yourself (and household members if they are willing).

8. To Keep or Not to Keep

Purpose: To take a very small part of your house and apply some basic guidelines for reducing clutter.

Stuff! Stuff! And more stuff! Papers, magazines, clothes, CDs, videos, tools, and toys. It can be overwhelming. With this activity, you will chip away at this pile of stuff and learn how you can gradually gain control.

My plan:

_____

_____

_____

The results:

_____

_____

_____

_____

Recommendations:

_____

_____

_____

_____

Figure 13–9 Easier errands

But begin with one thought: it took you many years to accumulate all of this stuff, so don't expect to get it under control in a day.

Choose a realistic space—maybe two drawers, or your desk, or the top of a work table piled with papers. Don't choose a closet or a whole room unless you feel that it is already fairly well organized, since you want to see how easy and fun this process is. Then start your plan with the ABCs.[3]

Anticipate your needs: Plan to have available cleaning supplies, a trash can, and two or three boxes for discards on hand.

Bar the door: Do not leave your space until the job is finished; if something needs to be moved to another room, just set it by the door so you can do that later. If you are interrupted, come back immediately.

Concentrate: Stay focused on your task. For example, if you are cleaning out a stack of magazines, do not be tempted to read them. That would be a "Noted: Schedule for Later" task.

With these standards in mind, you are ready to start. As you sort through your stuff, divide everything into three piles: keep, discard, and not sure.

Keep: If it belongs in this room, plan to put it in its place immediately, or before this exercise is finished. This is usually a

_____

[3] Pipi Campbell Peterson, *Ready, Set, Organize: Get Your Stuff Together* (Indianapolis, IN: Park Avenue Productions, 1996).

case of "do it now." If it goes in another room, put it in a box
marked "move." (Taking it to another space will be done later.)

Discard: If you haven't used it for some time, say a year or more, it
is probably a good candidate for discard. If you are hesitating,
ask yourself, "What would realistically happen if it were gone?"
If the answer is "Nothing," it's a discard.

Not sure: Are you saving it for sentimental purposes? Would a
picture of it be a satisfactory alternative? Do you know someone
else who could really use and appreciate it? Could you give it to
a thrift store? Wherever possible, keep this category to a
minimum.

So, how are you doing? Push the boxes marked "move" and "discard" closer to the door, out of your way. It's probable that some of the "keep" stuff is still out and visible. That's fine, if it's out for the sake of convenience. However, often it is out because you haven't found a place for it. Is there a convenient place in this room, a drawer, cupboard, or closet, in which the item could be stored? If it is out of sight yet has a storage space, you will feel more organized and in control of this space.

Review the items in the "not sure" pile, moving them to the discard pile if at all possible.

Congratulations! One space is finished. To finish the task you may now discard the items in the discard box and re-store the stuff in the "move" box.

Depending on the size of the space, and how often you use it, you can keep it organized with five minutes of attention every once in a while.

9. Daily Clutter Crew

Purpose: To set aside five to ten minutes a day to keep clutter to a minimum.

Daily decluttering can go a long way to helping you and your family feel organized. Designate a time—five to ten minutes each day—to put stuff away. This might include bills and mail, toys, clothes, dishes, and papers. Make this activity a cooperative one, including all household members. Even small children can play this game.

After one week, ask family members how they feel about the results. Write about your experiences in Figure 13–10, or report the result in class.

10. Parents on the Web

Purpose: To become familiar with Internet sites that provide parenting information that is age-specific, as well as suggestions on family time and resource management.

There are many Web sites on the Internet that can provide information, as well as sources of support via chat rooms. Several are listed here. Your task is to choose one, visit it, and evaluate it in Figure 13–11.

Parent Soup: Features advice to parents of infants through grown
children; reviews of children's toys, movies, and software; age-specific advice on homework, behavior, sex, health.
(http://www.parentsoup.com) (or keyword: parentsoup on
America Online).

_____
_____
_____
_____
_____
_____

Figure 13–10 My daily clutter crew experience

Web site: _____

What I learned:

_____
_____
_____
_____

How easy was it to get information?

_____
_____
_____
_____

Will you do this again? Why?

_____
_____
_____
_____

Figure 13–11 Evaluation: Parenting web site

Parent Time: A joint project of Time Warner and Proctor & Gamble, offers advice with articles from experts on child rearing, household care; links to sites with age-specific information. (http://www.parenttime.com).

Disney's Family.com: Specializes in the under-twelve crowd. Includes family-related information on computing, travel, activities, food, and learning. Features a local section to help find resources in your region. (http://www.family.com).

National Parent Information Network: From the ERIC Clearinghouse on Urban Education, one of the few Web sites that focuses on the needs of minority parents. Provides solid information and an area where you can submit questions. (http://ericps.crc.uiuc.edu/npin/npinhome.html).

FamilyEducation Network: Offers expert advice about helping children to learn from a pediatrician, a family therapist, and a special-needs expert. (http://www.familyeducation.com/).

11. Cut Back Television

Purpose: To assess television watching as a potential time waster, and to create personal or household limits.

A major use of leisure time is to watch television. This activity asks you to gather information about television viewing from a personal perspective or from a general audience perspective. Much information is available about the hours spent by the average person, the number of commercials viewed, and the affect of television violence on individual emotional levels. If you select the personal route, keep a log for a week of what you watch, how you feel before and after, and how long you watch.

Based on the result of this research and a review of your goals, establish a standard for your television viewing. Include time and type of program. Implement this plan for two weeks, and write about the results in Figure 13–12.

EXPAND YOUR LEARNING

Lehmkuhl, Dorothy, and Dolores Cotter Lamping. *Organizing for the Creative Person: Right Brain Styles for Conquering Clutter, Mastering*

Figure 13–12 My television viewing

Time, and Reaching Your Goals. New York, NY: Crown Trade Paperbacks, 1993.

McCurdy, Shelia G. *Clutter Stop: The Permanent Solution.* Rancho Cucamonga, CA: Multi Products & Services, 1997.

Peterson, Pipi Campbell. *Ready, Set, Organize: Get Your Stuff Together.* Indianapolis, IN: Park Avenue Productions, 1996.

GROUP ACTIVITIES

1. What Messages Did You Learn About Time as a Child?

Purpose: To help students discover that their ideas about the use of time were influenced by their family values and childhood experiences.

Begin by *individually* recording messages, ideas, or clichés that come to mind when you read each word or phrase:

Promptness
Being early
Being late
Being the first one there
Duty first
Knowing when to leave
Dawdling
Clocks

Now join together with three or four other people and share the results of this questionnaire. Then discuss among yourselves:

1. Are there other messages about time that come to mind?
2. Have *any* of these messages affected your current time management style?
3. How do you feel about these messages?

Have a group member share the results with the rest of the class.

2. Time and Philosophy

Purpose: To allow students an opportunity to see how the concept of time affects our lives.

Form groups of four students each. Within each group, choose someone as *facilitator,* to keep the discussion going; someone as *recorder,* to take notes; someone as *timekeeper,* to keep you on track; and someone as *reporter* to share the results with the whole class.

There are three questions to be answered about the group topic:

1. What does it mean?
2. Do you agree?
3. What are examples of this situation or your position?

The topic can be selected by the teacher, by the students, or at random. Topics include but are not limited to:

"Time is a method or way of communicating."
"A sense of urgency often distorts priorities."

"Man created clocks to master time. Now time has become the master."

"Lack of time is a reality, as opposed to a perception."

"Success means accomplishing whatever you want out of life."

After adequate time for this process, reporters share the results with the class.

Chapter 14

Managing Money

Are you feeling rich today? Consumers in the United States and Canada are finishing the millennium with more goods and services than any other group of people at any time in history. For most readers of this book, the basic needs of food, clothing, and shelter have been met over and above the bare minimum required to maintain daily routine. By the standards of the majority of the world's population, you probably *are* rich. Why don't you feel like it?

INCOME AND THE PROBLEM OF SCARCITY

We all have **needs**, items required for survival, and **wants**, desires above and beyond what is needed. Quickly, think of five things you want. That probably wasn't too difficult, since wants can be unlimited. Once wants are fulfilled, they are often replaced by two or three more, creating what economists call the problem of scarcity. In all systems, there is *scarcity*, a situation where we do not have enough resources to fulfill all our needs and wants.

Most discussions on scarcity are logical, filled with facts and statistics. But that approach ignores the emotional impact that money has on our lives. Feelings about money are often wrapped up with a person's self-belief. Our society judges success by the amount of our income and the type of our possessions. Right or not, the same criteria is often used to judge a person's inner worth as well. This results in using money to fulfill emotional needs, a process that is rarely successful, because what is needed is inner personal development.

To this point, this book has focused on the scarcity of personal energy, skills, and time. Now we'll turn to money, since it is the vehicle for obtaining many of our wants and goals. This is a huge subject, worthy of its own book. Therefore, this chapter can only introduce some of the basics. More information is included as part of the activities.

Why Have a Plan?

Most adults recognize that money is a scarce resource. Yet the idea of sticking to a monthly spending plan, or **budget**, has negative connotations for many. As a result, one out of three families do not use a plan. However, those who do create one report that the effort is very worthwhile because it helped them feel secure and reach long-term goals. Creating a budget may require us to reconcile our emotional selves with our rational selves. One way to do that is to visualize the five benefits of money management.

1. *Money management helps you get what you want.* If you have a plan, you avoid purchasing haphazardly; hence, you avoid

wasting money on unused and unsuitable goods, and on the cost of credit.

2. *You live within your income.* There is never enough money to "buy it all." Applying the decision-making process to money management allows you to live your values and priorities.

3. *It can help maintain a harmonious home.* Studies repeatedly show that a major problem in households is failure to agree on a spending plan, leading to arguments and often divorce.

4. *It helps with future planning.* Budget records can assist in calculating taxes and may minimize your tax bill. Records are also useful when questions arise regarding product warranties.

5. *It puts you in control and helps you stay there.* The interest charges for credit diminish the amount of money available for other spending. Planning reduces the need for credit and allocates your money to your primary goals.

MONEY MANAGEMENT

Money management helps you control not only your money but your life as well. This section will apply systems thinking to money management. Figure 14–1 begins with input: accounting for your income and expenses. It then proceeds to transformation: analyzing your situation and implementing your action plan. As with all systems, feedback will identify areas requiring adjustment.

Accounting for Income and Expenses

The first step toward a sound financial plan is to get a clear picture of where you are now. Begin with your **gross income**, the total amount of money coming in. This includes your salary, as well as things such as child support payments, student loans, tax refunds, and gifts. Of course,

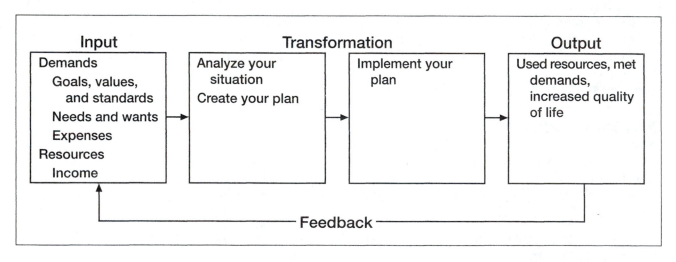

When thinking about money management, the typical input of goals, values, and standards generates needs, wants, and expenses. Income is the major resource.

Figure 14–1 Systems thinking and money management

not all of this is available for spending because an employer withholds amounts to pay taxes, social security (FICA), group insurance payments, and other deductions. This leaves **net** or **disposable income**, which is also commonly called take-home pay.

Most people can fairly accurately estimate their income. It is far more difficult to identify where the money has gone, and that's why a spending record is essential for planning. The simplest way is to keep paper and pencil or a small notebook handy for each family member to jot down *daily* how much money he or she spends. To make record keeping easier, you can divide expenses into categories such as food, rent, utilities, transportation, entertainment, and so on. Or you can make copies of the figure in Individual Activity 1 in this chapter. At the end of the month, add your expenses by category.

Analyzing Your Situation

Group your spending categories into two chunks: fixed expenses and variable expenses. **Fixed expenses** are regular, predictable, definite, and frequently the same each month. **Variable expenses** differ from one period to another and usually include food, clothing, entertainment, gifts, and education.

Next, consider how this month differs from others. Look to see whether periodic fixed expenses such as automobile insurance or taxes are reflected in your one-month spending record. You may need to consult checking and charge card records, as well as previous tax returns, for those figures.

Now you have gathered the information you need to analyze your situation. Were you able to meet all your fixed expenses? Did your spending exceed your income? If so, why? Did you pay off all your credit card balances, or just the minimum payment? Did you save toward short-term and long-term goals?

In regard to savings, are you protected by an emergency fund? Everyone should expect to face unexpected expenses such as the need to repair a car or broken appliance, or to pay for illness or accident. Families who declare bankruptcy or lose their homes because of a financial crisis often indicate that it was a "little emergency" that pushed them over the brink.

At minimum, an individual or family should have two months' income saved as an emergency fund. Many experts recommend three or more. Are you prepared?

Allocating

Now you are ready to match future income to future expenditures and create a spending plan, commonly called a *budget*. Using decision-making skills, your goal is to have a monthly spending plan that meets all your expenses. Keep in mind this is a dynamic process and may require that you move back and forth from one step to another until all your needs are met within the limits of your resources.

First, calculate how much money you must allocate to pay your fixed expenses, including those that you pay quarterly, semiannually, or annually. For example, if you have an annual $300 tax bill, you will need to allocate $40 *each* month toward that expense.

Next, review the status of your emergency fund. If you and your family could withstand unemployment for six months, then you are prepared. If not, begin to bring your fund up to the necessary level. Allocate a specific amount each month.

Now evaluate your spending on variable expenses. Is there money here that could be used in another way? Are you getting what you really need? Is a vacation more important than weekends at the movies? Is it worth giving up new carpeting to get a new car? Are your needs for insurance and retirement being adequately met? Allocate money toward your variable expenses based on your goals, values, and priorities. Figure 14–2 is a visual representation of priorities based on the recommendation of professional financial planners. The foundation of the pyramid is your values and goals, allowing you to budget for your basic needs.

After basic needs, your next concern is saving for emergencies as well as short- and long-term goals. Figure 14–2 shows that insurance is of equal importance to protect you, your family, and possessions. Types of

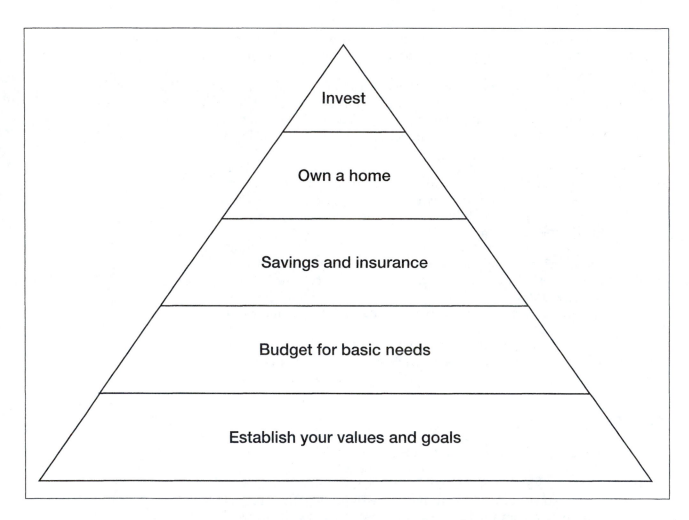

Source: Robert Throop and Marion Castellucci. *Reaching Your Potential.* 2nd ed. Albany, NY: Delmar Publishers, 1998.

It is important to establish your values and goals and to use them as a basis for budgeting for daily needs. Savings for emergencies and goals, as well as insurance, must also be budgeted. After that, long-range goals, such as owning a home or investing, can be achieved.

Figure 14–2 Financial pyramid

insurance that are needed include health, disability, automobile, property, and, for those with dependents, life insurance.

So, there really are an unlimited number of needs and wants, but with financial planning, you can have what you need. It involves critical thinking and conflict resolution and requires sacrifices, but it results in satisfaction from reaching your most important goals.

Adjusting Your Plan

Like any plan, a budget will need adjusting when it is implemented. You may have forgotten something, or you may have under- or overestimated an item. Your expenses and income will change. Therefore, like any system, you will need to keep an eye out for feedback and be prepared to adjust when necessary.

PLANNING FOR THE FUTURE

To this point, we have been looking at your current financial circumstances. As you may recall from Figure 14–2, it could be called "budgeting for basic needs." The next level on the financial pyramid is savings and insurance. These are needs and should be fixed expenses in your budget. Almost regardless of your goals, part of your savings needs to be for retirement purposes. People are living longer, are experiencing more periods of self-employment, and may be working for companies with limited pension plans. Even people as young as their early twenties need to take advantage of tax laws and invest in plans such as an Individual Retirement Account (IRA). A net-worth analysis will help you determine your financial position over time. Look at the activities section of this chapter for more information on these topics.

CREDIT

Even a brief discussion of money management would not be complete without some comments on credit. An estimated 1.1 million individuals filed for bankruptcy in 1996, up 27% from the previous year. What does this mean? A record number of people are drowning in debt, while others are definitely in over their heads. Why? There is a multitude of factors, including the availability of "easy credit." One factor is a lack of understanding about the cost of credit, and that problem can be remedied here.

Cost of Credit

Consider this question: if you owe $1,000 on a store credit card, the annual percentage rate is 21% interest, and you make each monthly minimum payment and charge no more merchandise, when will the bill be paid off? The answer depends upon which of three systems that specific store uses to credit your account. The earliest the bill can be paid will be in about seven and one-half years, and the least amount you will have paid will be around $2,000.

Will you still remember what you bought, and will you still be using it seven or eight years from now? Besides the interest fees, credit costs include your freedom. Sometimes the price is worth it in order to handle a medical emergency or a car repair. Other legitimate uses include a short-term loan for appliances or an automobile. But buying an expensive item impulsively that will bust your budget or borrowing when there is no likelihood of being able to pay the money back are not acceptable reasons for using credit. Your goal is to keep debt light and to use credit only when necessary.

Rights and Responsibilities

Credit, like all inventions, is neither all bad nor all good. Used wisely, it can be more of a benefit than a burden. Understanding your rights and responsibilities in regard to credit will allow you to make wise choices. Let's start with the responsibilities.

Your first responsibility is to inform yourself about the costs and benefits of using credit, the sources of credit, and the terms of credit. Your second responsibility is to only assume a debt that you can reasonably manage. Third, you need to maintain records and pay in a timely way. And fourth, if you experience difficulty repaying, you need to immediately contact the creditor to work out a solution.

As a consumer, you also have certain rights. You are entitled to full disclosure of the terms and costs of credit, and you are entitled to be granted credit impartially, without discrimination. You have the right to obtain a copy of your credit record and to know which businesses have seen it in the last six months. If your record contains inaccuracies, you have the right to have the matter investigated and corrected. You are especially protected under the Fair Credit Billing Act against billing errors, defective goods, and lost or stolen credit cards. The Fair Debt Collection Practices Act prevents debt collectors from calling you at work, or at home late at night. It also protects you from debt collection calls that contain obscene language or threats of violence.

SPECIAL ISSUES DURING YOUR LIFE

Once you have your expenses under control and have a created a plan for your future income, you might think it would be time to move on to other issues. And that's probably true, at least for awhile. But, as we've seen, life events have a way of coming upon us. Some of them are predictable parts of the life cycle, such as meeting the needs of growing children and supporting education for teens after high school. Others might be unpredictable, such as divorce, remarriage, and child support expenses.

There are other situations that we should also anticipate. One is caring for elderly parents. Because of increasing longevity, most adults will be responsible for at least one elderly parent or relative. Often this happens just when families are trying to send children off to college, creating two major expenses in the family budget. "Sandwich generation" aptly describes the feelings of those caught in the middle.

Planning for retirement and perhaps life as a single elder is also important. For those readers who are in midlife, it is essential to review your resources to ensure the lifestyle of your choice in the future. Assessing net worth and investigating insurance and investment options are the first steps for all adults to be prepared. Activities in this chapter focus on these needs.

INDIVIDUAL ACTIVITIES

1. Add It Up

Purpose: To keep track of income and expenses for one month in order to have accurate data for creating a financial plan.

As mentioned, this is really the first step to getting control of your money. If you live on your own, or totally control all the spending, this will be an easier task for you than for those of us who share income and expenses with others. If you do share income and expenses, you may need to be at your most persuasive to elicit their cooperation. Careful money management will make your money go farther—it can feel like you have received a ten percent raise. Try this argument with reluctant household members. Make it a game to be as accurate in tracking income and expenses as possible.

Figure 14–3 has been provided for you as a place to keep track of income and spending. Be sure to include even small expenses, such as a cup of coffee. Round numbers up or down for simplicity.

2. Analyze and Allocate

Purpose: To analyze the results of your one-month spending record, and to create a monthly budget based on all annual expenses.

If you got through the month with all bills paid and money left over, this is a good sign. If you didn't, you are probably saying, "This was an unusual month." The purpose of this activity is to minimize unusual months, to plan ahead for expected expenses, to build in a cushion for emergencies, and to allot money toward important goals.

Analyzing Your Situation. Review your income to determine whether it was typical. Then group your spending categories into two chunks: fixed expenses and variable expenses.

Now, consider how this month differed from others. Look to see whether periodic fixed expenses such as automobile insurance or taxes were reflected in your one-month spending record. You may need to consult checking and charge card records, as well as previous tax returns, for those figures.

After you have gathered this information, you need to analyze your situation.

Were you able to meet all your fixed expenses?
Did your spending exceed your income? If so, why?
Did you pay off all your credit card balances, or just pay the minimum payments?
Did you save toward short-term goals such as a holiday, tuition, or a vacation?
Did you save toward long-term goals such as a car, a house, or retirement?
Are you adequately covered by insurance?

Write about your situation here:

In regard to savings, are you protected by an emergency fund that is two to three months' income? If your job has irregular pay, such as construction or self-employment, then you will need more. The object is

| Income and Expenses for the Month of _____ | | | | | | | | | | | | | | | | | |
Date	Income	Food	Clothing and laundry	Housing (rent)	Household expenses	Utilities (gas, water, etc.)	Transportation	Insurance	Medical	Education	Recreation	Contributions and gifts	Credit card costs	Other	Savings	Daily spending total
1																
2																
3																
4																
5																
6																
7																
8																
9																
10																
11																
12																
13																
14																
15																
16																
17																
18																
19																
20																
21																
22																
23																
24																
25																
26																
27																
28																
29																
30																
31																
Amount spent																
Amount planned																
	Income grand total							Spending grand total								

Figure 14–3 Recording monthly income and expenses

that you and your family are prepared to withstand unemployment for six months. This money needs to be **liquid**, that is, readily available. Some of it can be in a savings account or an interest-earning checking account. Larger amounts can be in a money market fund that has a checking component.

Write about your savings situation:

Allocating. Now you are ready to create a spending plan, or *budget,* that meets all your expenses. Figure 14–4 provides a form for that purpose.

First, calculate how much money you must allocate to pay your fixed expenses, including those that you pay quarterly, semiannually, or annually. For example, if you have an annual automobile insurance bill of $800, you will need to allocate $67 *each* month toward that expense.

Next, review the status of your emergency fund. If it is not sufficient, begin to bring your fund up to the necessary level. Allocate a specific amount to it, and treat that as a fixed expense. Also review your insurance commitments, and be sure to include allocations for health care and other necessary insurance (disability, household, and so on) as fixed expenses.

Now review your credit practices. If you do not pay off each credit card balance in full every month, can you at least pay more than the minimum? (See Activity 3 for more information on this topic.)

Now allocate money toward your variable expenses based on your goals, values, and priorities. Don't forget gifts, holidays, entertainment, and personal expenses such as haircuts.

Plan to provide each person in the family with some personal money that they can spend in any way they choose. This allows some freedom and independence for everyone, and it teaches children how to plan and budget for what they want.

Keep reviewing your budget to see that you have allocated money to your long-term goals such as buying a home, establishing a college fund, or planning for retirement. Even a small amount will make a big difference, and you have to start somewhere.

At this point, you may feel like you have more needs and wants than money. If you think back to the discussion of scarcity, you will really understand it now. Take the next step and apply this knowledge in your life by making the tough choices—the choices that will lead you to fulfilling important goals. This means you will need to "say no" to certain fun but trivial uses for money now, in order to meet the needs that will increase the quality of your life.

Adjusting Your Plan. Implement this plan for two months, then review it and adjust it where necessary.

3. Credit Card Caper

Purpose: To review credit card payment practices and current credit card debt load in order to free up money for other goals.

Step 1: Calculate income.

Income from jobs _____

Income from other sources _____

Total: _____

Step 2: Calculate fixed expenses.

Monthly

    House payment or rent _____

    Utilities _____

        Electric _____

        Gas _____

        Water _____

        Phone _____

    Installments

    _____

    _____

    _____

    Savings _____

    Other _____

Periodic

    Insurance

        Auto _____

        Health _____

        Household _____

        Life _____

Mortgage _____

Auto license _____

Taxes _____

Other _____

Step 3: Calculate emergency fund contribution. _____

Step 4: Calculate variable expenses.

Food and beverages _____

Clothing _____

Personal care _____

Household expenses _____

Transportation _____

Entertainment, recreation _____

Gifts, contributions _____

Credit _____

Other _____

_____

Step 5: Compare income and expenses.

Total all expenses _____

Compare with income _____

Readjust if necessary!

Figure 14–4 Monthly budget

A growing portion of consumer debt takes the form of what was once called **revolving credit**, and which is often termed **open-end credit**. This is credit that can be used over and over as long as the consumer does not exceed a prearranged borrowing limit. It includes bank and department store charge cards, and check overdraft accounts that allow you to write checks for more than your actual balance in the bank. Some home equity loans also function this way.

As already noted, there are advantages to using credit. However, the major disadvantage is the cost, or interest charged for credit. The costs are escalating because more people have more cards and are using them more often. Young adults just out of high school are offered bank cards as they register for their first term of college, in the hope that they will be loyal customers for life.

So, this activity asks you to review how you use credit so that you know what it is costing you, and so you can evaluate whether it is worth it.

> *Step 1—Determine What the Use of Credit Cards Cost You Last Year:* Add all the finance charges and cost of "membership" on each card if there is one. Finance charges were reported to you on the end of the year statement. Do you have those records? If not, call the Customer Service Department of each card and have them look it up.
>
> *Step 2—Determine Your Current Credit Card Debt Load:* Add all the balances.
>
> *Step 3—Determine How Long It Will Take You to Pay Off Each Balance in Total:* Use your budget as a reference to determine whether you can double up on payments.
>
> *Step 4—Research Your Loans:* Identify the cards that have the highest interest rate and aim to pay these off first. Also, read the back of your statement to determine which method is used for computing finance charges. The following text will explain the differences.
>
> *Step 5—Quit Using Credit Cards Until All Balances Are Paid Off:* People who pay with cash spend twenty percent less than those using credit, plus they don't owe the interest.

Now you have a sense of the cost of credit in your life. Did you discover that interest rates can vary from one card to another, some being at 12% annual percentage rate (APR) and others as high as 22% APR? Once this is discovered, some people decide to transfer a credit balance from a high interest card to a low interest card. This can be very attractive, especially since some banks will offer a very low introductory rate of perhaps 6% APR. Read the fine print carefully, though, since in six months that may zoom back up to a more typical 12 or 14%, which is still decidedly better than a 21% APR that is common with store cards.

Speaking of fine print, did you look at the back of your statement and read about the method of computing finance charges? Figure 14–5 shows the results of the three methods.

A quick look at the table suggests that the *adjusted balance* method is best for the consumer who routinely keeps a previous balance. As you select the card to pay off first, this might be a consideration. Of course, once you are in the habit of paying off the full balance each month, the cost of credit goes to zero, and all the benefits accrue to you.

Now that you know your situation, create a credit action plan for yourself. Decide what to pay off, and when. Plan to make future purchases with cash or check. Some people put away the credit cards, so that they aren't tempted to use them, while others cut them up. If you decide to do this and really want to close the account, notify the store or bank. This way any liability for a lost or stolen card will be eliminated.

4. Debt Load Analysis

Purpose: To determine your full debt load, to analyze whether it is appropriate to current and future needs, and to adjust it if necessary.

	Adjusted balance	Previous balance	Average daily balance
Monthly interest rate	1.5%	1.5%	1.5%
Previous balance	$400	$400	$400
Payments made on the fifteenth day	$300	$300	$300
Interest charge	$1.50	$6.00	$3.75
	($100 × 1.5%)	($400 × 1.5%)	(Average balance of $250 × 1.5%)

Source: Board of Governors of the Federal Reserve System. *Consumer Handbook to Credit Protection Laws.* Washington, D.C.

Figure 14–5 Three methods of computing finance charges on open-end (revolving) accounts

Not all debt comes in the form of credit cards. Other debts can be owed to banks, savings and loans, finance companies, family, friends, or the local pawnbroker. The purpose of this activity is to assess your total consumer debt load (and that of your family if applicable) and to see whether it falls within safe limits. You will analyze your debt sources, determine your debt load, compare it to safety guidelines, and draw conclusions. Record your information in Figure 14–6.

5. Saving Strategies

Purpose: To review possible strategies in order to increase savings.

You might want to save for a new car, a down payment on a house, or a vacation, or you might want to increase your emergency fund. Regardless of your goal, there are many ways to build your savings account. Your goal is to choose two of them and implement them.

The key to savings is to "pay yourself first." This means that you treat savings like a fixed expense, and it is the first "bill" you pay. Many people find the easiest way to adopt this strategy is through payroll deduction. That way you accumulate money for an emergency fund, holiday spending, or annual vacation without reconsidering the decision with each paycheck.

Once a set amount is being saved regularly, there are other strategies that are effective:

Deposit windfall money such as tax refunds, bonuses, and overtime pay.

Deposit money earned from a raise, rather than adding it to your budget.

Save "loose money" at the end of the day—all the quarters or single dollar bills—and watch them add up.

Have a "Rediscover Home Week"—spend no money on recreation, eating out, and so forth during the week, and deposit the savings.

Step 1: Analyze Debt Sources

Identify the sources and calculate the cost of consumer debt, excluding mortgages.

| **Source of credit** | **Monthly payment** | **Annual percentage rate** |

Loans

1. _____

2. _____

3. _____

Credit Cards

1. _____

2. _____

3. _____

4. _____

5. _____

6. _____

Step 2: Determine Your Current Debt Load

A. Determine disposable income per month. $ _____

B. List monthly debt payments.

    1. Automobile $ _____

    2. Appliances, stereos, etc.   _____

    3. Cash loans   _____

    4. Credit cards   _____

    5. Other   _____

    Total   _____

C. Calculate your monthly payment as a percentage of disposable income.

    Current debt load is _____ % of disposable monthly income.

Step 3: Compare Current Debt Load to Safe Guidelines

Circle the category that most fits your circumstance:

Percentage	**Description of debt load**
15% or less	within safe limits
15–20%	right at the limit
20–30%	overextended
above 30%	on the brink of disaster

Figure 14–6 My sources of debt

Step 4: Draw Conclusions

What would happen if you had to pay off all of these debts tomorrow?

How long would it take you to pay them off without eliminating basic needs?

What is the cost to you, monetary and otherwise, of owing this much money?

Complete the following sentences:

I think _____

_____

I feel _____

_____

Step 5: Plan for Yourself

I will _____

_____

and I will _____

_____

Time Plan for Action

Action you will take	Start date	Finish date

Figure 14–6 My sources of debt (cont'd)

Figure 14–7 Evaluating saving strategies

Say "no" to impulse purchases, since chances are, in a week the item won't seem so important.

Apply the Pareto principle (also known as the 80/20 rule) to all clothing, household, hobby, and recreational purchases, and save the money instead.

Quit smoking—a pack a day at $2 a pack is $730 annually.

Your task is to try two of these strategies. Some of them you will need to do more than one time, such as the "loose change" idea. When you've given these strategies a chance, evaluate their effectiveness in your life. Write your evaluation in Figure 14–7.

6. My Net Worth: Assets and Liabilities

Purpose: To determine your overall financial picture in order to establish specific financial goals.

After looking at the immediate day-to-day picture and planning a budget, the next important step is to determine your **net worth.** This shows the relationship between your assets and your liabilities. An **asset** is something you own; a **liability** is something you owe. The mathematical difference between assets and liabilities is net worth. A net-worth statement can be used to determine if your financial position is improving over time.

Complete Figure 14–8, then store it with your tax return statements. Annually, or when a major change occurs, recalculate your net worth to determine whether you are sufficiently obtaining your financial goals.

Young people often have a low net worth, or even a negative one. If that is your circumstance, don't be discouraged. As individuals move throughout the life cycle, their net worth usually rises steadily. When retirement approaches and income slows or stops, net worth begins to fall as assets are used to pay for living expenses.

Assets (what you own). Record the current cash value of each of the following items.

Cash on hand _____

    Checking account _____

    Savings accounts _____

Home _____

Other real estate _____

Automobile _____

Personal property (furniture, cameras, jewelry, and so forth) _____

Investments _____

    Certificates of deposit _____

    Savings bonds _____

    Stocks _____

    Bonds _____

    Mutual funds _____

    IRA/Keoghs _____

    Cash value of annuities _____

    Cash value of life insurance _____

    Pension plan _____

Total assets _____

Liabilities (what you owe) _____

Unpaid bills _____

    Charge accounts _____

    Utilities _____

    Other _____

Installment loans _____

    Automobile _____

    Other _____

    Other _____

Mortgage loans _____

Education loans _____

Other _____

Total liabilities _____

Net Worth (assets minus liabilities) = _____

Figure 14–8 My net worth statement

7. Financial Independence: Insurance and Investments

Purpose: To review your insurance and investment position in order to protect what you have and to ensure future goals.

Your experience with insurance and investments is somewhat correlated with your age. Each reader has needs that are unique to their circumstance. For example, young or midlife single individuals with no dependents have little need for life insurance. (Keep in mind that it only pays off upon death and is intended to support those left behind.) On the other hand, disability insurance is very important, since the chances of someone in their early twenties becoming disabled for at least three months are seven times greater than the chances of death.

And what about investments? Most young people feel that they have plenty of time to start saving, but everyone needs to fit this into their budget. And starting early can pay off *big*. For example, if you set aside $1,000 a year (that's $19 per week) from ages 20 to 29, and you do not invest another cent, your account will be worth $210,645 at age 60, assuming a 9% return. But if you wait until age 30 and invest $1,000 a year for 30 years, with the same rate of return, you will have only $142,441 at age 60. This is the magic of compound interest.

So, what is it you need to do? Investigate how much disability or life insurance you have at work? How much it would cost to buy this coverage if you need it? Comparison shop for renter's insurance? Decide where to invest $19 a week? Take advantage of the tax laws and establish an IRA (Individual Retirement Account)? Or do you need to move money from savings into mutual funds? Perhaps you need to diversify and expand your knowledge of the range of investments.

Just pick one of these tasks, or a related task. Use the decision-making process to determine your goal, gather information, and research options. You can do this using popular financial publications such as *Money* magazine, books at the library, or data gathered from the World Wide Web. Then decide what to do, and create an action plan that will make you more secure and move you to financial independence. Write about the process and describe the action plan in Figure 14–9.

8. Get Organized: Bills and VIPs

Purpose: To create a money center and devise a system for keeping track of bills and VIPs (very important papers).

Having a definite place for incoming bills and a safe place to store very important papers allows you to feel in control. Having a "money center" also helps to ensure that you are not late with payments, thereby avoiding extra finance charges.

Creating a money center can be fun and liberating and will save time and hassle in the long run. Look at office supply stores for colored folders, some of which you can see through. If you don't have a file cabinet, use a metal box, as it will better protect your papers in a disaster.

Establish a Work Center: First you need a work center with a place for writing, a place for supplies, and a place to store financial

My goal:

_____

_____

_____

_____

_____

_____

What I learned from my research:

_____

_____

_____

_____

_____

_____

What I decided:

_____

_____

_____

_____

_____

_____

My action plan:

_____

_____

_____

_____

_____

_____

Figure 14–9 Improving my financial independence

records. Usually a desk, a drawer, and a small portable file will be sufficient.

Stock It with Supplies: Envelopes, pens, tape, stamps, address book, checkbook, account book, and check ledger are examples.

Set Up a Filing System: Using accordion files or manila folders, label files with appropriate categories: for example, budget, salary statements, bills, sales receipts, canceled checks and bank statements, investment records, income tax records, automobile and automobile insurance, property and property insurance, credit cards, life insurance, health records, and pensions and social security.

Get a Safety Deposit Box. For around $25–35 each year, you can store valuable papers. This way, in case of a disaster, you still have original documents and insurance records. Include in such storage: property records, such as deeds, mortgages, and so on; insurance policies; birth and death certificates; passport; marriage and divorce papers; military discharge papers; automobile titles; wills and trust agreements; stocks, bonds, and negotiable securities; and household inventories, including videotaped records.

9. My Journal

Purpose: To explore attitudes about handling money in order to better understand your own money behavior.

By taking a look at what makes people want to spend or not spend, and attitudes about handling money, you can better understand your own behavior. For example, some people see money as a source of freedom, while others see it as a source of security or power, or as a way to enhance relationships.

Your task is to find at least one article about the emotional aspects of spending money. Such articles appear in the popular press, and the topic is the focus of several readily available books. After learning a little about this topic, think about the following: Why is money important to you? How do you feel when you make a major purchase? What would you do if you came into a lot of money? Write about your own attitudes and feelings about money in your journal.

10. Live a Simpler Life

Purpose: To re-examine your standards and definition of success, and to simplify some aspect of your life in order to reduce stress and enhance your financial situation.

The 1990s saw considerable discussion in the media about people choosing to simplify their lives in order to make more time to "smell the roses." Simplifying was one of the major trends of the decade. Changes people reported making included cutting back on daily and weekly routines such as cooking, shopping, cleaning, yardwork, and errands. Some people moved to smaller quarters and got rid of accumulated possessions. Others changed buying habits to reduce consumption of the earth's resources.

Are you aware of this "voluntary simplicity" movement? Have you tuned in to those who suggest that each of us already possesses whatever we need to be genuinely happy? Sarah Ban Breathnach, in *Simple Abundance,* says, "The simpler we make our lives, the more abundant they become."[1]

---

[1] Sarah Ban Breathnach, "January 12—There Is No Scarcity," *Simple Abundance: A Daybook of Comfort and Joy* (New York, NY: Warner Books, 1995).

Your first step is to identify the things that make your life complicated. Have family members join in, since they are part of your life. Remember that during brainstorming, no judging occurs. So, just because someone lists "having two dogs" as a complication does not mean they hate the dogs and want to get rid of them. The goal is to let the ideas flow, make a game of it, and list as many items as you can.

Well, how did it go? Did you get twenty-five items? Forty items? Seventy-two items? How many of these items are within your control? Elaine St. James, writing in *Living the Simple Life,* lists one hundred complications and marks only ten of these as being beyond personal control. She also points out that the basis for many items on the list is our drive to consume. With less consumption, there is less debt, less to insure and maintain, and less space needed for housing the stuff. Also with less consumption, we need to work less to pay for it. Finally, with less consumption, the world's resources will last longer.

So, that's a quick introduction to the issue, both at a personal level and at the macro level. Now, in order to generate internal motivation, learn a bit more about this topic. You can do this by interviewing someone such as an environmental biologist, by gathering information about the three Rs of recycling (reduce, reuse, recycle), or by reading an article or book on simplifying your life. (See the "Expand Your Learning" section in this chapter for suggestions.) Or you may want to browse the Internet for sites, for example, http://www.greenshopping.com.

Finally, create your action plan. What will you do to simplify your life that will have a positive impact on your finances? Write about your plan in Figure 14–10.

EXPAND YOUR LEARNING

Buchan, James. *Frozen Desire: The Meaning of Money.* New York, NY: Farrar Straus & Giroux, 1997.

Elgin, Duane. *Voluntary Simplicity: Toward a Way of Life That Is Outwardly Simple, Inwardly Rich.* New York, NY: William Morrow and Co., Inc., 1981.

Figure 14–10 Simplifying my life

Englander, Debra Wishik. *Money 101: Your Step-by-Step Guide to Enjoying a Secure Future*. Ricklin, CA: Prima Publishing, 1997.

Felton-Collins, Victoria, and Suzanne Blair Brown. *Couples and Money: Why Money Interferes with Love and What to Do About It*. New York, NY: Bantam Books, 1990.

Morris, Virginia. *How to Care for Aging Parents: A Complete Guide*. New York, NY: Workman Publishing, 1996.

Tyson, Eric. *Personal Finance for Dummies,* 2nd ed. Foster City, CA: IDG Books Worldwide, Inc., 1996.

GROUP ACTIVITIES

1. Special Issues of the Life Cycle

Purpose: To form a support group of people in the same stage of the life cycle who have like needs, then to share research and information to make life easier.

Depending upon your age and your stage in the life cycle, you have particular financial needs. Gather together with others in your same circumstance. You may all be young singles, single parents, young parents, members of blended families or the sandwich generation, nearing or in retirement, single elders, or part of any other group that is relevant.

Each person is obligated to find some information related to money or other resource management that will make this stage of life easier. The source might be a newspaper or magazine article, or a useful book. The Internet has many options, for example, http://www.plan.ml.com/family or http://www.nces.ed.gov.pubs98/fathers. Look for information about budgeting, selecting insurance, investing, use of credit, balancing work and family, and the like. Another Internet option is http://www.co.la.ca.us/consumer-affairs. Sponsored by the Los Angeles County Department of Consumer Affairs, this site offers numerous Fact Sheets on credit, fraud, and buymanship.

Each person should make a copy of the information for group members, plus briefly summarize the content when the group meets.

Chapter 15

Preparing for Your Career

As we approach the end of this book, it is important to discuss a life management skill that is frequently omitted from college curricula, that is, preparing to obtain a job. One-third of your day is spent at work. Therefore, the more pleasant this experience can be, and the closer it suits your needs and values, the happier you will be.

Some of you may be approaching the end of a school term and will be hunting for your first professional position. Others of you may be seeking an advancement or planning to switch careers. Some of you may be unemployed and discouraged from a lengthy job search. Regardless of your current situation, in the new millennium, understanding the job market and having job search skills are essential for survival.

What you will learn in this chapter will be used several times in your life. The career that you love in your twenties, you may tire of ten years later. You might begin in business management and years later switch to design, or you might start in teaching and later begin your own business. The point is that you will undoubtedly work for several employers, and you will probably change occupations several times in your life. Knowing how to make these transitions makes it possible for you to take charge of your destiny.

UNDERSTANDING THE JOB MARKET

Although you may prefer to begin thinking about a job search from a personal perspective, it is first necessary to know what is happening in the job market at the time you are seeking employment. How long it will take you to find a job, what type of work is available, and at what pay are all a function of supply and demand. The labor market is a dynamic, ever-changing entity, and so your degree of success is dependent upon knowing current conditions. You will need to set aside time to prepare for your job search, and then know that the search itself could take several months. But like all things, preparation pays off in the end.

Supply of Workers

Let's begin our review of the labor market by exploring the **supply** of workers. The size of the labor force is partially a matter of demographics. For example, the Baby Boomers, a large population cohort, began to enter the labor force in the mid-1960s. By now many of them are in the middle of careers, and those with college educations are competing with each other for limited numbers of upper management positions.

This large supply of workers has allowed employers to restructure their companies, resulting in early retirement packages for experienced workers who have been in the labor force longer than Boomers, but perhaps have less formal education. The cohort that followed the Boomers, often called Generation X, is smaller in numbers and will find sufficient entry-level positions. However, particularly in large structured organizations, they may find their career advancement slowed due to the glut of Boomers ahead of them on the rungs of the career ladder.

But supply is more than just demographics; it is a matter of the knowledge and skills that are available in the labor pool. The supply of college-educated workers, particularly women, has been on the rise in the last two decades. Only half the women who drop out of high school are in the labor force, as compared to four-fifths of those with college degrees. This, too, has greatly increased the competition for middle-management and staff positions.

As you might anticipate, when supply rises, competition increases. The type of jobs taken by those who have not finished a college degree is now similar to the employment pattern of those with only a high school education. And worth noting, as competition increases, compensation decreases.

Demand for Workers

The other factor of the labor market is the **demand** for employees, that is, which employers will be hiring, and how many people they will hire. By paying attention to future demand, you can position yourself to offset any unfavorable demographics.

The United States Department of Labor forecasts the fastest-growing industries and specific fast-growing jobs within industries. Similar forecasts are available on a regional level. For example, you have probably already heard about the projected growth in the medical field and in high-tech industries. What does it mean?

Well, first, it means that you need to select a career where there will be *some* demand. There needs to be someone who will pay you to do a task, so, for example, you probably shouldn't prepare to manufacture buggy whips. On the other hand, don't choose a field only because it is projected to grow. Most job openings occur because someone quits, is fired, or retires. It's just that, with all other things being equal, finding a job in a growth area is easier.

Labor market forecasts are readily available at your campus or community library. Don't stop with just one source! College counselors are also a valuable resource. Seek out information from professional organizations that are related to your field. Many have Web pages, and some of them will lead you to local chapters of their organizations. Then you can talk with people currently doing the work you want. Individual Activity 1 provides more direction on how to access labor market forecasts.

PREPARING FOR YOUR SEARCH

If you haven't narrowed your career choice by previous job experience or other means, it's time to turn back to the Explorations section at the end of Unit 2. It will introduce you to a way to analyze careers in terms of field and function. Keep in mind that the purpose of narrowing the choice is so that you can find a job. This is one of those areas in which you can try out a decision and change your mind about it later. Just because you become an accountant, or an office manager, or an environmental biologist doesn't mean you will have to stick with that exact job for the rest of your life. Just picture what you want to do in the near future. Once you've imagined it, the challenge is to prepare for the job search.

Your Work Environment

More than likely the type of work you have selected can be performed in many different settings. Would the ideal environment for you be in a big company or a small one? A formal or a casual one? Would it be situated in a major downtown area or out in the country? And geographically speaking, where would it be?

When discussing where jobs can be found, it is essential to consider where the specific industry is located. If you want to be a farmer, you will probably need to be in a rural area. Otherwise, it is probably easier to find a job in a metropolitan area with more specialized businesses and services.

In terms of values, how important is job security? Could you be content with a job that would be short-term, with being hired for one project at a time? Or would you prefer to have a longer contract? What is the minimum salary you want?

Many people leave jobs because of a mismatch in the job and the individual's personality and temperament. We looked at temperament in Chapter 3 when we used the True Colors assessment. An analysis of that assessment suggests that on a particular job, if there are many rules that must be followed precisely, then a "gold" temperament might be the ideal, while an "orange" would be less comfortable. Matching your style to the working environment is an important part of the job search.

Matching You to the Job

Take a look at the description of the job you've selected. It's time to match your own education and skills, interests, and personality to what is required in the industry of your choice. You want to have the best answer for the interviewer who says, "Tell me about yourself and describe why I should hire you."

The first thing you want to show is your ability to do the task, to produce the results the job requires. You need to review your education, including classes that you took and projects that you did. Could you show these to the interviewer? Although a **portfolio** is commonly developed by artists, interior designers, and similar visually oriented people, others can do so as well. Your portfolio can include a list of your coursework and examples of reports, notebooks, and projects.

Remember that most jobs require communication and interpersonal relation skills. The ability to think on your feet, negotiate in a crisis, and see the big picture by using systems thinking are all highly valued, but rarely taught in school. The SCANS competencies introduced in Chapter 1 identify those skills and others that you will want to prove you possess. By including the Competency Matrix from the Appendix of this book in your portfolio, you can show achievement in many SCANS skills.

Employers will appreciate knowing about your interests that might not be directly related to the job. If you have been involved in a community choir or band, volunteered at your child's school, coached an athletic team, or participated in an internship, you have possibly shown dedication, commitment, initiative, and leadership. All of this can enhance the overlap in the job description and your background (see Figure 15–1).

Make Your First Impression Count

Depending on the business or industry and your approach to job hunting, there are four basic tools, or ways, that you can use to present yourself to a prospective employer. All of them must be ready to make the best statement about you. These tools include your resume, your cover letter, the application, and *you.*

A **resume** is a short, concise summation of what you have to offer an employer in regard to a specific job. It is a necessary and useful tool if you are seeking a professional or managerial position. Its intent is to make a good first impression, accurately reflect your education and experience, and reflect your personality. The goal of a resume is not to get you a job but to get you an interview.

The resume should stimulate interest in meeting you; it need not include everything about you. It should confirm that you meet the job qualifications, focus on your achievements, and suggest how you might be of value to the employer. It must have a professional appearance and be attractive, and it must be easy to skim, since most people only spend about thirty seconds looking at a resume. There are several common resume formats, so you will want to select one that will best suit you and

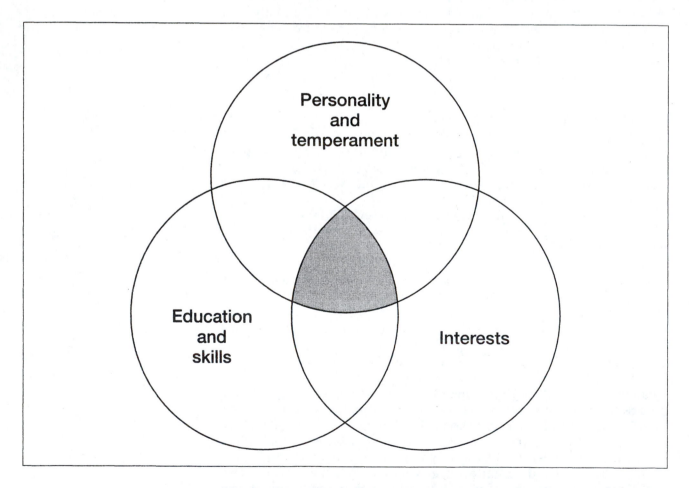

An appropriate job would match the integration or overlap of your education and skills, personality and temperament, and interests.

Figure 15–1 Matching you to the job

the circumstance. Many books are available with full directions, and they are packed with numerous examples.

In addition to a resume, a **cover letter** is usually needed. This letter should be directed to a specific person. This person may be the one who placed the job announcement, or the manager of the department in which you want to work. The intent of the cover letter is to personalize the resume even more, to introduce you, and to ask for an interview. It should have a "feel" that is similar to that of the resume. A cover letter should always accompany a resume.

The **application** is the employer's formal and required record of your employment history. This must be accurately filled out in black ink, since many advertisements today require a FAX response.

Sometimes an application is supplied a few minutes before an interview, as a partial test of your organizational skills. Therefore, you need to take all records with you, such as a list of previous employers with addresses and phone numbers, a list of all schools attended with addresses, and a list of references with addresses and phone numbers.

Regarding references, be sure to ask people in advance if you can use them as a reference. Then provide them with a resume and describe the position you are seeking. Also remind them of your achievements so that they are prepared to say positive things about you.

Your final tool is *you*. Now is the time to review the dress code for your future job. What type of clothing is worn by others in the job you are seeking? By their bosses? You will want to select a conservative version of these "looks" for the interview. If typical work clothes are very casual, consider wearing more business-like apparel to the interview. This makes a stronger statement of your purpose and mission.

Now is also the time to review your own standard of personal appearance. Check personal hygiene, grooming, and the condition of your accessories. Run-down heels and dirty fingernails suggest slovenly work habits. When there is competition, people with a poor appearance get passed over.

Your school Placement Office might offer seminars on resume writing, appropriate wardrobe, and interview techniques.

GETTING THE JOB

As mentioned earlier, research on the job market and preparation for the job search take time. But as with all planning, you will save time later. Now that you know what types of jobs are available and you are ready to make a great first impression, it's time to find job openings.

Finding Jobs

Each year about thirty percent of the jobs in this country become open and available. The trick is to find them. While you are engaged in that process, you need to recognize that this is a numbers game. You need to find and apply for as many jobs as possible in order to obtain as many interviews as possible. This process can take three to six months. In time, a match will be made.

As you pursue your goals, you will need to keep records. One way to do this is to establish a notebook. Then you will always know where you stand. Individual Activity 3 has more details.

Many jobs are never listed in the classified ads but, instead, are advertised person to person. Therefore, you need to be **networking**, that is, telling anyone and everyone what type of job you are seeking and what you have to offer. Although it would be a natural assumption that the recommendation of a mere acquaintance, someone who may only have met you once, would carry little weight, this turns out not to be true.

Networking can begin with family and friends but needs to extend to owners, managers, and executives who have the power to hire and the knowledge to refer you to others similarly positioned. Make many appointments for **referral interviews** of about ten minutes in length. At a referral interview, you are not applying for a job, but only seeking advice and information about openings in the industry from the expert with whom you have the interview. See Individual Activity 4 for more information on this technique.

Once you have arrived at this stage, you may want to consider making a **cold call**. This is a common strategy used in sales, and it means that you walk into a suitable business unannounced and ask to talk with someone "for only five minutes" about opportunities in the company. A cold call functions like a referral interview—because many jobs are not advertised to the public, these methods are surprisingly effective, particularly if you have a portfolio.

Your job search should leave no avenue unexplored. Talk with your *current employer* for possible job opportunities in other divisions or different sites of the company. Visit the school *Placement Office* and interview the director or manager to see what services are available to you. Search *classified ads* in general newspapers, in trade papers, and on the Internet. Also investigate *government agencies* that might offer opportunities, many of which are announced on the Internet.

The Interview

The interview is what you want, as it is a chance to showcase your skills. But it is even more than that. An interview needs to be a two-way communication, with you asking as many questions as you answer. Only preplanning will allow you to do that effectively.

You can anticipate questions that will be asked about your background and your possible contribution to the company. The key to success here is to practice, practice. Role play with someone, so that you are comfortable with your answers.

Finally, you need to immediately follow up the interview with a thank-you note. If you do not get offered the job, it can be very helpful to get feedback about the reason. Such feedback can lead you to make a change or acquire a skill that will get you the job in the future.

Don't get discouraged. It's a big country. Part of the secret to finding a job is making hundreds of calls, having numerous interviews, and being in the right place at the right time.

INDIVIDUAL ACTIVITIES

1. Forecasting Future Job Demand

Purpose: To understand how to gain information about the current job market in order to prepare for a job search.

Forecasts for labor market demand are available on a general basis, by job field, and to some extent by job function and title. A good place to seek this information is a college Career Center. Another source of information is campus and public libraries. (Since most of the books you will use in any of these sites cannot be checked out, it usually won't matter if you are a member of the student body or reside in the city.) What you will find at these centers are extensive collections of occupational directories, with job descriptions and forecasts of future demand.

On your first visit, describe your quest to the reference librarian, whose expertise lies in finding specialized information. He or she is familiar with the major directories, government publications, and so forth and, therefore, can save you immense amounts of time.

As you become more familiar with the field, you will be able to identify professional associations that can also be sources of information. Many have established Web sites that highlight current trends, describe national activities and meetings, and list local chapters or individual contact members. All of this information can help you understand your field and lead you to job opportunities.

Following your search, summarize your findings in Figure 15–2.

2. Participating in Networking

Purpose: To practice networking in order to pursue your job search.

As previously mentioned, many jobs are never advertised to the general public but, instead, are advertised person to person. This is because there is a greater feeling of confidence in a referral, as people have a sense that the qualifications of the potential employee have been prescreened.

Therefore, you need to be networking. This entails meeting as many people as possible and making them aware of your desire for a job. Opportunities are best at meetings of professionals in your particular field, but do not overlook general interest groups such as the Chamber of Commerce, the PTA, your church or temple, your friends and family, their friends and family, and so on *ad infinitum*.

Clearly, you need to use your interpersonal skills—shake hands, state the job title or a very brief description, and provide the individual with a way to contact you. This may mean that you will need to have some business cards printed. In some fields, a creative, handmade business card may be acceptable. Consider it a small investment in your future.

My job and field _____

The future demand

_____

_____

_____

_____

_____

_____

Figure 15–2 My labor market forecast

Your task for this activity is to plan to participate in two networking opportunities. Wherever possible, collect business cards from the people you meet, and annotate them on the back with reminders such as the date, meeting, and other useful information. Follow up any referrals or suggestions. When you have had your two meetings, write in Figure 15–3 about your experience and what you plan to do next.

3. Create a Job Search Notebook

Purpose: To maintain a record of contacts with potential employers in order to ensure effective follow-up.

After you begin networking and referral interviews, you will find that you need an organized way to keep all of your information together. One way to do this is with a Job Search Notebook, with one page for each company that you contact.

Figure 15–4 provides an example of a form for this purpose. Make two copies to get started, and plan to make more as you need them.

4. Participating in a Referral Interview

Purpose: To practice obtaining and participating in a referral interview in order to pursue your job search.

The intent of a referral interview is to expand your information search and multiply your contacts in the field. Therefore, you want to meet with owners, managers, and executives who have the power to hire people in the job you are seeking. The purpose is not to get a job, but just to seek information about the field and businesses like this one. Therefore, the person with whom you will speak has no obligation and will be inclined to be objective about your qualifications.

What I did

_____

_____

_____

What I learned

_____

_____

_____

What I will do next

_____

_____

_____

Figure 15–3 My network experience

Company _____

Contact _____

Contact title _____

Address _____

Telephone _____

Fax _____

Referred by _____

Initial contact

    Letter or phone? _____   Date _____

    Result _____

Follow-up #1

    Letter or phone? _____   Date _____

    Result _____

Follow-up #2

    Letter or phone? _____   Date _____

    Result _____

Resume submitted

    Yes or no_____   Date _____

    Result _____

First interview

    Date _____

    Result _____

    Thank-you note sent _____

Second interview

    Date _____.

    Result _____

    Thank-you note sent _____

Comments:

_____

_____

_____

_____

_____

Figure 15–4 Job search notebook

First, you would write a note and ask for ten minutes of their time. Explain that you want to hear from an expert, a leader in the field, about the current local labor market. Say that you will call shortly to discuss arrangements.

Remember, the goal is to meet in person whenever you can. So be prepared to explain that you want to see general working conditions or something of that sort and that, therefore, a phone conversation will not be sufficient. A professional meeting might also give you a chance to explain your situation.

How do you find a person for a referral interview? By *networking*. Don't overlook the telephone operator or receptionist at the company as a source of information to help you identify any people that you and this manager have in common. Why would such a person want to help you? It is in the self-interest of managers and executives to meet qualified newcomers. Most managers trade names of qualified people and help each other find employees.

Your major goal is to make a fabulously favorable impression on the manager. Unless you do that, nothing else will come of this effort. Clearly, your best appearance, manners, and communication skills are essential.

If this person judges you to be serious and capable, he or she may refer you to others. If you get no such referral, carefully and tactfully ask for one. "Is there someone you would recommend that I meet and talk with in your company, or in another company?" If this does not yield a referral or leads to a suggestion that you seek more education or pursue further reading, you probably have been judged as not yet qualified for what you are seeking. If you are sent to someone else within the company, congratulations! You have been judged to be suitable and a potential employee.

After the interview, be sure to send a thank-you letter. Personalize it by mentioning one or two key points that were useful. Summarize what you have learned in Figure 15–5.

5. Practice Cold Calling

Purpose: To practice cold calling as a way to extend your information and job search.

A cold call is similar to a referral interview, only without the appointment. It may be suitable for medium- to large-sized businesses, government agencies, or educational institutions. It is particularly useful if you have a portfolio, something for people to review.

On the other hand, cold calling can be time-consuming, tiring, and quite discouraging, since there will be a certain number of people who will not speak with you or who have no openings. The odds of a small business having an open position of the sort you seek are worse than for a large business.

Cold calling in person or by phone tends to pay off at a higher rate than sending out unsolicited written resumes and cover letters. Yet the former approach leads to a more painful rejection for most people.

With this in mind, decide to commit a certain amount of time every day to cold calling, either by phone or in person. Select the company, and ask to speak to the person who does the hiring. Then mention the job you are seeking and two of your qualifications. Keep in mind that

What I did

_____

_____

_____

What I learned

_____

_____

_____

What I will do next

_____

_____

_____

Figure 15–5 My referral interview experience

the goal is a job interview, not to be interviewed over the phone. Keep a record of who you talk with and when, as well as their comments and recommendations.

Do not hesitate to call back a month or so later, as an opening may have occurred. Consider yourself successful if you obtain one interview for about thirty targeted phone calls.

After five days, write about your experience in Figure 15–6, noting what you have learned and your level of success.

6. Form a Job Searchers Team

Purpose: To form a support group who will help maintain morale and provide ideas and suggestions.

Depending upon how long your job search extends, it may prove to be a discouraging experience. How ironic, that just when you have almost reached an important goal and you need your most optimistic attitude, depression can set in.

To combat the natural anxiety that accompanies a job search, form a support group of other searchers. Chances are you know others who are looking for a job, but who are not looking for the same job you are. This group will meet regularly, perhaps weekly, to encourage and support. No griping allowed!

You can meet to exchange advice and leads, and to swap learning experiences and interview tips. It also is very productive for everyone to set goals and then report on their accomplishments at the next meeting. For example, goals might include making twenty calls this week, going to see a specific list of people, and so on.

Form a support group, and after two weeks, list in Figure 15–7 five positive results that have come from the group.

_____

Figure 15–6 My job search: Cold calling

1. _____
2. _____
3. _____
4. _____
5. _____

Figure 15–7 Positive results from my support group

7. Preparing for the Interview

Purpose: To research typical interview questions and to prepare answers in advance of the interview.

The interview is the time when your education, previous job experience, and personal qualities will be scrutinized and evaluated. In order to exude a confident attitude, you want to be enthusiastic. Preparation will make that possible.

Interviews can vary widely, from casual conversations to demonstrations of technical skills. Some interviews are highly structured, allowing questions only at the very end. Ask about the format so that you can rehearse.

Most interviews cover four basic issues:

1. *What type of person are you?* This subject is often approached by a request to "Tell me about yourself" or "Describe a difficult decision you had to make." Be prepared with details that can be favorably tied back to job performance and attitude to work.

2. *Why did you choose this company?* To answer this question effectively, you will need to know the company's goals and business strategies. Examine the annual report or a press release kit. Your friend, the reference librarian, can help you with this.

3. *What are your career goals five years from now?* Employers are impressed with people who have concrete goals, so here you are already.

4. *Are you good at what you do, and do you want to learn more?* Provide specific, measurable examples of what you can do. Also, plan your answer to show initiative and interest in learning more.

Now, it's your turn to prepare. Think about how you would answer each question—about the specific, measurable examples you would use to support your position. Then write out your answers in Figure 15–8.

Now find two friends and, at two different times, role play with them. Have them ask questions that will cover each of the four key points, but be sure that they ask them in their own, original way. Your challenge is to answer the questions they ask. After each role play, work together to evaluate your responses.

8. Doing More Research

Purpose: To learn more about resumes, cover letters, and the overall job search process through reading.

The topic of job search is detailed enough to warrant an entire book. There are several good ones available at most libraries or bookstores. Find one that appeals to you. Read it and compare the information to the ideas presented here.

Then, using the guidelines found in your reading, create a resume that does justice to your accomplishments. Write a sample cover letter.

9. What Can Your School Do for You?

Purpose: To explore the services at your school (or in your community) to assist people in finding a job.

Whether you are a student or are reading this book on your own, there are many resources available to you at your school or in your community to help you find a job. The list might include campus or public libraries, job fairs and seminars, on-campus recruiters, college or job counselors, and career centers. Some regions might have a job search Web site. For example, there is Job Smart in California, which can be reached at http://jobsmart.org. Access is provided free at California public libraries.

Your task is to locate as many support services as possible. Gather brochures and pamphlets. Then, make a chart that lists each agency and what they provide, and identify any restrictions on who can use the services.

Share this chart with a group of people at school, church, or community.

10. Create a Personal Portfolio

Purpose: To utilize a personal portfolio approach to preparing for an interview.

In the past, portfolios were used during interviews primarily by people in the visual arts. Today there is a growing interest in showing proof of accomplishment, performance, and work history by collecting a variety of

1. What type of person are you?

_____

_____

_____

_____

_____

2. Why did you choose this company?

_____

_____

_____

_____

_____

3. What are your career goals five years from now?

_____

_____

_____

_____

_____

4. Are you good at what you do, and do you want to learn more?

_____

_____

_____

_____

_____

_____

Figure 15–8 Interview answers

documents. These documents can originate from work, school, community, or personal efforts, and they would include such items as transcripts, certificates of achievement, letters of reference, and actual projects.

Transcripts: This is an official copy of your college courses, number of credits, and letter grades. You may also supplement this with a list of courses taken for your major.

Certificates of achievement: You may receive something of this nature for volunteering your time in the community, achieving a certain grade point average, serving as an officer in an organization, or completing a self-improvement seminar. Include the Competency Matrix in the Appendix of this workbook.

Letters of reference: Gathering letters of reference should be an ongoing process. Ask for letters of reference when you are about to leave a company. Do not count on going back three years later for one, since your boss may no longer be there. The same is true of professors. If you have become well-acquainted with your instructor and you are doing exceptionally well in class, ask for a letter of reference. Your accomplishments need to be fresh in someone's mind in order for them to create a personal, glowing letter.

Actual projects: Collect and preserve projects that show your highest skill level. Such a project might be application, where you show you can do the task, or something higher such as analysis, synthesis, or, finally, evaluation. The projects you would include might be written papers, charts, or evaluations of your experiences. They could be some of the things you created while completing this workbook. They might be your action plans and proof of their implementation.

Find an attractive, professional carrying case for these materials. Practice showing them to someone, explaining their significance.

EXPAND YOUR LEARNING

Bolles, Richard Nelson. *What Color Is Your Parachute? A Practical Manual for Job Hunters and Career-Changers.* Berkeley, CA: Ten Speed Press, 1998.

Josefowitz, Natasha. *Paths to Power: A Woman's Guide from First Job to Top Executive.* Reading, MA: Addison-Wesley Publishing Co., 1990.

Moreau, Daniel. *Take Charge of Your Career: Survive and Profit from a Mid-Career Change.* Washington, DC: Kiplinger Books, 1996.

Richardson, Bradley G. *JobSmarts for Twentysomethings.* New York, NY: Vintage Books, 1995.

Rosenberg, Howard. *How to Succeed Without a Career Path: Jobs for People with No Corporate Ladder.* Manassas Park, VA: Impact Publications, 1995.

GROUP ACTIVITIES

1. Begin the Job Search: A Team Approach

Purpose: To begin with a team of people who are all interested in searching for jobs in similar or related fields.

There are many resources and agencies that can be utilized as you begin a job search. If people work together to locate them, everyone can benefit and save time.

The idea is that you gather with three or four other people who are looking for a job in a field similar to yours—for example, art, marketing, fashion, interior design and architecture, health, and so forth. Then you brainstorm resources, and each person will be responsible for finding the address, phone number, and procedures for using one of the services.

A list of resources might include the college placement office, the state Employment Services Office, a union or apprenticeship program, appropriate professional organizations, journals and newsletters for professionals, a veteran's placement office, private employment and temporary agencies, personnel offices of larger companies, and on-line databases.

All of the information will be compiled and shared with all members in the group.

Bring It All Together

Since you are reading this page, my guess is that you have read much of the rest of this book and have completed your self-paced or classroom study. If you completed a few activities in most chapters, experimented with the ideas, and applied the strategies to help you take charge of your life, congratulations on your achievement!

What happens now? If you've begun to use systems thinking, you can probably guess that it's time for *feedback*. So, take a minute to reflect on who you are today, and what is different about you and your life compared to when you first looked at this book.

Chances are you completed goals and adopted some new habits. This is just the beginning. As you have undoubtedly discovered, life management is a process, not a result. It's a journey, not a destination. And what an exciting journey it will be—filled with even more successes, adventures, and challenges. You will have many opportunities to learn and be creative, and using your planning tools, you can choose any path you wish. You have come full circle and can begin again. The challenge and the fun is to stick with it.

MAINTAINING MOMENTUM

As you know, intrinsic motivation is what really drives people to achieve their goals. And intrinsic motivation is what causes personal development and change. Here are some suggestions for keeping on track.

Maintain a Positive Attitude

A positive attitude makes all the difference, wouldn't you say? As the old saying goes, if you believe you can do something, you can, and if you believe you can't, you are also right. A positive attitude is so powerful because it precedes action, as well as directs action.

You can maintain a positive attitude by creating and using positive self-talk. You did this particularly with your "Change of Habit" activity in the Explorations section at the end of Unit 3. Did you support the change you made by visualizing the desired result? Visualizing works just like a simulator, the equipment that test pilots use to practice and prepare for combat. Picture the result you want, repeat your positive affirmations, and get amazing outcomes. Remember, attitude is altitude.

Focus on What You Have

All of us are blessed with an abundance of wonderful possessions—generally over and above our basic needs. But because we are in a consumer-oriented culture, it is easy to have a huge list of wants. A funny thing happens, though, when one of our wants is met: it gets crossed off our "want list," and two more things are added in its place.

Does that sound familiar? It seems that even though we get what we want, we still aren't happy. What isn't always clear is that happiness is obtained by focusing on what we have rather than on what we want. The next time you wish for a bigger television screen, take a mental step back and be grateful that you have a television. Instead of complaining about your boss, be happy that you have a job. When you start feeling sad that you can't take a vacation, consider the wonderful things you can see and do right at home. Have you really seen all the parks, museums, architecture, and historic sites in your state? Have you read all the super books or seen all the interesting videos available to you at your public library?

Vow to switch to a new way of thinking. Make a mental note each day about something wonderful you already have. Imagine that you thank someone for what they have shared with you. Spend a few minutes each day feeling grateful for what you have, and odds are you will feel more satisfied with your life.

Keep Building on Your Strengths

You are unique and have so many wonderful talents, skills, and personal qualities. This workbook has attempted to help you identify these, and has shown you ways to use them to greater advantage. This isn't always easy. You may have had great success with some of the activities but, after some time, quit using the new habits or tools.

That's understandable. We have covered a lot in this workbook. But, after all, you still have it. You can review these activities that you found valuable and rework some of them. They will work again, sometimes with even quicker and better results. Or you may want to try different activities this time.

Many other good ideas are to be found in the books listed in each chapter. Some of the books explore topics in much greater depth than was possible here. The point is to continue to grow, use your study skills, and build on your strengths.

Try Something New

There is much to be discovered about yourself. One approach is to try something new—something that you have never done before, something that you believe you can't do, something that is opposite from your usual pattern.

What type of thing? Well, consider which multiple intelligences are your weakest, and choose something from that category. Try a sport that's new, especially if you believe yourself to be "nonathletic." Go to the symphony, especially if you are "not musical." Take a drawing class, especially if you "couldn't draw a straight line." The point is to take a chance, a risk—to stretch yourself.

Take Time for Yourself

However you do it, you need to find time for *you alone*. You need to regenerate your energy and excitement about life, whether it's by fitting in Fives and Fifteens to reduce stress, sitting for ten minutes doing nothing, meditating, reading a book, or taking a walk.

The best way to be sure this happens is to plan it as part of your routine. Busy people will always be busy. The point is to accept fewer requests from others and to schedule yourself into your life. You choose; you take charge.

Give Back

Giving to others brings so much joy into our own lives. It can be as simple as a smile or a greeting. It can be a "random act of kindness" like putting a quarter in a stranger's parking meter. It can be listening to a friend and choosing not to talk about yourself. It can be something larger, like volunteering in your community or giving to charity.

Giving back becomes easy once you see the many opportunities. You can pay someone a genuine compliment, or thank them for something that you appreciated. You can offer your seat on the bus or train to someone who needs it more. You can pick up litter as you walk. Each day you will find endless opportunities to give back, indirectly, to your family and community. Your life will be happier for it, since "what goes around, comes around."

Make Plans

By now you have selected certain planning tools that you like, and you are developing your skills with them. Continue to work toward mastery of goal setting, time management, and planning. Create your own ways to track your multiple goals and integrate your action plans. The more you use these skills, the better you will get at them, and the more control you will have over your life. Take charge!

INDIVIDUAL ACTIVITIES

1. Competency Matrix

Purpose: To again review the Competency Matrix in the Appendix and to rate your expanding knowledge and skills in regard to life management.

Here you are at the end of this workbook, and so you will want to re-evaluate your current levels of achievement on the Competency Matrix found in the Appendix.

You have accomplished so much! Consider sharing your knowledge and skills with friends, family, and in community settings. By teaching others, you will advance your level of understanding.

If there are areas that you still want to explore or improve, choose the appropriate activities throughout this workbook or consult the reading lists in each chapter.

2. Writing or Recording

Purpose: To maintain momentum by continuing to record personal thoughts regarding life management.

Throughout this workbook, there have been many opportunities to record, in writing, audio, or pictorial form, your responses to using life management strategies and tools. One way to keep up the momentum is to continue articulating your thoughts and feelings.

You can use audiotapes, drawings and pictures, a journal, or letters. You can choose to keep all of this private, or you can share some or all of it with others.

The value of writing or recording messages to others is enormous. You can choose to send the messages, keep them, or destroy them afterward. The result is that you get to articulate and, therefore, better understand your own feelings. You also get practice in communication skills.

Don't worry if you don't know what to say in your journal or letter. It doesn't need to be lengthy or complicated, or perfect. Even if you just sit down for five minutes each day and write whatever comes to mind, you will be amazed that soon it becomes easy, you look forward to it, and your writing begins to make great sense.

3. Good Time for a Life Recap

Purpose: To take a look at where you've been so that you can plan where to go next.

Now it's time for feedback, so that you can plan the next part of your journey and direct your path to the destination of your choice. One way to get feedback is to visualize or record your life up to this point. Would you prefer to do this in writing, with audio/video, or by drawing or charting? The object is to include *key* events, decisions, and changes. It is not necessary to be totally inclusive, just the highlights will do. The length is really up to you. Most people enjoy sharing their life recap with family members, and it turns out to be a valuable family treasure.

Writing: Tell your story from the beginning until now. This is your autobiography, and you may write it any way you want. Some people like to illustrate it with photos, drawings, or other objects.

Audio/video: Talk into an audiotape, or choose to do your audio commentary as you videotape locations, people, and objects that are relevant.

Drawing/chart: You can create a drawing or photo album, or chart the important events on a timeline.

As you recapitulate your life and recall the key events and people, ask yourself:

What events do I remember the clearest?
What people really stand out?
What smells do I remember?
What were the most emotional events or times—the happiest, the saddest?
What were the significant changes?
Which experiences had the greatest influence on my life?
What important decisions did I make? Which do I regret? Which do I feel happy about?

Incorporate this information in your life recap. Evaluate the results, and use them for your next round of goal setting. Make them the basis of planning your future. Go for it!

Appendix

Competency Matrix

One way to evaluate how well you are learning something is to chart your progress on a Competency Matrix. Just as a stopwatch tells the sprinter how fast they can go today, a matrix can reveal your level of understanding or knowledge and your ability to apply the information that you have today.

The matrix also allows you to chart your progress, as you gradually develop a deeper understanding of life management skills. Practice will allow for mastery, and you will be able to see that happen over time.

If you are taking a class, your teacher may ask you to chart your level during the early days of the term. Then, periodically there will be a chapter activity that asks you to re-evaluate yourself. Remember that this matrix can be used in your career to show life skills, something in demand by employers today.

Competency	Competency Breakdown	Knowledge		Know-How		Wisdom	
		Did I hear it?	Did I understand it?	Could I use it?	Could I explain it?	Could I teach it?	Could I evaluate it?
Values	Definition						
	Source of values						
Value clarification	Definition						
	Reason for						
	Steps/process						
Self-belief/ esteem	Definition						
	Importance						
	How to increase						
Affirmation	How it works						
	How to write one						
	How to use one						
Goal setting	Definition and identification of goals						
	Establishment of goals						
	SMART goals						
Decision making	Steps in the process						
	Application of the steps						
Systems	Definition						
	How they function						
	Circle of influence						
Intrapersonal	Multiple intelligences						
	Learning styles						

Competency	Competency Breakdown	Knowledge			Know-How		Wisdom	
		Did I hear it?	Did I understand it?	Could I use it?	Could I explain it?	Could I teach it?	Could I evaluate it?	
	True colors							
	Motivation							
Interpersonal	Cohorts							
	Assertion model							
Study skills	Brain research							
	Mind-mapping							
	Organizing							
Planning your education	Choosing							
	Creating a plan							
Nutritional health	Six forms of nutrients							
	Food pyramid							
	Eating disorders							
	Weight management							
Physical fitness	Five aspects of physical fitness							
	Drugs and alcohol							
	Tobacco							
Change of habit	Process							
	Application							
Communication	Process							
	Definition of effective communication							
	Nonverbal communication							

Competency	Competency Breakdown	Knowledge		Know-How		Wisdom	
		Did I hear it?	Did I understand it?	Could I use it?	Could I explain it?	Could I teach it?	Could I evaluate it?
	Barriers to communication						
	Cultural differences						
	Differences in genders						
Listening	Process						
	Active listening						
Speaking	Speech qualities						
Leadership	Definition						
	Effective leadership						
Conflict resolution	Levels or alternatives						
	Negotiation						
Delegating	Process						
	Barriers to delegating						
Stress management	Definition of stress						
	Causes of stress						
	Management strategies						
Time management	Setting goals and priorities						
	Swiss cheese						
	80/20 rule						
	Handle it once						
	Learn to say "no"						

Competency	Competency Breakdown	Knowledge		Know-How		Wisdom	
		Did I hear it?	Did I understand it?	Could I use it?	Could I explain it?	Could I teach it?	Could I evaluate it?
	"What's the best use of my time?"						
	Job expands to time available						
	Buffer time						
	Prime time and circadian rhythm						
	Open door policy						
	Procrastination						
Multiple roles	Definition						
	Application to own life						
	Strategies for managing						
	Effect on workplace						
Money management	Terminology						
	Budget						
	Net worth						
	Financial pyramid						
	Personal goals						
Career planning	Choosing						
	Job search						

Glossary

Accepting differences   In a conflict, both sides accepting the right of the other to choose and make an independent decision.

Action plan   A chronological list of tasks, supplies, and due dates necessary in order to reach a goal.

Active listening   An emotional and intellectual activity that takes concentration and energy and is usually interactive.

Aerobic exercise   Movements using the large muscle groups that make the heart and lungs work at top capacity, for example, brisk walking, running, biking, swimming.

Alcohol   A depressant on the brain and central nervous system.

Anger   An emotion that signals that your body is prepared for a fight.

Anorexia nervosa   An eating disorder that involves self-denial of food, sometimes to the point of death.

Anxiety   A normal feeling due to worries, anxiousness, or nervousness.

Application   A form that is required by employers or colleges that provides a record of education and employment.

Assertion model   A three-step process to being more assertive (I feel . . ., I want . . ., I vow . . .).

Assertiveness   The ability to express needs and desires while still showing respect for the rights of others.

Asset   Something you own, such as a car, a house, or a savings account.

Authority   In delegation, the right to obtain materials, use equipment, instruct others, and make decisions about procedures.

Backward planning   After creating a plan, beginning at the end, at the time of the event, and working backward to schedule activities in order to ensure that enough time has been allowed for all the necessary tasks.

Baseline assessment   A quantification of current behavior in order to measure change.

Behavior goal   A response or action that a person wants to exhibit more frequently or less frequently.

Bodily-kinesthetic   Expertise in using one's body to express ideas and feelings.

Boundaries   The lines drawn or standards set to help individuals preserve their self-respect and sense of control.

Brain dominance   The study of the brain that focuses on tasks that are directed by the right hemisphere, such as spatial tasks, and those that are directed by the left hemisphere, such as linguistic tasks.

Brainstorming   Generating ideas and suggestions without judging or evaluating them.

Bread group   One of the five food groups. This one includes whole grain breads, cereals, tortillas, pastas, and brown rice. Less desirable examples include donuts, cookies, and muffins.

Budget   Same as *spending plan*. A plan for allocating income based on annual expenses.

Buffer time   Unscheduled time between other activities to eliminate rushing and feeling stressed.

Bulimia   An eating disorder characterized by bingeing on thousands of calories and then purging them by vomiting or using laxatives.

Carbohydrates   Nutrients that provide energy, particularly for the brain and nervous system, and fiber for digestion. Complex carbohydrates come from breads, cereals, and grain products.

Cholesterol   A fatty acid found in animal products such as meat, cheese, and eggs that seems to increase the risk of heart disease.

Chunking   Organizing information into short lists or groups as a memory aid.

Circadian rhythm   An inner daily clock that governs the operation of our bodies.

Circle of influence   A visual representation of an individual's relationship to systems, such as family and community, and a reminder that there is more control over the systems that are closest to us.

Cold calling   Visiting a company without an appointment, and with little prior research.

Communication   A continuous, two-way process that can include verbal and nonverbal information. When effective, the receiver attaches the same meaning to the message as does the sender.

Competency matrix   A list of skills or capabilities that have been scored to indicate a person's level of mastery.

Compromise   In a conflict, both parties' choice of an acceptable, but lower priority, alternative.

Conversion   In a conflict, one side persuasively convincing the other to change their position.

Cost/benefit analysis   Part of the self-change model, an analysis in which a person weighs the costs and benefits of making a change.

Cover letter   A letter accompanying a resume and addressed to a specific person that should introduce you and ask for an interview.

Decision-making process   A simple process that is consciously followed in order to make better decisions.

Decoding   In communication, the process of interpreting verbal and nonverbal messages.

Delegation   See *Effective delegation*.

Demand In economics, the need for a product, resource, or asset in the marketplace, such as the need or demand for teachers.

Demands In a system, part of the input that includes goals, values, standards, needs, wants, and daily events.

Depression A disorder characterized by sadness and difficulties with eating, sleeping, and concentrating.

Disposable income Also called *net income* or *take-home pay.* The amount of money available for spending after deductions for taxes, FICA, group insurance, and the like.

Dominance In a conflict, one side getting what it wants through the use of fear, threat, or abuse.

Eating disorders Abuse of food caused by psychological problems. Includes anorexia nervosa and bulimia.

Economic resources All forms of money, credit, and possessions that can be sold for money.

Educational plan A sequencing of required courses with dates they will be taken. This is necessary to complete educational goals in a timely way.

Effective delegation Assigning additional duties and authority to another person to work toward goals that are mutually developed and agreed upon.

80/20 rule Also known as the *Pareto principle.* A rule that says that 80% of the result comes from 20% of the effort.

Emergency fund A minimum amount of money set aside for unexpected repairs, periods of unemployment, or other unplanned and necessary expenses. The recommended amount varies from three to six months' income.

Encoding In communication, the process of putting thoughts into words and actions.

Environmental resources Social resources such as schools and police and fire protection, and natural resources such as clean air and water and wildlife.

Extraction A beginning, or understanding, stage of committing something to long-term memory.

Fats Nutrients that provide a concentrated store of energy in the body and assist with insulation and the utilization of certain vitamins. These are found in their pure form in oils and butter, and in foods such as meat and cheese.

Feedback In a system and in communication, information that develops as a result of the output, and which becomes input.

Field One of two ways to categorize jobs, this one emphasizes a major category of information, such as law or health care.

Financial pyramid A visual representation of monetary priorities based on the recommendations of financial planners.

First impression   The image a person presents in a first meeting. It is formed in ten to fifteen seconds and is based upon appearance.

Fitness   A state that can be achieved with regular activity, including aerobic exercise, muscle strengthening and endurance, and flexibility.

Fixed expenses   Regular, predictable expenses for rent or mortgage, loan payments, credit cards, and utilities.

Flexibility   The ability to move a joint through its full range of motion.

Flexible expenses   See *Variable expenses.*

Food Guide Pyramid   A visual representation of the recommended range of servings of the five major food groups.

Fruits   One of the five food groups. Many fruits are a primary source of vitamin C.

Function   One of two ways to categorize jobs, this one is based on the major activity or responsibility.

Givens   Assumptions about how a system operates. Two of these givens are that change is constant and that there is increasing complexity as a system develops.

Goal   A result or achievement toward which effort is directed—the "What?" of life.

Gross income   The total amount of money coming into a household or business.

Hostility   Being ready for a fight all the time.

Human resources   Time, energy, skills, knowledge, and talents.

Input   Information entering a system, including demands and resources.

Integration   In a conflict, all parties striving for mutual gains and arriving at a "win-win" position.

Interference   Something that diminishes the effectiveness of communication, such as noise or a lack of trust.

Intermediate goal   Something a person intends to accomplish within one to five years.

Internalization   The final stage of committing something to long-term memory.

Interpersonal   The ability to notice and respond appropriately to the moods, temperaments, motivations, and desires of other people.

Intrapersonal   The capacity for self-knowledge—to detect and discern among one's own feelings—and the ability to use that knowledge for personal understanding.

Leadership   A set of behaviors, beliefs, and values that enable one person to persuade others to act.

Left brain   The hemisphere of the brain that is analytical, verbal, sequential, and the seat of reason.

Liability   Something owed, such as a credit card bill or a car loan.

Linguistic The capacity to use words effectively in writing or in speech.

Liquid assets Assets that are cash or can readily be transformed into cash.

Listening See *Active listening*.

Logical-mathematical The ability to use numbers effectively, to solve problems using logical patterns.

Long-term goal A goal that a person plans to accomplish five or more years from now.

Long-term memory Apparently limitless storage of information in the brain, use of which is limited only by our ability to retrieve the information.

Management The purposeful use of resources to achieve valued goals.

Meat group One of the five food groups and a primary source of protein as well as fat.

Message In communication, the verbal and nonverbal information that is transmitted.

Milk group One of the five food groups and a primary source of calcium, vitamin D, protein and fat. The best choices are reduced or low-fat milk, nonfat yogurt, and cheeses with a lower fat content.

Mind-mapping A learning technique that organizes information in a bubble drawing format and serves as a visual outline.

Minerals Nutrients that are essential for strong bones and teeth and for healthy muscles and blood, and which assist with the formation of many enzymes and hormones.

Mission statement A verbal expression of one's unique purpose in life that can focus on specific areas of one's life, such as family, career, and so on.

Mnemonics A category of strategies that aid in memory retrieval, including acronyms and rhymes.

Multiple intelligences (MI) A theory by Howard Gardner that there are seven intelligences or capacities: linguistic, logical-mathematical, musical, spatial, bodily-kinesthetic, intrapersonal, and interpersonal.

Muscle strengthening and endurance A type of exercise that can prevent fatigue and increase good posture and energy.

Musical The capacity to perceive, express, or discern musical forms.

Myers-Briggs Type Indicator (MBTI) An assessment commonly used to determine personal temperament and which provides a clue to preferred learning styles.

Needs Things that are essential for survival, such as basic food, clothing, and shelter.

Net Income See *Disposable income*.

Networking Meeting and talking with others for mutual gain.

Net worth   The relationship between a person's monetary assets and liabilities.

Nonverbal communication   Conveying information without words. This can include facial expressions, posture, and gestures.

Norms   Standards or rules that measure behavior.

Nutrient   A major element that is essential to nourish our bodies. There are six: carbohydrates, protein, fats, vitamins, minerals, and water.

Open-end credit   Also called *revolving credit*. A line of credit that can be used over and over as long as the consumer follows the prearranged borrowing limit and makes minimum monthly payments.

Output   The end result, particularly in reference to a system.

Paradigm shift   A change in a belief or a set of beliefs commonly accepted by a large group of people.

Pareto principle   Also known as the *80/20 rule*. A principle that says that 80% of the result comes from 20% of the effort.

Parkinson's Law   A principle that says that a job will take as long as the time allotted to it.

Pitch   The level of sound on a musical scale.

Planning   The process of deciding what to do and how and when to do it.

Portfolio   Prepared for use during job hunting, it contains proof of one's skills. It can include lists of courses and examples of reports, notebooks, and projects.

Positive affirmations   Positive statements said to oneself to achieve high self-belief.

Prioritize   To organize or rank in order of importance.

Priority   The most important item.

Procrastination   A strategy of delay, often to the point of crisis.

Protein   A nutrient that primarily meets the body's need for growth, maintenance, and repair. Major sources include meat, fish, poultry, beans, eggs, nuts, and dairy products.

Pyramid   See *Food Guide Pyramid* or *Financial pyramid*.

Recall   A self-initiated search of long-term memory for information.

Receiver   In two-way communication, the person who intercepts the information or message.

Recognition   Retrieving something from long-term memory; a judgment that what has been presented to one is familiar.

Referral interview   A short interview with an industry expert to discuss job opportunities in the field.

Relaxation   Time to reduce tension and anxiety and incorporate a sense of joy into our lives.

Renewal   A time to listen to our inner voice and consider our purpose and contributions to life.

Repetition   A powerful tool for learning that requires frequent practice or exposure to an idea or application.

Resources   In a system, part of input that includes assets that are available to use to reach our goals, such as money, time, skills, and energy. There are three types of resources: human, economic, and environmental.

Rest   Essential for functioning mentally, emotionally, and physically. Most adults need at least eight hours of sleep each night.

Resume   A short, usually one-page, summation of education and work experience to show what you can offer to an employer.

Revolving credit   See *Open-end credit*.

Right brain   The hemisphere of the brain that is holistic, spatial, simultaneous, and the seat of dreams and passion.

Role   A set of expected behaviors for a particular position.

SCANS   An acronym for Secretary's Commission on Achieving Necessary Skills. A U.S. Department of Labor report identified foundation skills and workplace competencies that adults need for success in the workplace.

Self-change model   A five-step action plan for creating a behavior change.

Self-belief   Also called *self-esteem*. A person's perception of his or her personal worth.

Sender   In communication, the person who transmits the information or message.

Sensory memory   A response in the brain to something in the environment.

Sexually transmitted diseases (STDs)   Also called *venereal diseases (VD)*. Diseases that include AIDS, chlamydia, genital herpes, genital warts, gonorrhea, hepatitis B, and syphilis.

Short-term goal   Something one intends to accomplish within the next year.

Short-term memory   A temporary, no more than thirty-second, storage of information in the brain.

SMART   An acronym that stands for specific, measurable, achievable, relevant, and time-framed—concepts that are used to make goals more clear.

Spatial   The capacity to perceive the visual-spatial world accurately.

Spending plan   See *Budget*.

Standard   A measurable guideline or criteria—the "How?" of life.

Stress   A physical and psychological reaction to events, people, and the environment.

Study aids   Tools that include such things as mind maps, flash cards, and flow charts as well as purchased items like dictionaries, manuals, and office supplies.

Supply In economics, the availability of a product, resource, or asset, such as the number of teachers that are looking for jobs.

Swiss cheese A term that describes the process of breaking a large task into smaller, more manageable, and less intimidating pieces.

System In a specific environment, members of a group who have a unique set of procedures—who interact with each other through input, transformation, output, and feedback.

Systems thinking A way of thinking about a situation that acknowledges the interconnectedness of those in a system with each other and their environment.

Take-home pay See *Disposable income.*

Tobacco A product that contains nicotine, a stimulant, to which people become both physically and psychologically addicted.

Tone In conversation, the inflection that reveals mood and feelings.

Transcripts An official copy of school records that lists courses, number of credits, and letter grades.

Transformation In a system, planning the allocation of resources and implementing the plan.

True colors A trademarked assessment that simplifies the Myers-Briggs Type Indicator and assigns the names of colors to temperaments.

Value clarification A process of reviewing, evaluating, and revising one's values.

Values Learned beliefs that arouse strong emotional as well as intellectual responses—the "Why?" of life.

Variable expenses Also called *flexible expenses.* Expenses that vary from month to month to cover the needs of food, clothing, entertainment, gifts, and education.

Vegetables One of the five food groups. Selections from this group have such high nutritional value that you can eat as much as you want unless the item is fried or canned.

Venereal diseases (VD) See *Sexually transmitted diseases (STDs).*

Visualization To create a mental picture of the outcome that one desires.

Vitamins Nutrients that provide trace amounts of elements for life and growth.

Voluntary submission In a conflict, one side giving in to another because of a lack of interest or because they believe they will not get what they want anyway.

Wants Desires above and beyond what is needed.

Water A nutrient that is essential for the transport of other nutrients and for waste removal in the body.

Index